D1408657

CREATED BY **JOSS WHEDON**

GREG **PAK**   DAN **McDAID**   LALIT KUMAR **SHARMA**
DANIEL **BAYLISS**   MARCELO **COSTA**

firefly™

BLUE SUN RISING PART TWO

Published by

Series Designer
Marie Krupina

Collection Designer
Scott Newman

Assistant Editor
Gavin Gronenthal

Executive Editor
Jeanine Schaefer

Special Thanks to **Sierra Hahn**, **Becca J. Sadowsky**, and **Nicole Spiegel** & **Carol Roeder**.

Ross Richie CEO & Founder
Joy Huffman CFO
Matt Gagnon Editor-in-Chief
Filip Sablik President, Publishing & Marketing
Stephen Christy President, Development
Lance Kreiter Vice President, Licensing & Merchandising
Arune Singh Vice President, Marketing
Bryce Carlson Vice President, Editorial & Creative Strategy
Kate Henning Director, Operations
Spencer Simpson Director, Sales
Scott Newman Manager, Production Design
Elyse Strandberg Manager, Finance
Sierra Hahn Executive Editor
Jeanine Schaefer Executive Editor
Dafna Pleban Senior Editor
Shannon Watters Senior Editor
Eric Harburn Senior Editor
Sophie Philips-Roberts Associate Editor
Amanda LaFranco Associate Editor
Jonathan Manning Associate Editor
Gavin Gronenthal Assistant Editor
Gwen Waller Assistant Editor
Allyson Gronowitz Assistant Editor
Ramiro Portnoy Assistant Editor
Kenzie Rzonca Assistant Editor
Shelby Netschke Editorial Assistant
Michelle Ankley Design Coordinator
Marie Krupina Production Designer
Grace Park Production Designer
Chelsea Roberts Production Designer
Samantha Knapp Production Design Assistant
José Meza Live Events Lead
Stephanie Hocutt Digital Marketing Lead
Esther Kim Marketing Coordinator
Breanna Sarpy Live Events Coordinator
Amanda Lawson Marketing Assistant
Holly Aitchison Digital Sales Coordinator
Morgan Perry Retail Sales Coordinator
Megan Christopher Operations Coordinator
Rodrigo Hernandez Operations Coordinator
Zipporah Smith Operations Assistant
Jason Lee Senior Accountant
Sabrina Lesin Accounting Assistant
Lauren Alexander Administrative Assistant

BOOM! STUDIOS   20th TELEVISION

FIREFLY: BLUE SUN RISING Volume Two, May 2021. Published by BOOM! Studios, a division of Boom Entertainment, Inc. © 2021 20th Television. Originally published in single magazine form as FIREFLY No. 23-24, FIREFLY: BLUE SUN RISING No. 1. © 2020 20th Television. BOOM! Studios™ and the BOOM! Studios logo are trademarks of Boom Entertainment, Inc, registered in various countries and categories. All characters, events, and institutions depicted herein are fictional. Any similarity between any of the names, characters, persons, events, and/or institutions in this publication to actual names, characters, and persons, whether living or dead, events, and/or institutions is unintended and purely coincidental. BOOM! Studios does not read or accept unsolicited submissions of ideas, stories, or artwork.

BOOM! Studios, 5670 Wilshire Boulevard, Suite 400, Los Angeles, CA 90036-5679. Printed in China. First Printing.

ISBN: 978-1-68415-693-1, eISBN: 978-1-64668-237-9

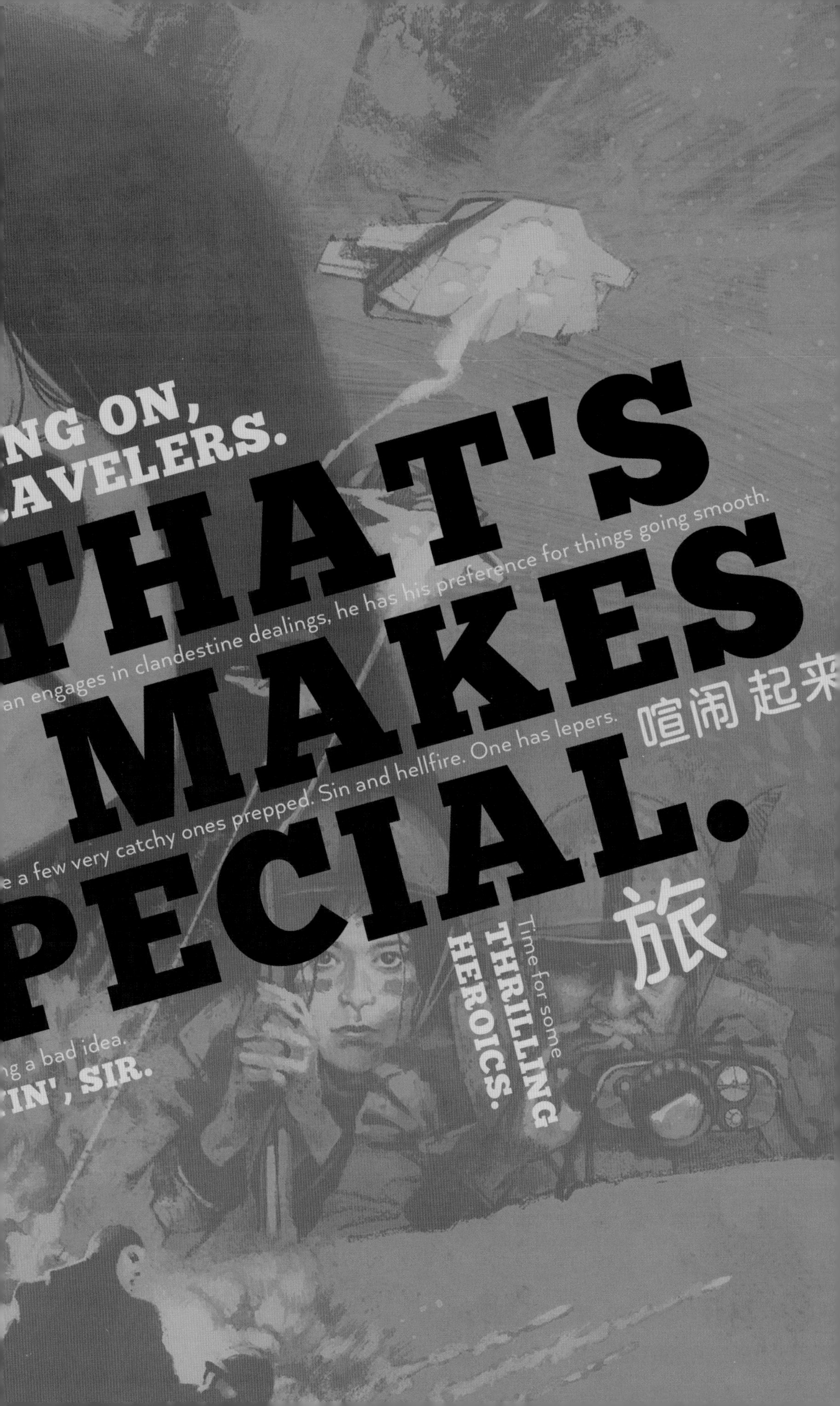
NG ON,
AVELERS.
THAT'S
an engages in clandestine dealings, he has his preference for things going smooth.
MAKES
e a few very catchy ones prepped. Sin and hellfire. One has lepers.
喧闹 起来
PECIAL.
旅
Time for some
THRILLING
HEROICS.
ng a bad idea.
IN', SIR.

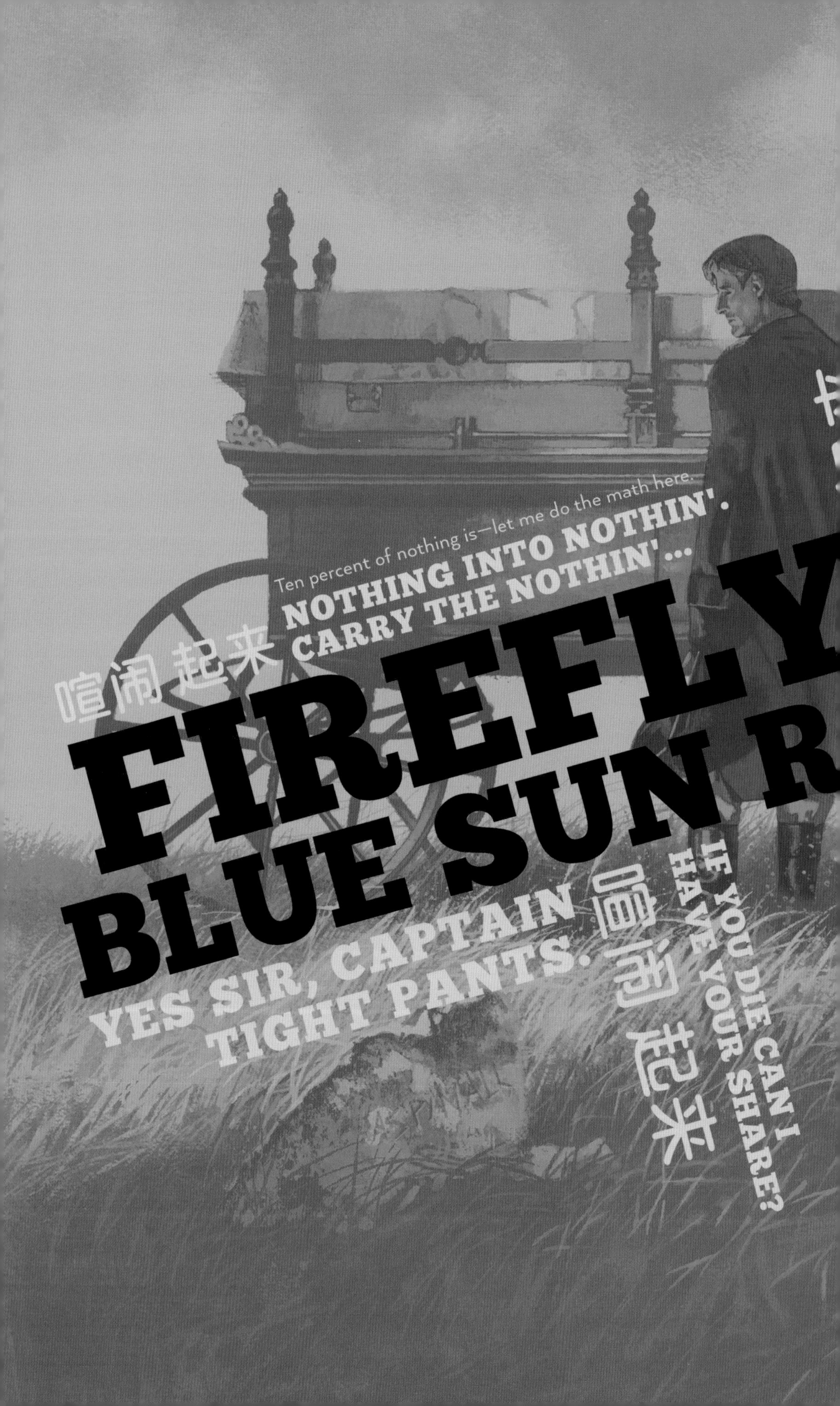
Ten percent of nothing is—let me do the math here.
NOTHING INTO NOTHIN'.
CARRY THE NOTHIN'...
喧闹起来
FIREFLY
BLUE SUN R
YES SIR, CAPTAIN TIGHT PANTS.
喧闹起来
IF YOU DIE CAN I HAVE YOUR SHARE?

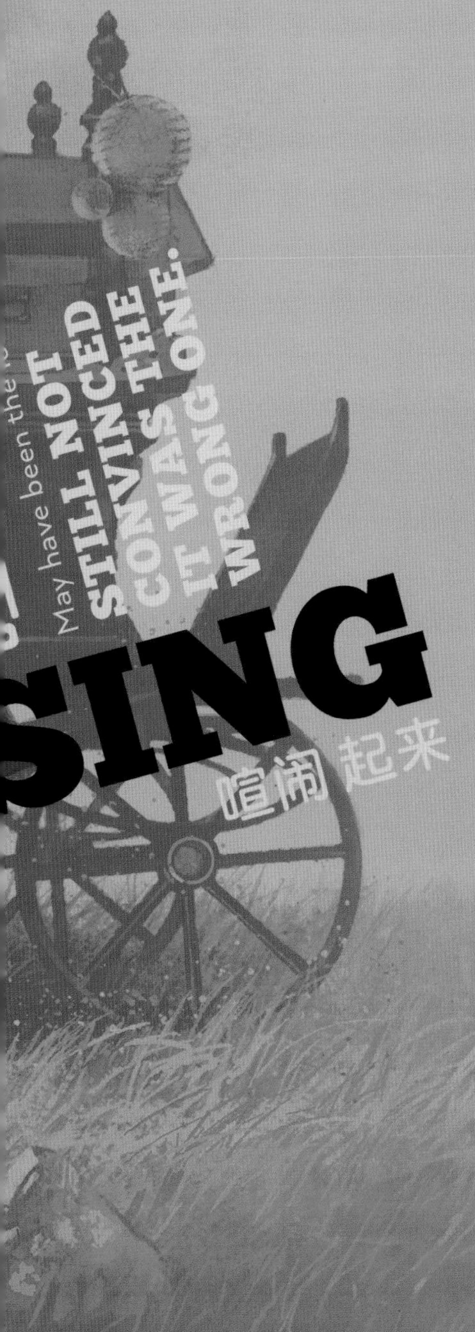
May have been the
STILL NOT
CONVINCED
IT WAS THE
WRONG ONE.
SING
喧闹起来

Created by
Joss Whedon

Blue Sun Rising Part Two

Written by
Greg Pak

Illustrated by
Dan McDaid
With inks by **Vincenzo Federici**
Lalit Kumar Sharma
Daniel Bayliss

Colored by
Marcelo Costa

Lettered by
Jim Campbell

Cover by
Nimit Malavia

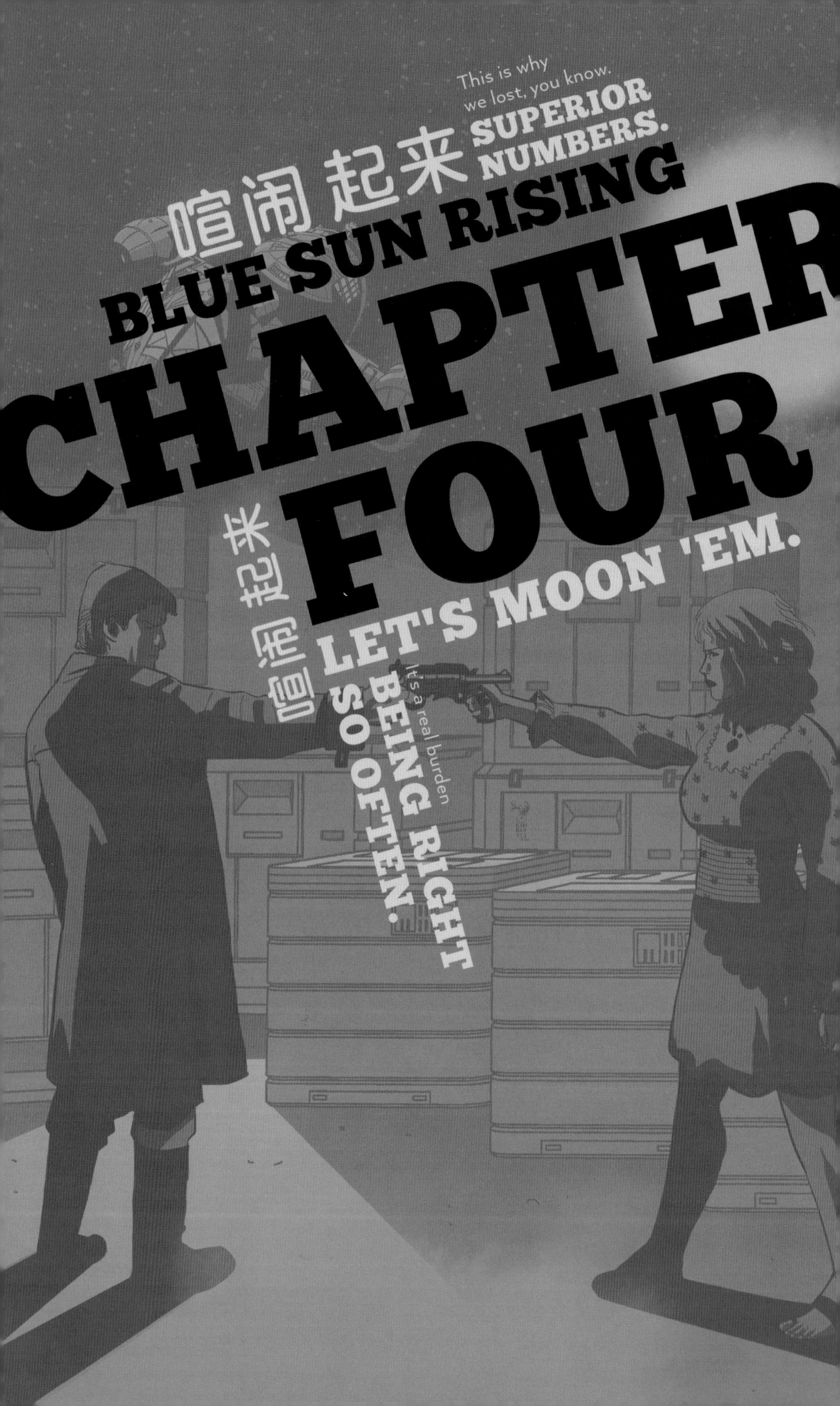
This is why we lost, you know.
SUPERIOR NUMBERS.
喧闹起来
BLUE SUN RISING
CHAPTER FOUR
喧闹起来
LET'S MOON 'EM.
It's a real burden
BEING RIGHT SO OFTEN.

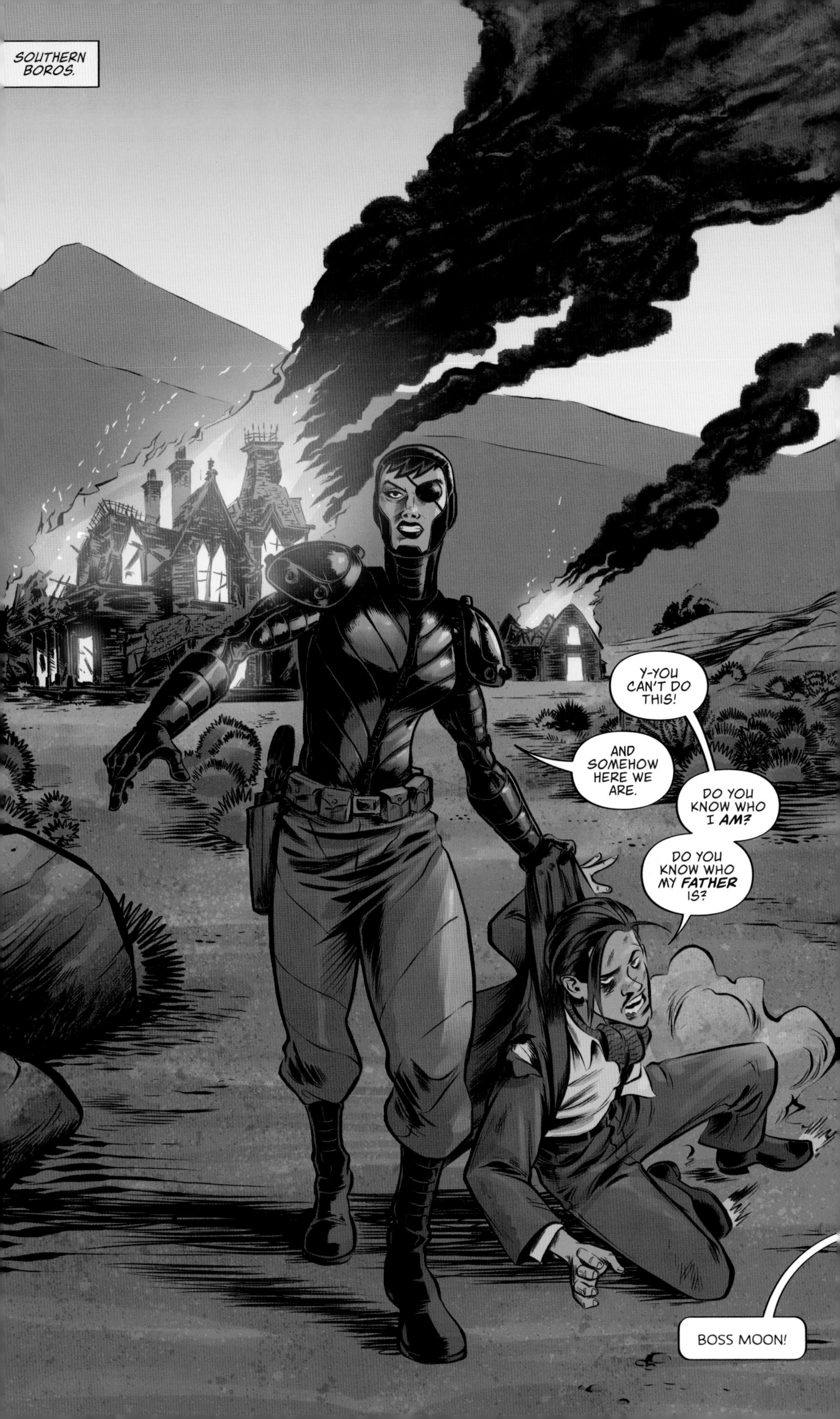
SOUTHERN BOROS.
Y-YOU CAN'T DO THIS!
AND SOMEHOW HERE WE ARE.
DO YOU KNOW WHO I **AM?**
DO YOU KNOW WHO MY **FATHER** IS?
BOSS MOON!

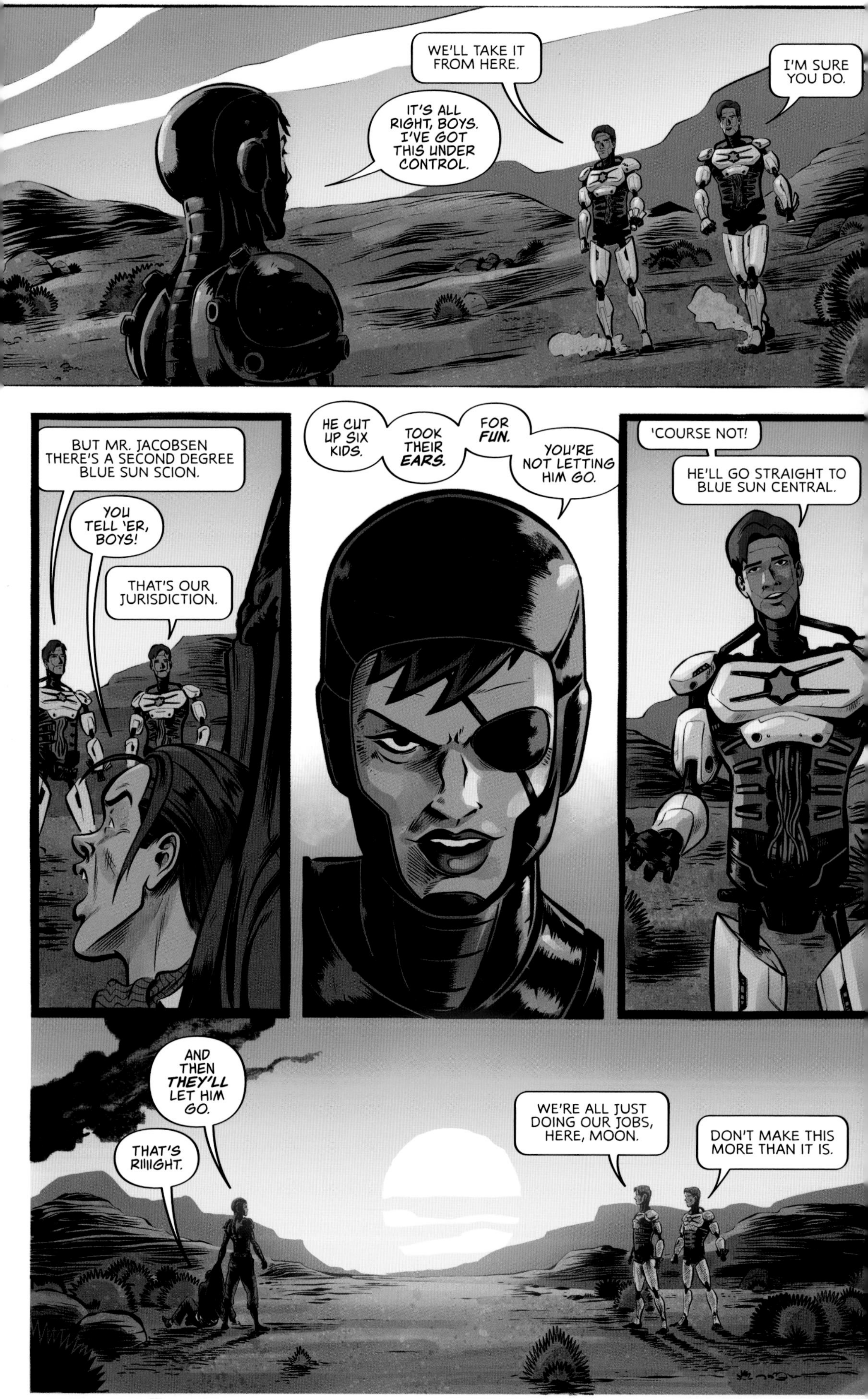
WE'LL TAKE IT FROM HERE.
IT'S ALL RIGHT, BOYS. I'VE GOT THIS UNDER CONTROL.
I'M SURE YOU DO.
BUT MR. JACOBSEN THERE'S A SECOND DEGREE BLUE SUN SCION.
YOU TELL 'ER, BOYS!
THAT'S OUR JURISDICTION.
HE CUT UP SIX KIDS.
TOOK THEIR EARS.
FOR FUN.
YOU'RE NOT LETTING HIM GO.
'COURSE NOT!
HE'LL GO STRAIGHT TO BLUE SUN CENTRAL.
AND THEN THEY'LL LET HIM GO.
THAT'S RIIIIGHT.
WE'RE ALL JUST DOING OUR JOBS, HERE, MOON.
DON'T MAKE THIS MORE THAN IT IS.

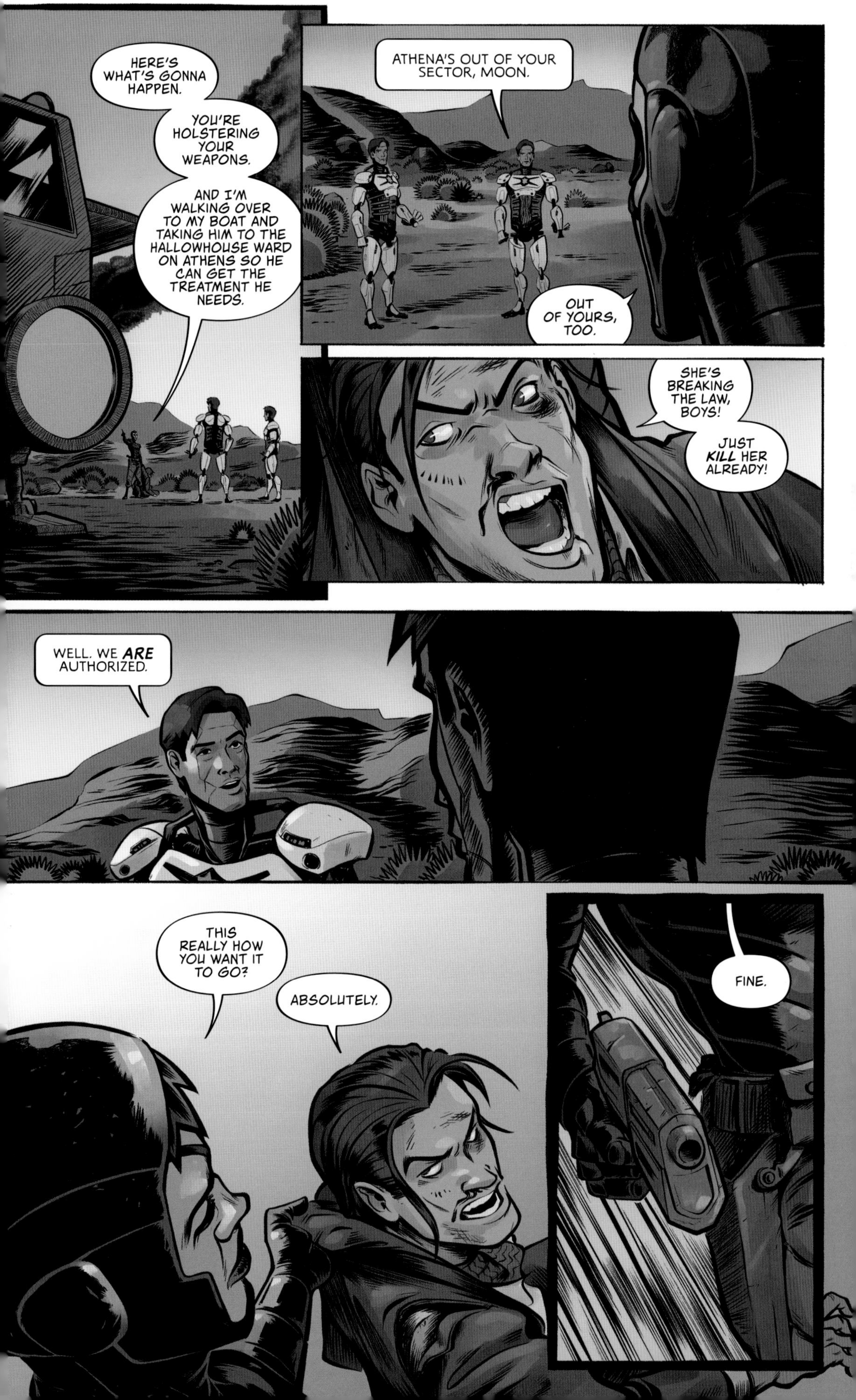
HERE'S WHAT'S GONNA HAPPEN.
YOU'RE HOLSTERING YOUR WEAPONS.
AND I'M WALKING OVER TO MY BOAT AND TAKING HIM TO THE HALLOWHOUSE WARD ON ATHENS SO HE CAN GET THE TREATMENT HE NEEDS.
ATHENA'S OUT OF YOUR SECTOR, MOON.
OUT OF YOURS, TOO.
SHE'S BREAKING THE LAW, BOYS!
JUST KILL HER ALREADY!
WELL. WE ARE AUTHORIZED.
THIS REALLY HOW YOU WANT IT TO GO?
ABSOLUTELY.
FINE.

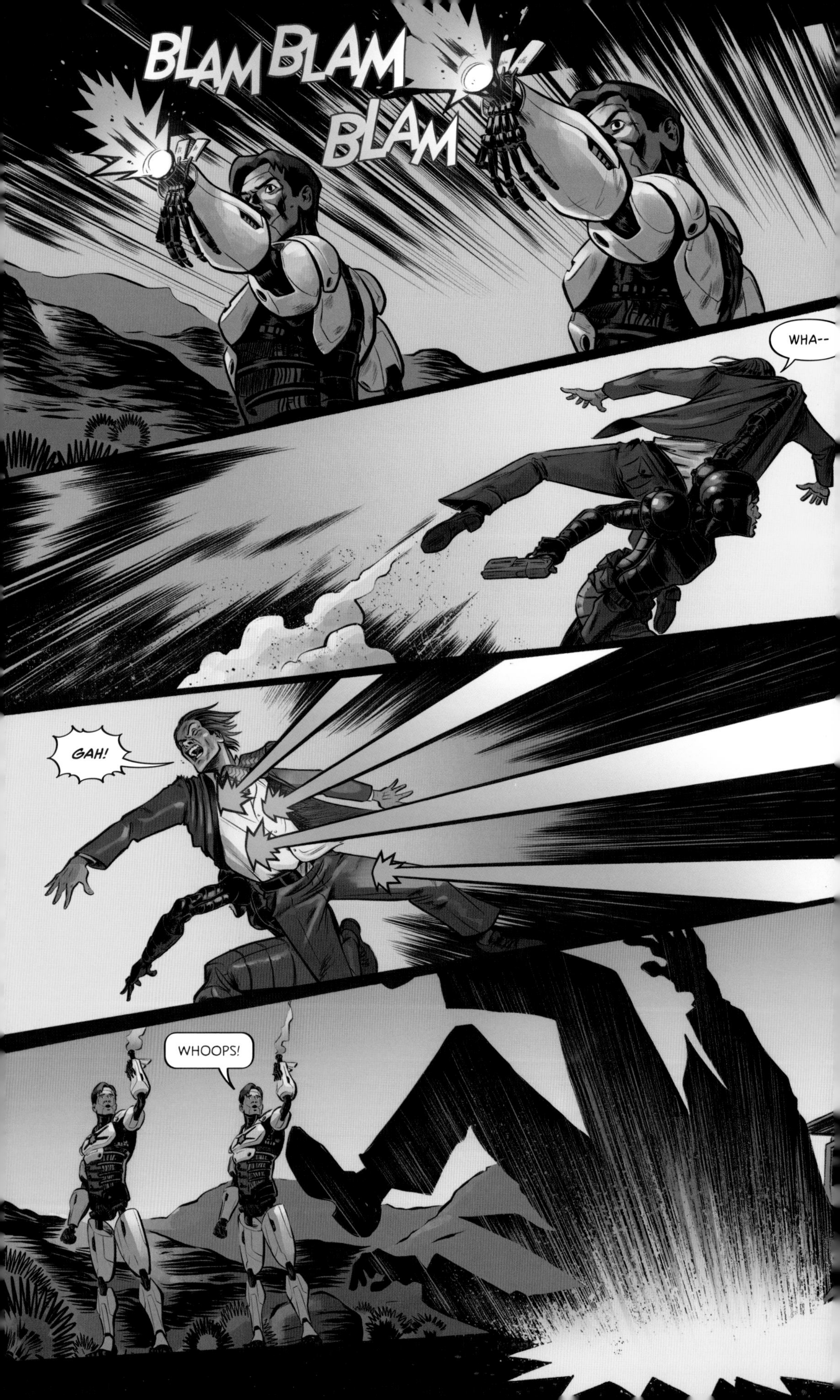
BLAM BLAM
BLAM
WHA--
GAH!
WHOOPS!

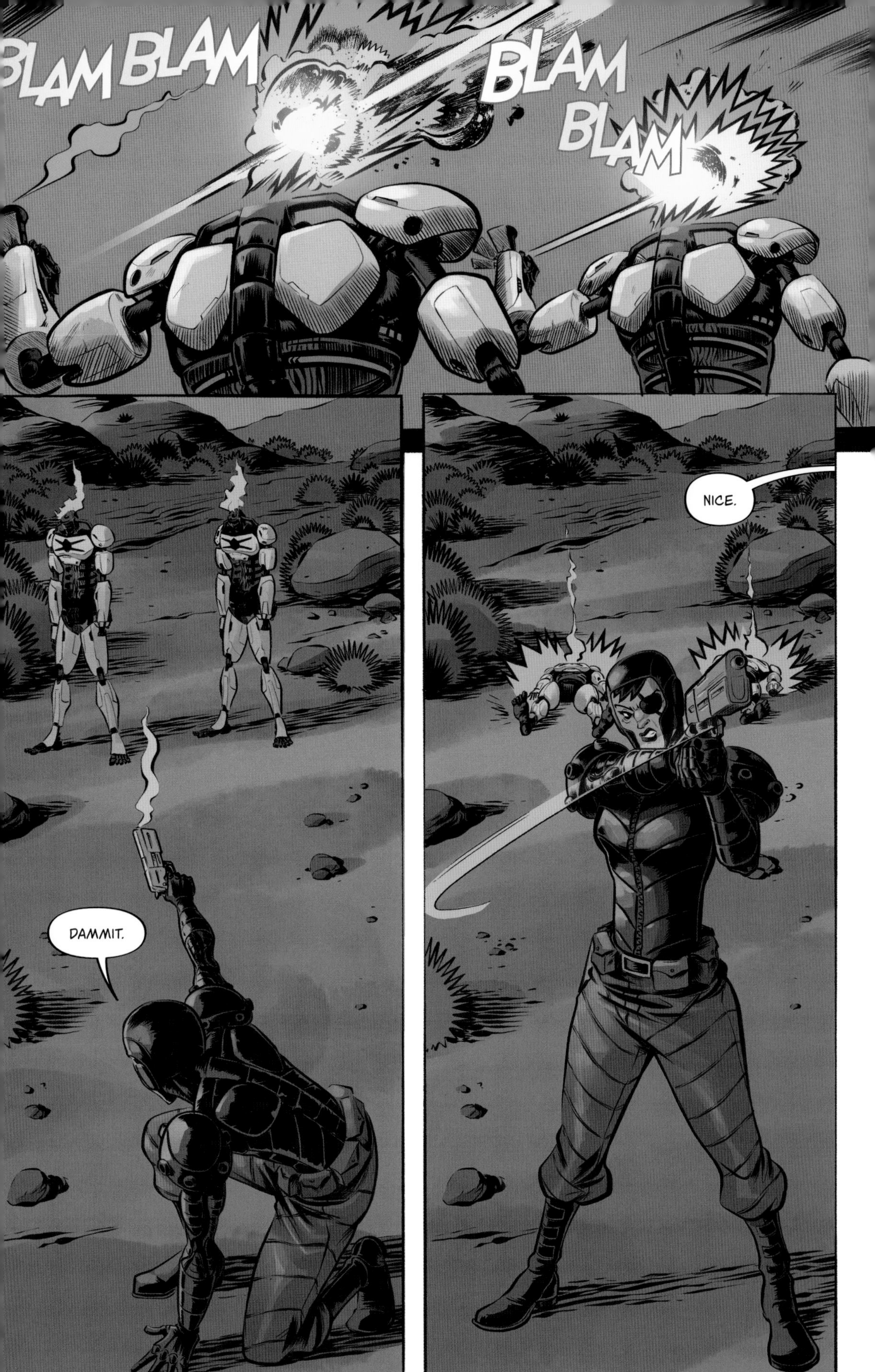
BLAM BLAM
BLAM
BLAM
DAMMIT.
NICE.

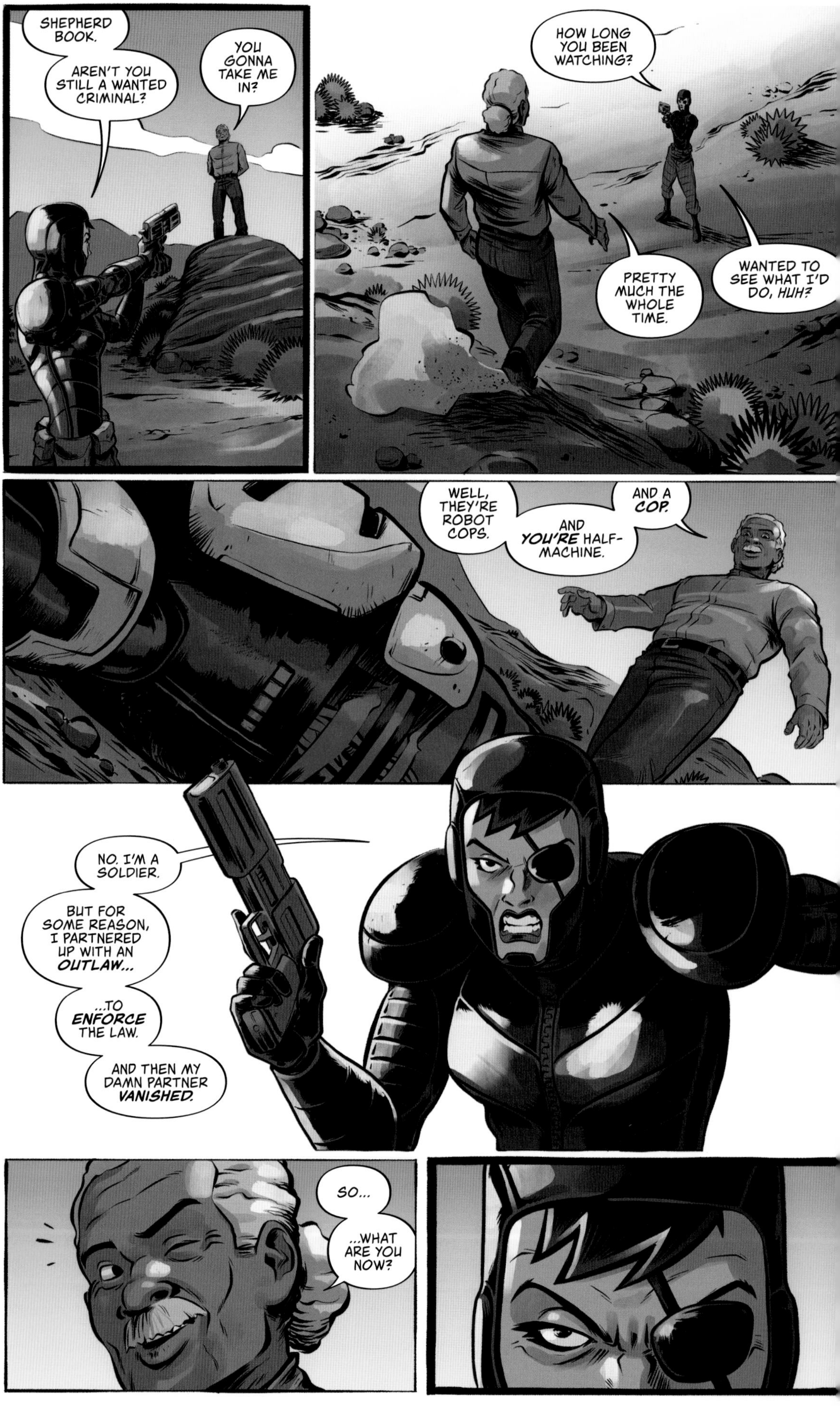
SHEPHERD BOOK.
AREN'T YOU STILL A WANTED CRIMINAL?
YOU GONNA TAKE ME IN?
HOW LONG YOU BEEN WATCHING?
PRETTY MUCH THE WHOLE TIME.
WANTED TO SEE WHAT I'D DO, *HUH?*
WELL, THEY'RE ROBOT COPS.
AND *YOU'RE* HALF-MACHINE.
AND A *COP.*
NO. I'M A SOLDIER.
BUT FOR SOME REASON, I PARTNERED UP WITH AN *OUTLAW...*
...TO *ENFORCE* THE LAW.
AND THEN MY DAMN PARTNER *VANISHED.*
SO...
...WHAT ARE YOU NOW?

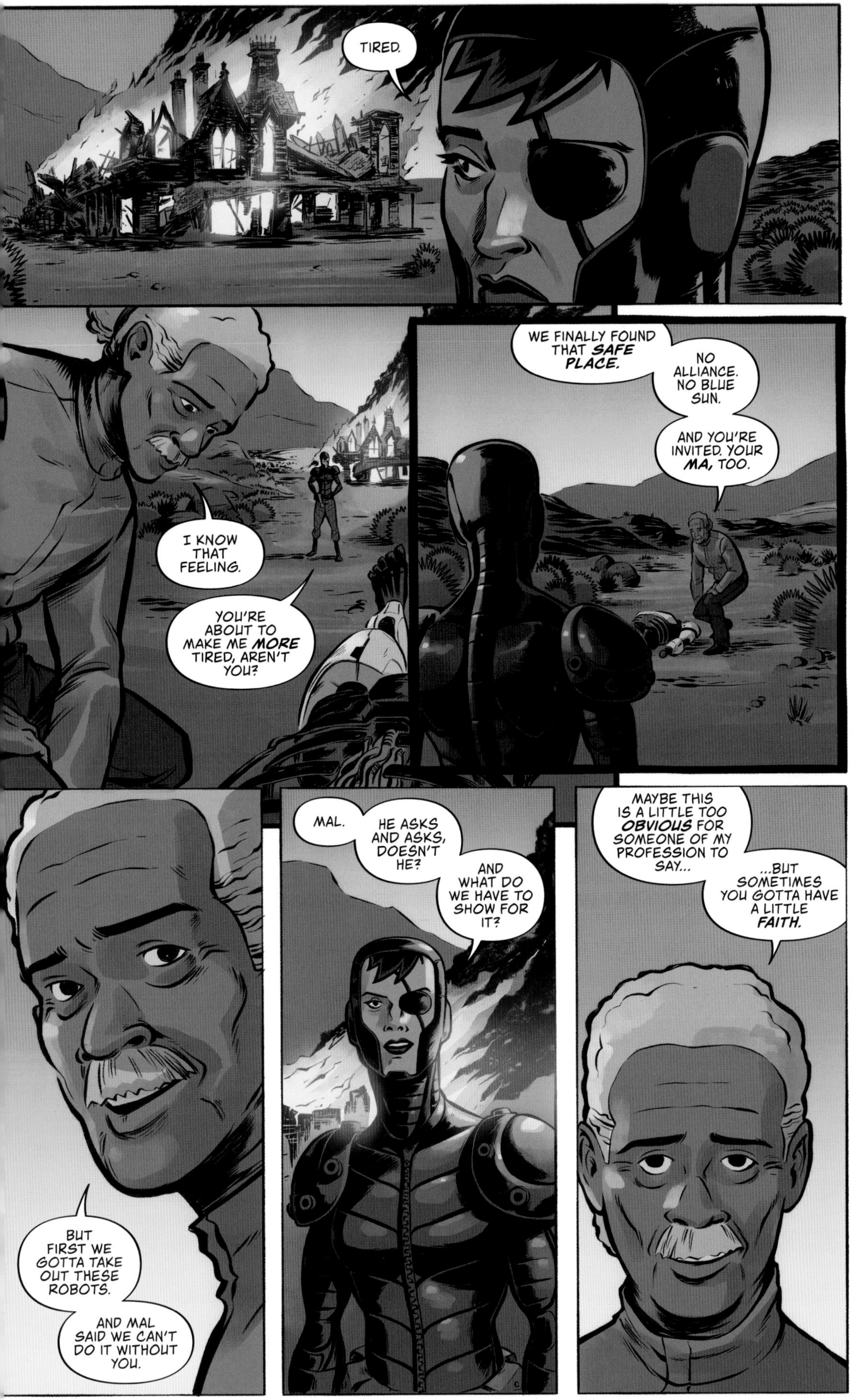
TIRED.
WE FINALLY FOUND THAT SAFE PLACE.
NO ALLIANCE. NO BLUE SUN.
AND YOU'RE INVITED. YOUR MA, TOO.
I KNOW THAT FEELING.
YOU'RE ABOUT TO MAKE ME MORE TIRED, AREN'T YOU?
BUT FIRST WE GOTTA TAKE OUT THESE ROBOTS.
AND MAL SAID WE CAN'T DO IT WITHOUT YOU.
MAL.
HE ASKS AND ASKS, DOESN'T HE?
AND WHAT DO WE HAVE TO SHOW FOR IT?
MAYBE THIS IS A LITTLE TOO OBVIOUS FOR SOMEONE OF MY PROFESSION TO SAY...
...BUT SOMETIMES YOU GOTTA HAVE A LITTLE FAITH.

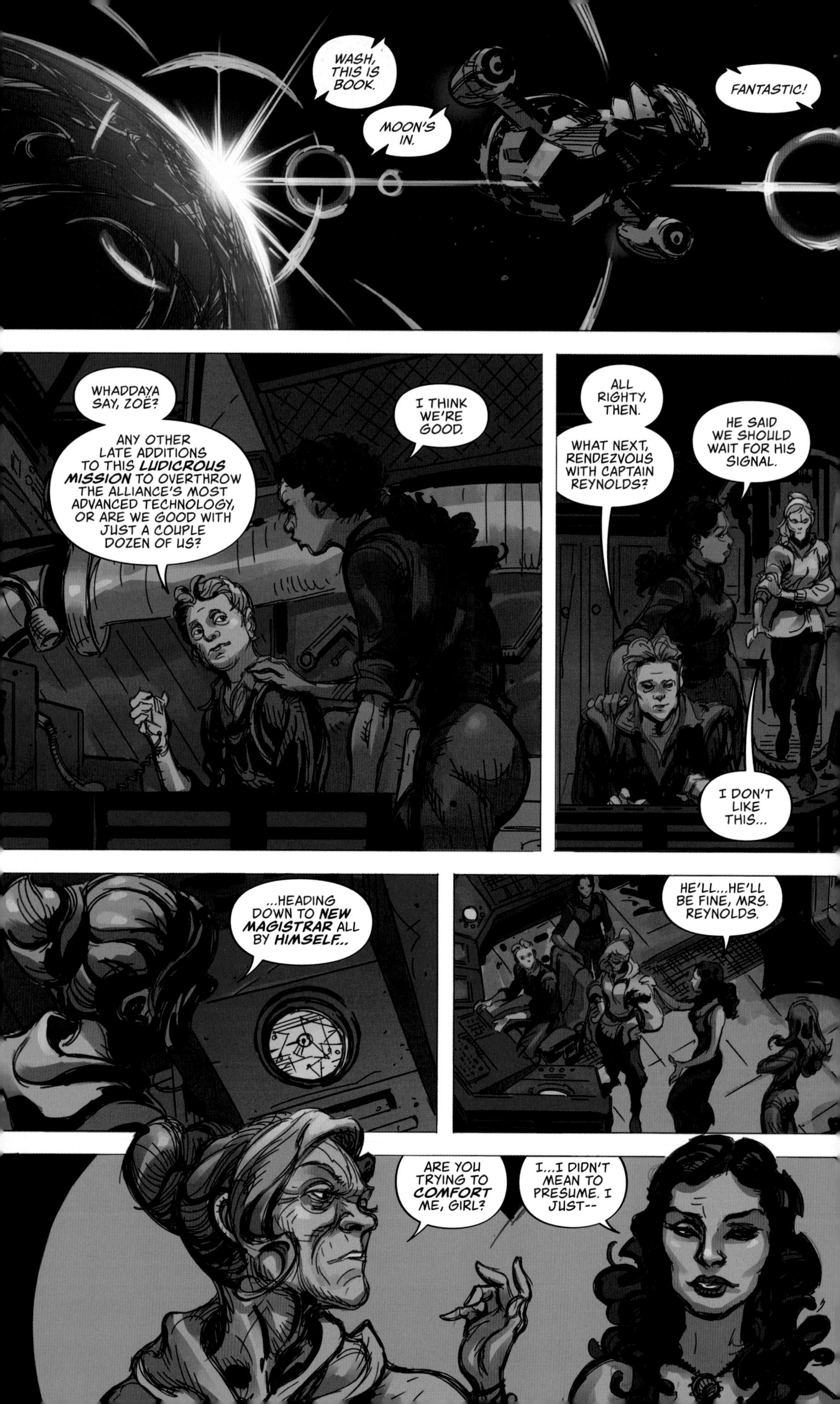
WASH, THIS IS BOOK.
MOON'S IN.
FANTASTIC!
WHADDAYA SAY, ZOË?
ANY OTHER LATE ADDITIONS TO THIS LUDICROUS MISSION TO OVERTHROW THE ALLIANCE'S MOST ADVANCED TECHNOLOGY, OR ARE WE GOOD WITH JUST A COUPLE DOZEN OF US?
I THINK WE'RE GOOD.
ALL RIGHTY, THEN.
WHAT NEXT, RENDEZVOUS WITH CAPTAIN REYNOLDS?
HE SAID WE SHOULD WAIT FOR HIS SIGNAL.
I DON'T LIKE THIS...
...HEADING DOWN TO NEW MAGISTRAR ALL BY HIMSELF...
HE'LL...HE'LL BE FINE, MRS. REYNOLDS.
ARE YOU TRYING TO COMFORT ME, GIRL?
I...I DIDN'T MEAN TO PRESUME. I JUST--

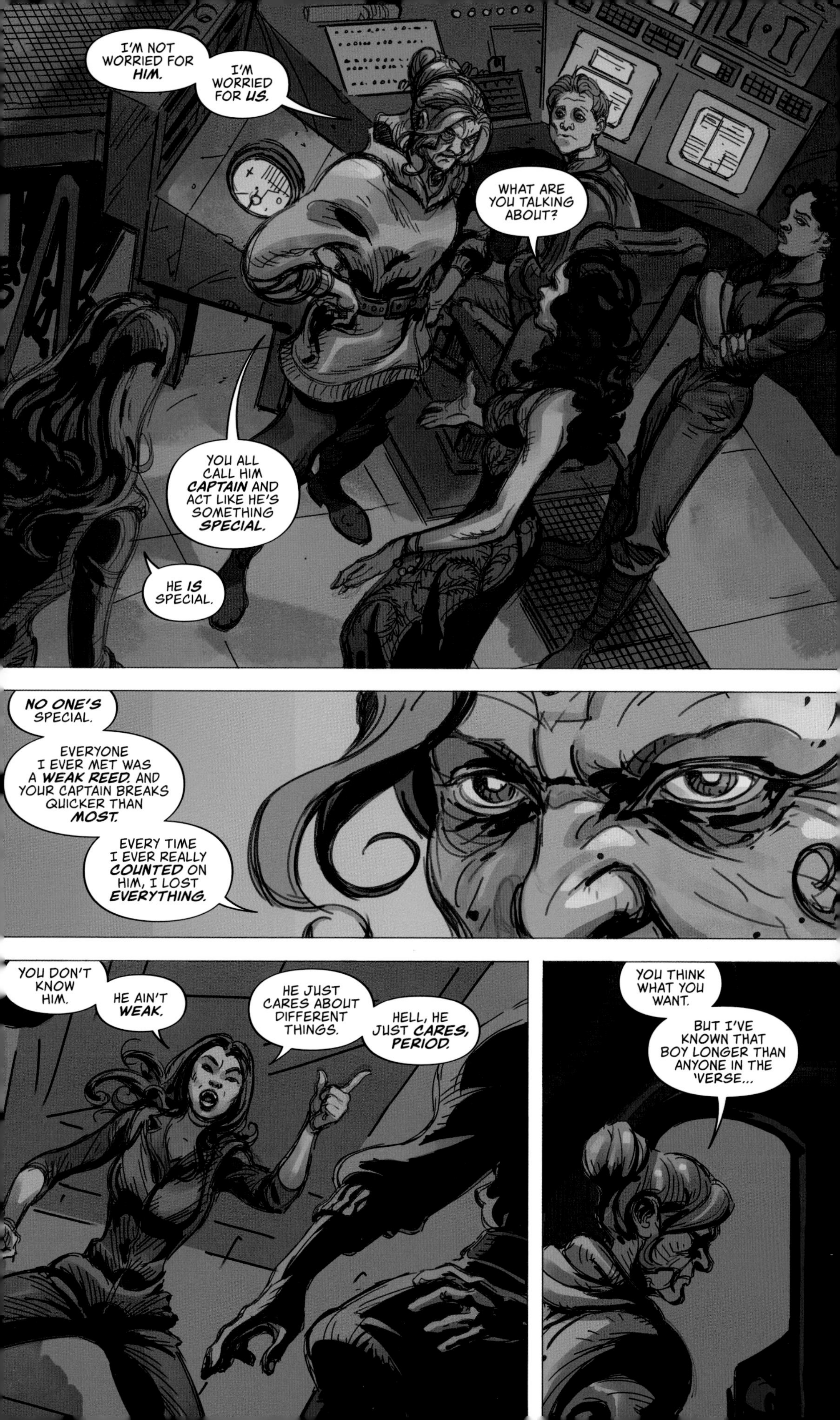
I'M NOT WORRIED FOR **HIM.**
I'M WORRIED FOR **US.**
WHAT ARE YOU TALKING ABOUT?
YOU ALL CALL HIM **CAPTAIN** AND ACT LIKE HE'S SOMETHING **SPECIAL.**
HE **IS** SPECIAL.
NO ONE'S SPECIAL.
EVERYONE I EVER MET WAS A **WEAK REED.** AND YOUR CAPTAIN BREAKS QUICKER THAN **MOST.**
EVERY TIME I EVER REALLY **COUNTED** ON HIM, I LOST **EVERYTHING.**
YOU DON'T KNOW HIM.
HE AIN'T **WEAK.**
HE JUST CARES ABOUT DIFFERENT THINGS.
HELL, HE JUST **CARES, PERIOD.**
YOU THINK WHAT YOU WANT.
BUT I'VE KNOWN THAT BOY LONGER THAN ANYONE IN THE 'VERSE...

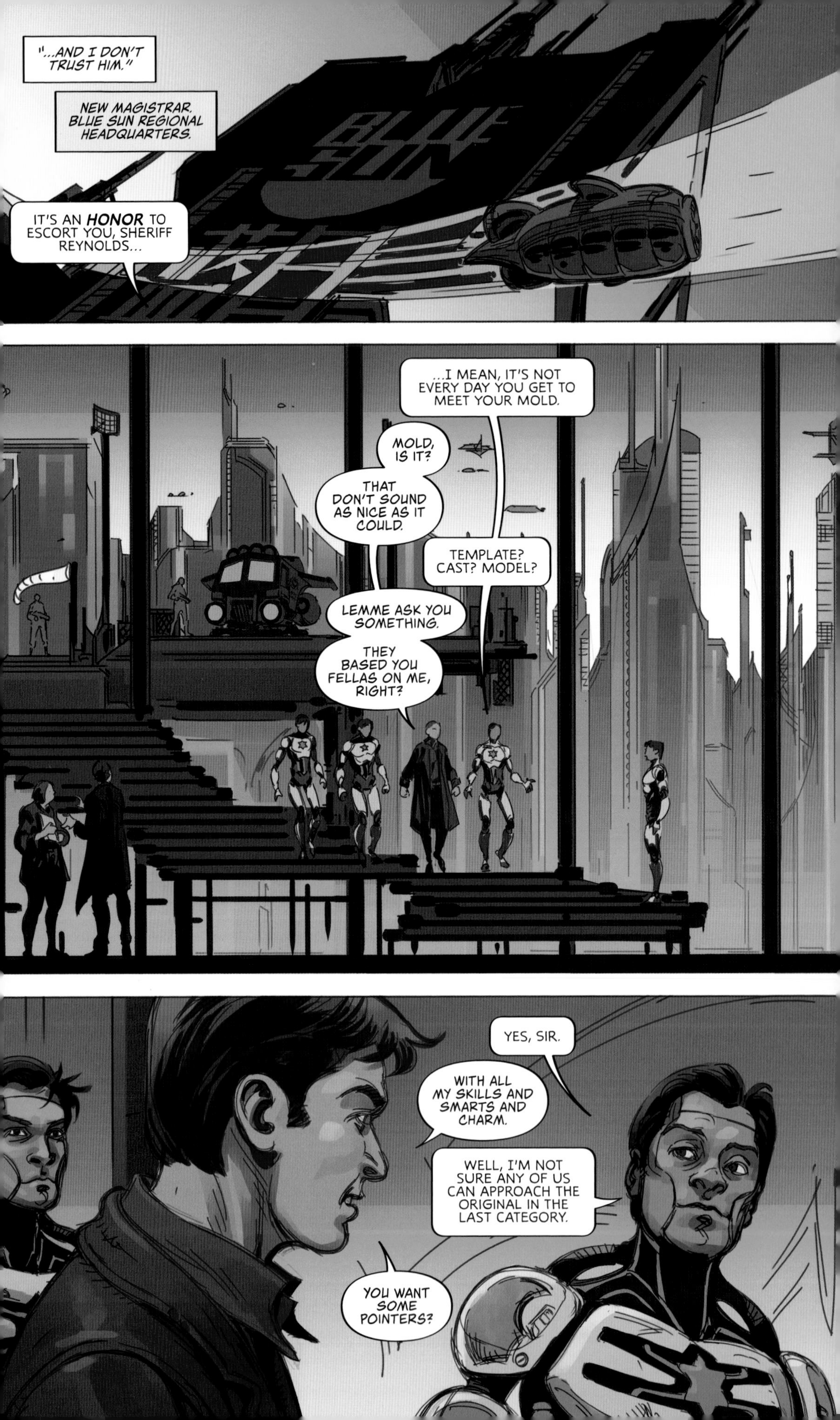
"...AND I DON'T TRUST HIM."
NEW MAGISTRAR. BLUE SUN REGIONAL HEADQUARTERS.
BLUE SUN
IT'S AN **HONOR** TO ESCORT YOU, SHERIFF REYNOLDS...
...I MEAN, IT'S NOT EVERY DAY YOU GET TO MEET YOUR MOLD.
MOLD, IS IT?
THAT DON'T SOUND AS NICE AS IT COULD.
TEMPLATE? CAST? MODEL?
LEMME ASK YOU SOMETHING.
THEY BASED YOU FELLAS ON ME, RIGHT?
YES, SIR.
WITH ALL MY SKILLS AND SMARTS AND CHARM.
WELL, I'M NOT SURE ANY OF US CAN APPROACH THE ORIGINAL IN THE LAST CATEGORY.
YOU WANT SOME POINTERS?

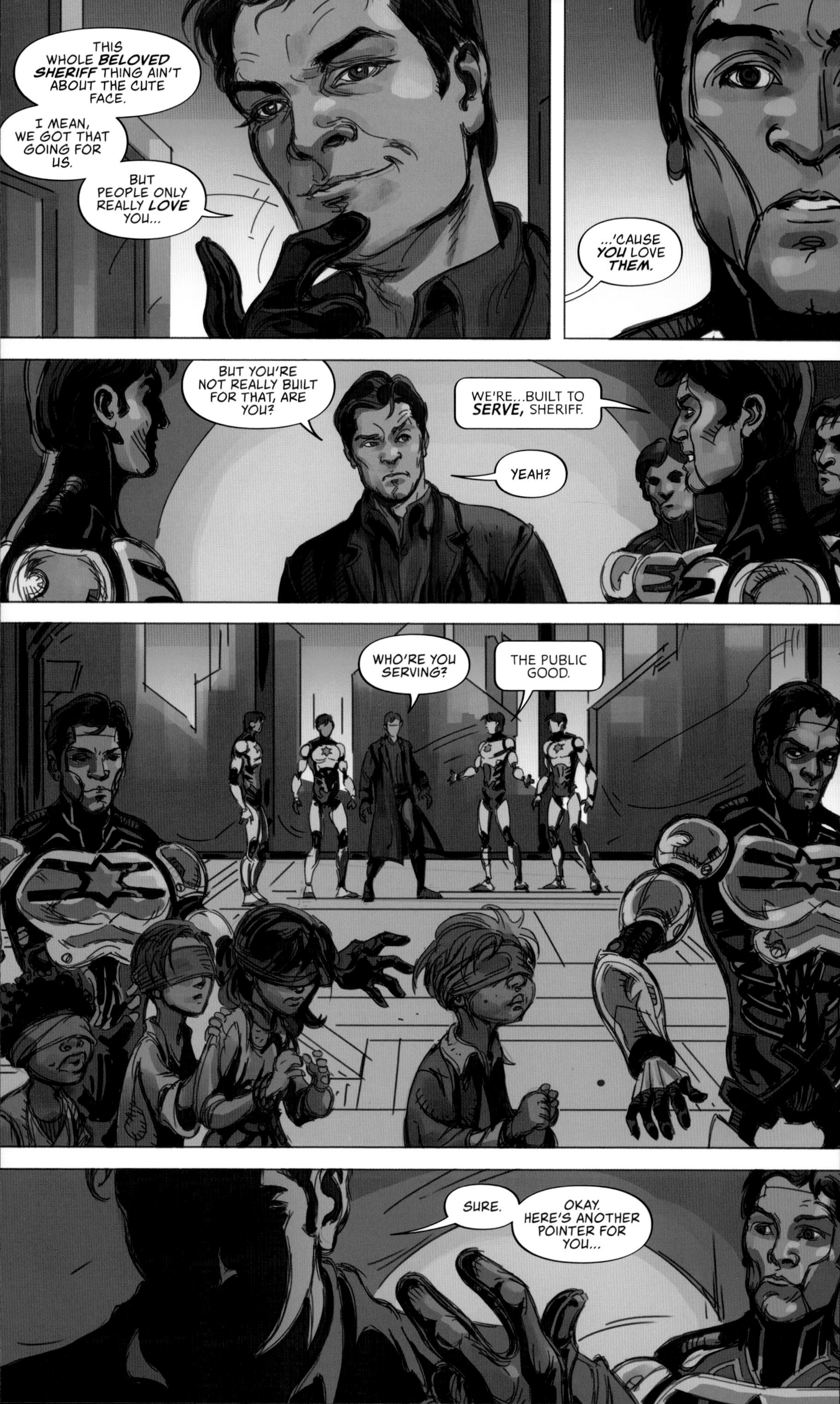
THIS WHOLE BELOVED SHERIFF THING AIN'T ABOUT THE CUTE FACE.
I MEAN, WE GOT THAT GOING FOR US.
BUT PEOPLE ONLY REALLY LOVE YOU...
...'CAUSE YOU LOVE THEM.
BUT YOU'RE NOT REALLY BUILT FOR THAT, ARE YOU?
WE'RE...BUILT TO SERVE, SHERIFF.
YEAH?
WHO'RE YOU SERVING?
THE PUBLIC GOOD.
SURE.
OKAY. HERE'S ANOTHER POINTER FOR YOU...

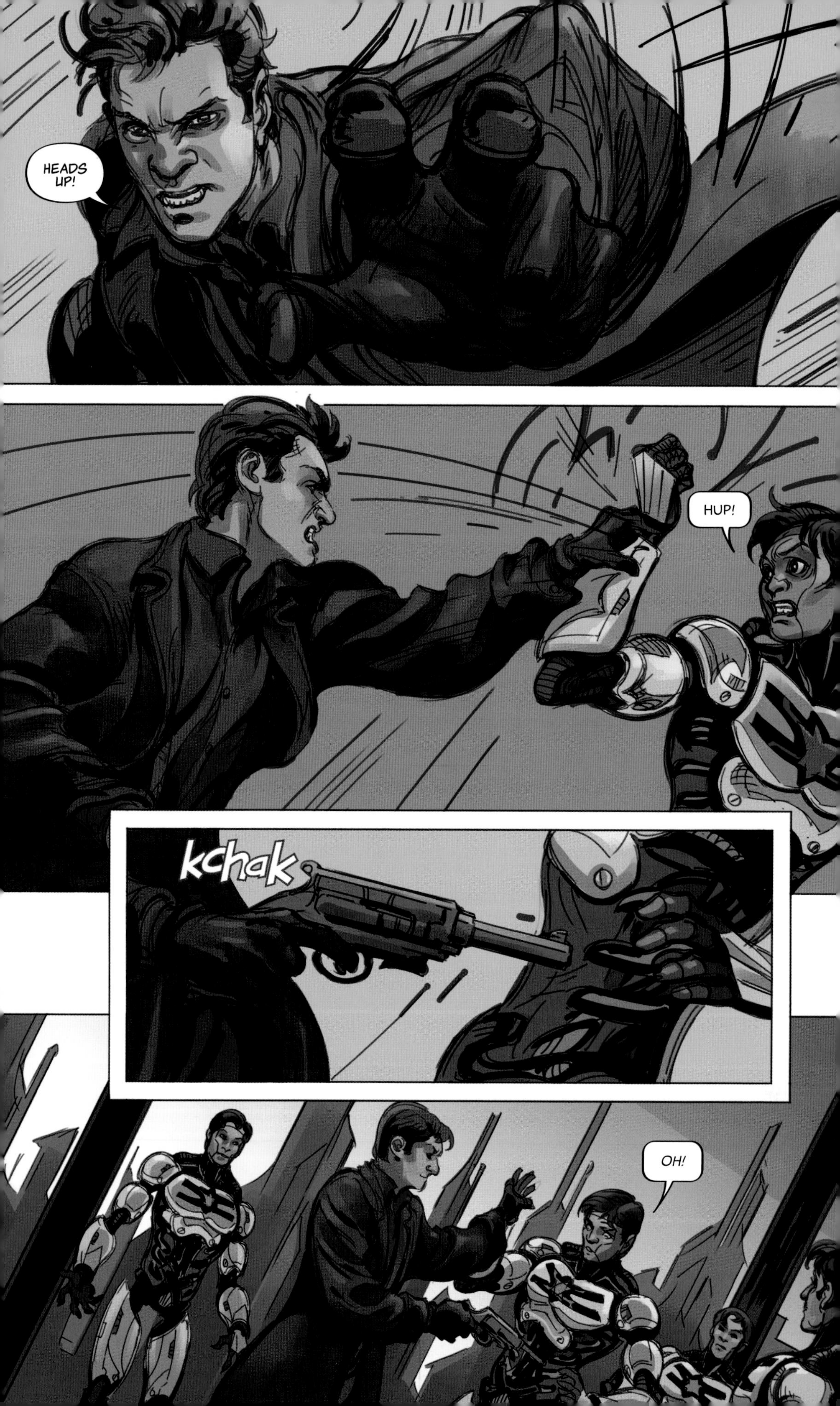
HEADS UP!
HUP!
kchak
OH!

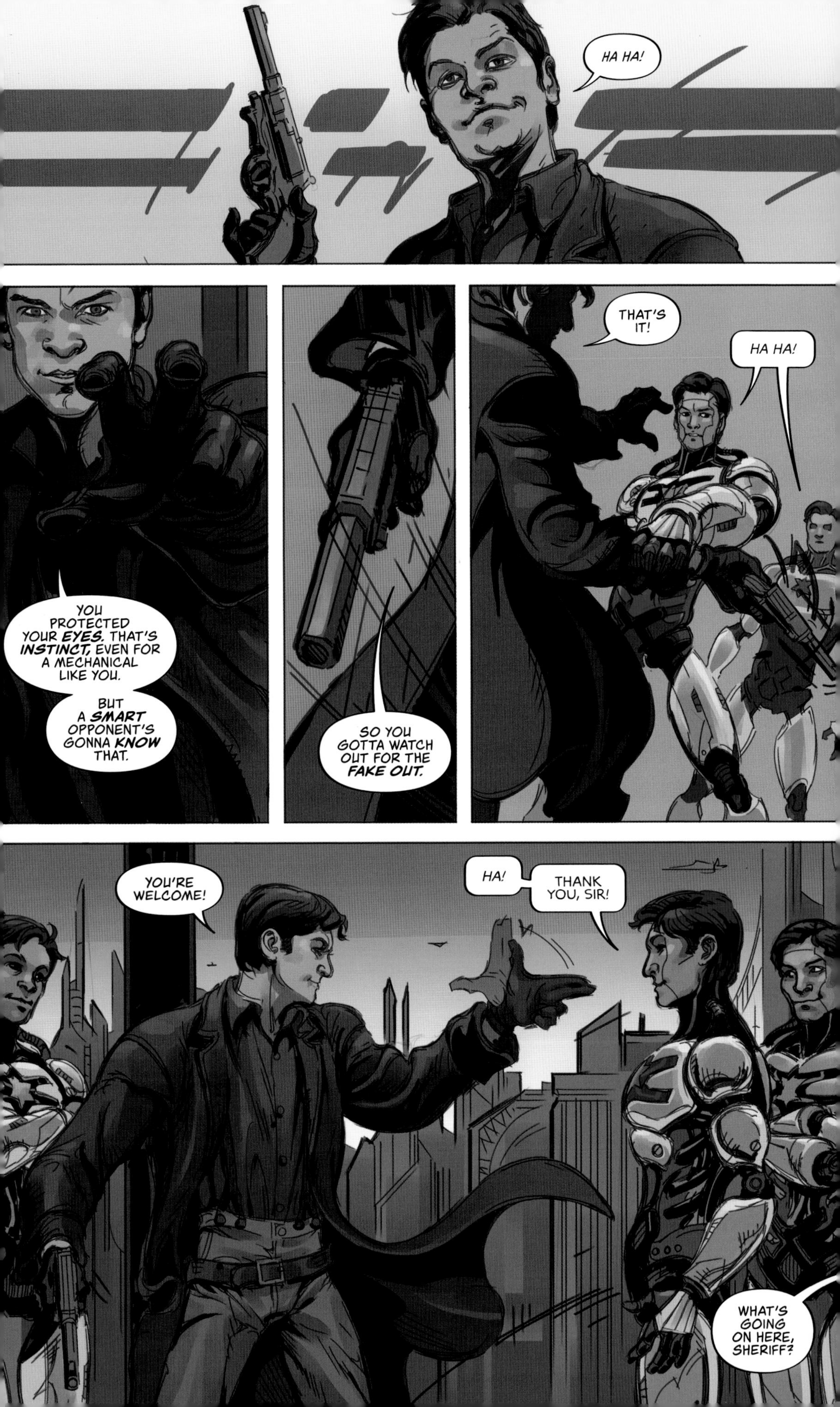
HA HA!
YOU PROTECTED YOUR EYES. THAT'S INSTINCT, EVEN FOR A MECHANICAL LIKE YOU.
BUT A SMART OPPONENT'S GONNA KNOW THAT.
SO YOU GOTTA WATCH OUT FOR THE FAKE OUT.
THAT'S IT!
HA HA!
YOU'RE WELCOME!
HA!
THANK YOU, SIR!
WHAT'S GOING ON HERE, SHERIFF?

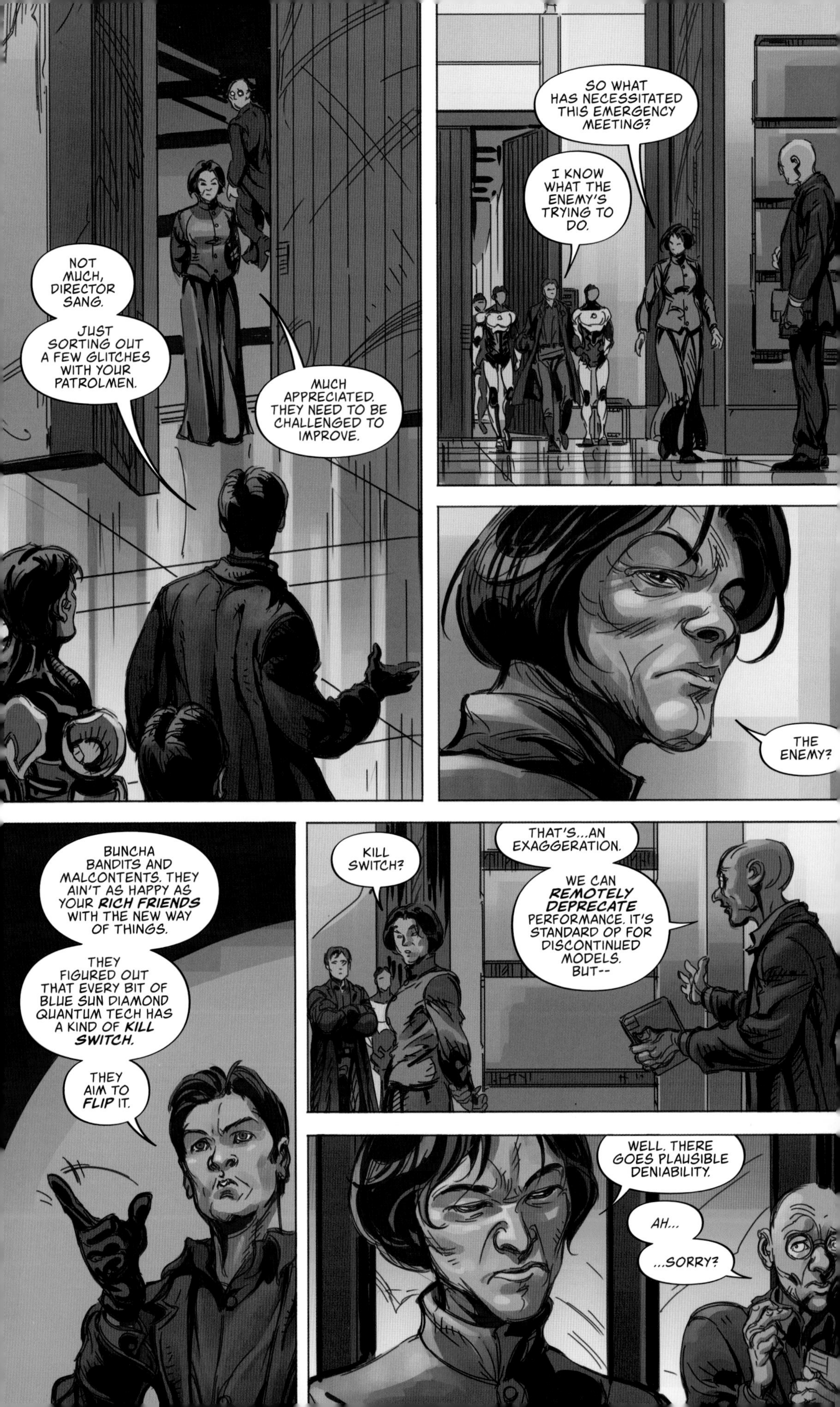
NOT MUCH, DIRECTOR SANG.
JUST SORTING OUT A FEW GLITCHES WITH YOUR PATROLMEN.
MUCH APPRECIATED. THEY NEED TO BE CHALLENGED TO IMPROVE.
SO WHAT HAS NECESSITATED THIS EMERGENCY MEETING?
I KNOW WHAT THE ENEMY'S TRYING TO DO.
THE ENEMY?
BUNCHA BANDITS AND MALCONTENTS. THEY AIN'T AS HAPPY AS YOUR **RICH FRIENDS** WITH THE NEW WAY OF THINGS.
THEY FIGURED OUT THAT EVERY BIT OF BLUE SUN DIAMOND QUANTUM TECH HAS A KIND OF **KILL SWITCH.**
THEY AIM TO **FLIP** IT.
KILL SWITCH?
THAT'S...AN EXAGGERATION.
WE CAN **REMOTELY DEPRECATE** PERFORMANCE. IT'S STANDARD OP FOR DISCONTINUED MODELS. BUT--
WELL. THERE GOES PLAUSIBLE DENIABILITY.
AH...
...SORRY?

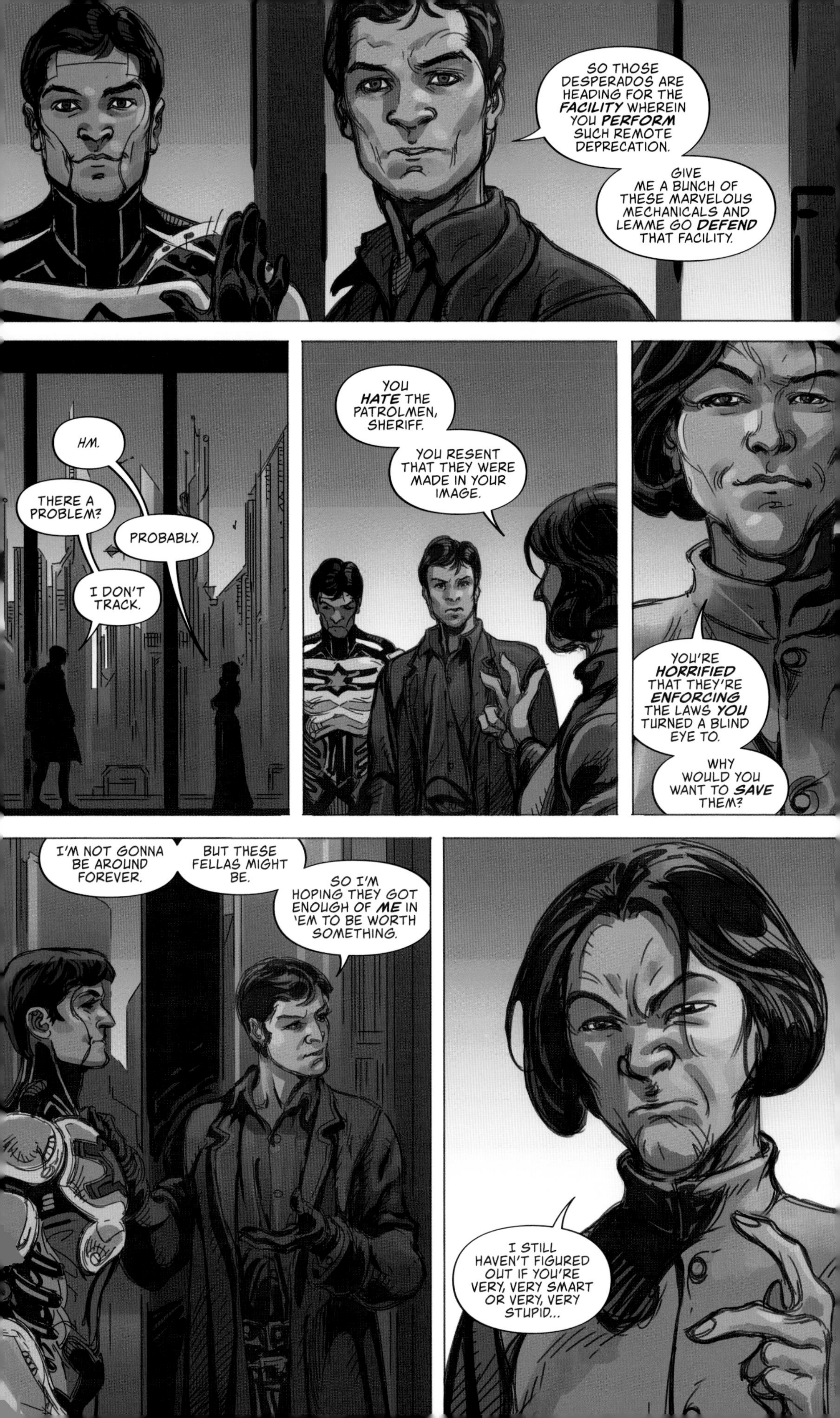
SO THOSE DESPERADOS ARE HEADING FOR THE FACILITY WHEREIN YOU PERFORM SUCH REMOTE DEPRECATION.
GIVE ME A BUNCH OF THESE MARVELOUS MECHANICALS AND LEMME GO DEFEND THAT FACILITY.
HM.
THERE A PROBLEM?
PROBABLY.
I DON'T TRACK.
YOU HATE THE PATROLMEN, SHERIFF.
YOU RESENT THAT THEY WERE MADE IN YOUR IMAGE.
YOU'RE HORRIFIED THAT THEY'RE ENFORCING THE LAWS YOU TURNED A BLIND EYE TO.
WHY WOULD YOU WANT TO SAVE THEM?
I'M NOT GONNA BE AROUND FOREVER.
BUT THESE FELLAS MIGHT BE.
SO I'M HOPING THEY GOT ENOUGH OF ME IN 'EM TO BE WORTH SOMETHING.
I STILL HAVEN'T FIGURED OUT IF YOU'RE VERY, VERY SMART OR VERY, VERY STUPID...

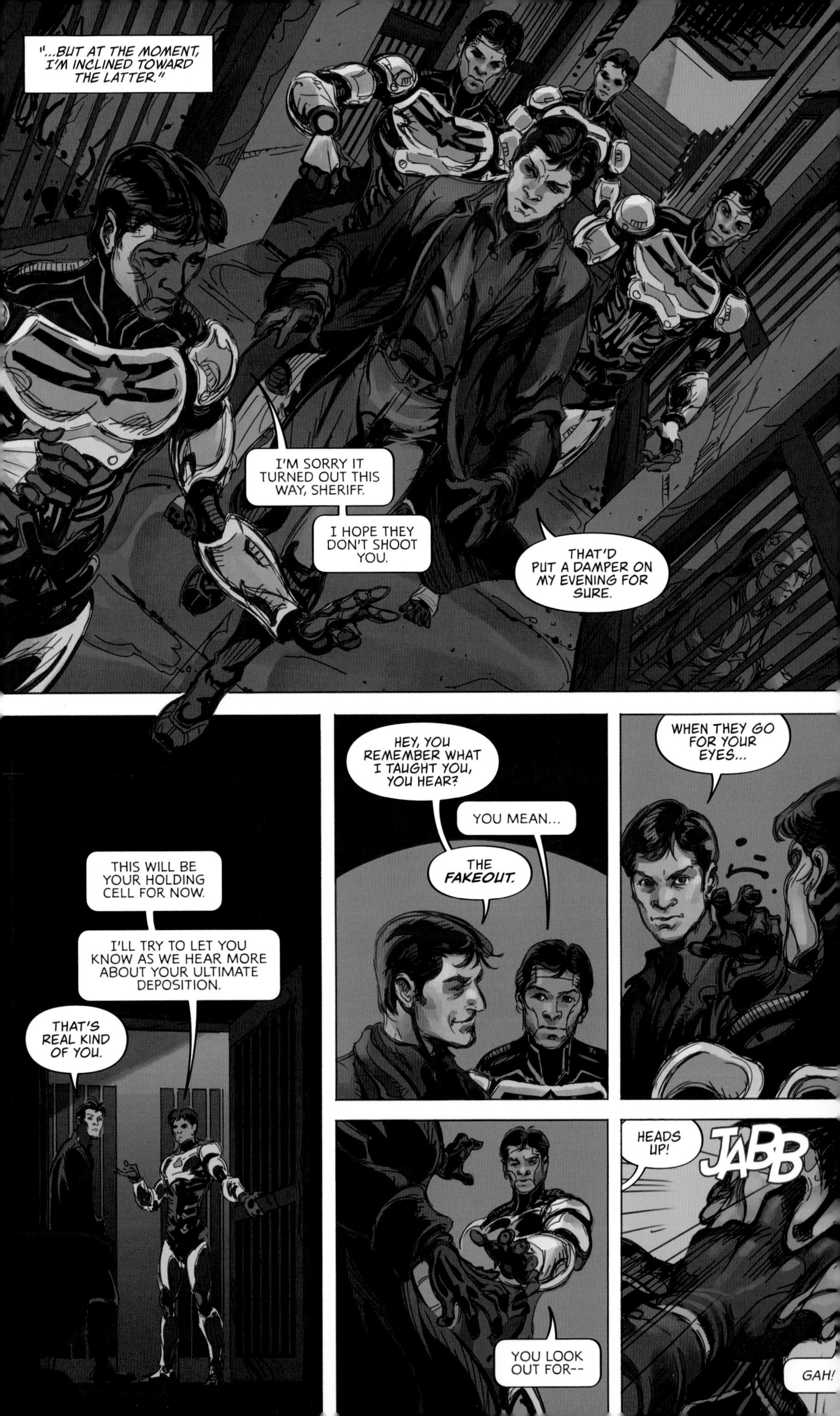
"...BUT AT THE MOMENT, I'M INCLINED TOWARD THE LATTER."
I'M SORRY IT TURNED OUT THIS WAY, SHERIFF.
I HOPE THEY DON'T SHOOT YOU.
THAT'D PUT A DAMPER ON MY EVENING FOR SURE.
THIS WILL BE YOUR HOLDING CELL FOR NOW.
I'LL TRY TO LET YOU KNOW AS WE HEAR MORE ABOUT YOUR ULTIMATE DEPOSITION.
THAT'S REAL KIND OF YOU.
HEY, YOU REMEMBER WHAT I TAUGHT YOU, YOU HEAR?
YOU MEAN...
THE *FAKEOUT.*
WHEN THEY GO FOR YOUR EYES...
YOU LOOK OUT FOR--
HEADS UP!
JABB
GAH!

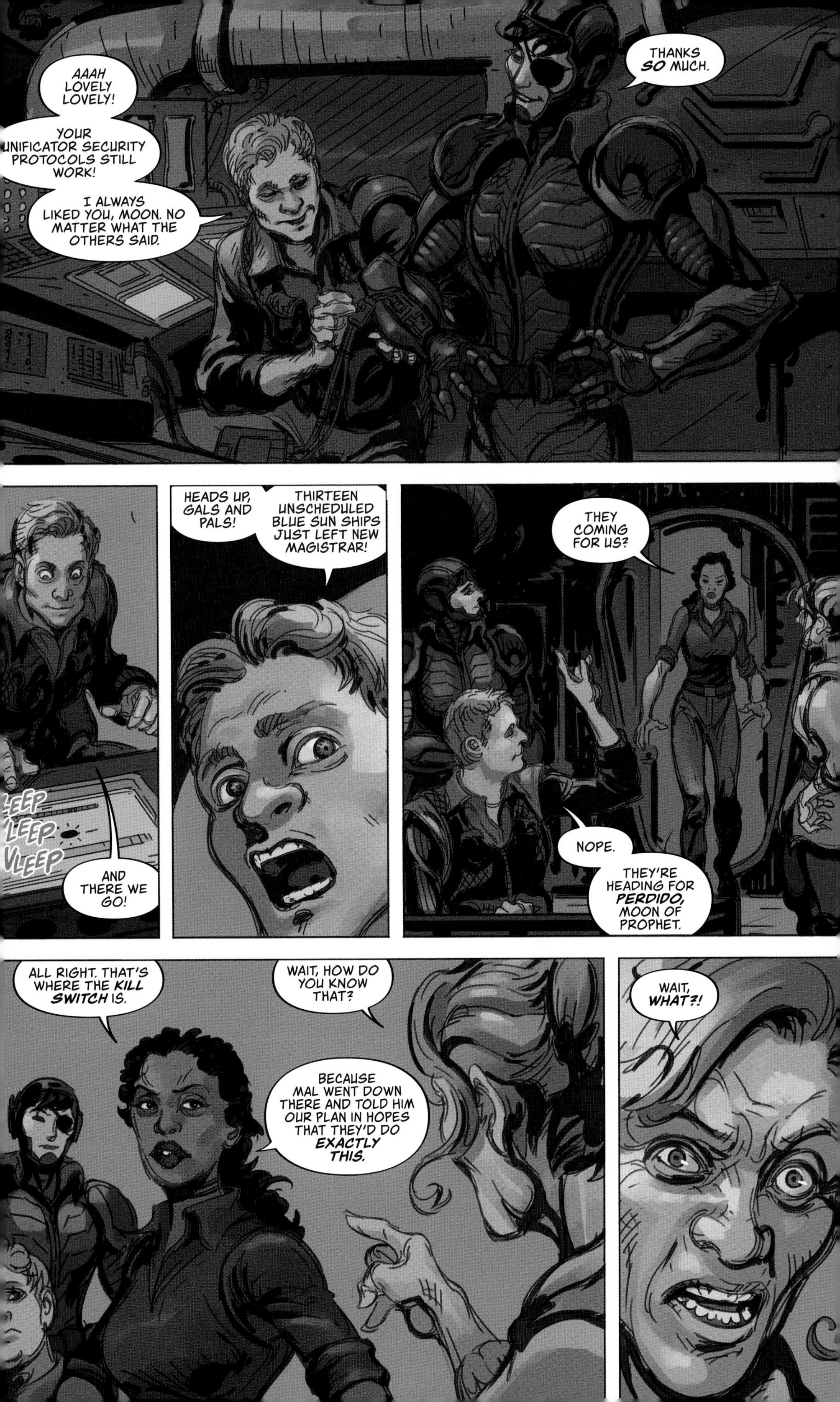
AAAH LOVELY LOVELY!
YOUR UNIFICATOR SECURITY PROTOCOLS STILL WORK!
I ALWAYS LIKED YOU, MOON. NO MATTER WHAT THE OTHERS SAID.
THANKS SO MUCH.
VLEEP VLEEP VLEEP
AND THERE WE GO!
HEADS UP, GALS AND PALS!
THIRTEEN UNSCHEDULED BLUE SUN SHIPS JUST LEFT NEW MAGISTRAR!
THEY COMING FOR US?
NOPE.
THEY'RE HEADING FOR PERDIDO, MOON OF PROPHET.
ALL RIGHT. THAT'S WHERE THE KILL SWITCH IS.
WAIT, HOW DO YOU KNOW THAT?
BECAUSE MAL WENT DOWN THERE AND TOLD HIM OUR PLAN IN HOPES THAT THEY'D DO EXACTLY THIS.
WAIT, WHAT?!

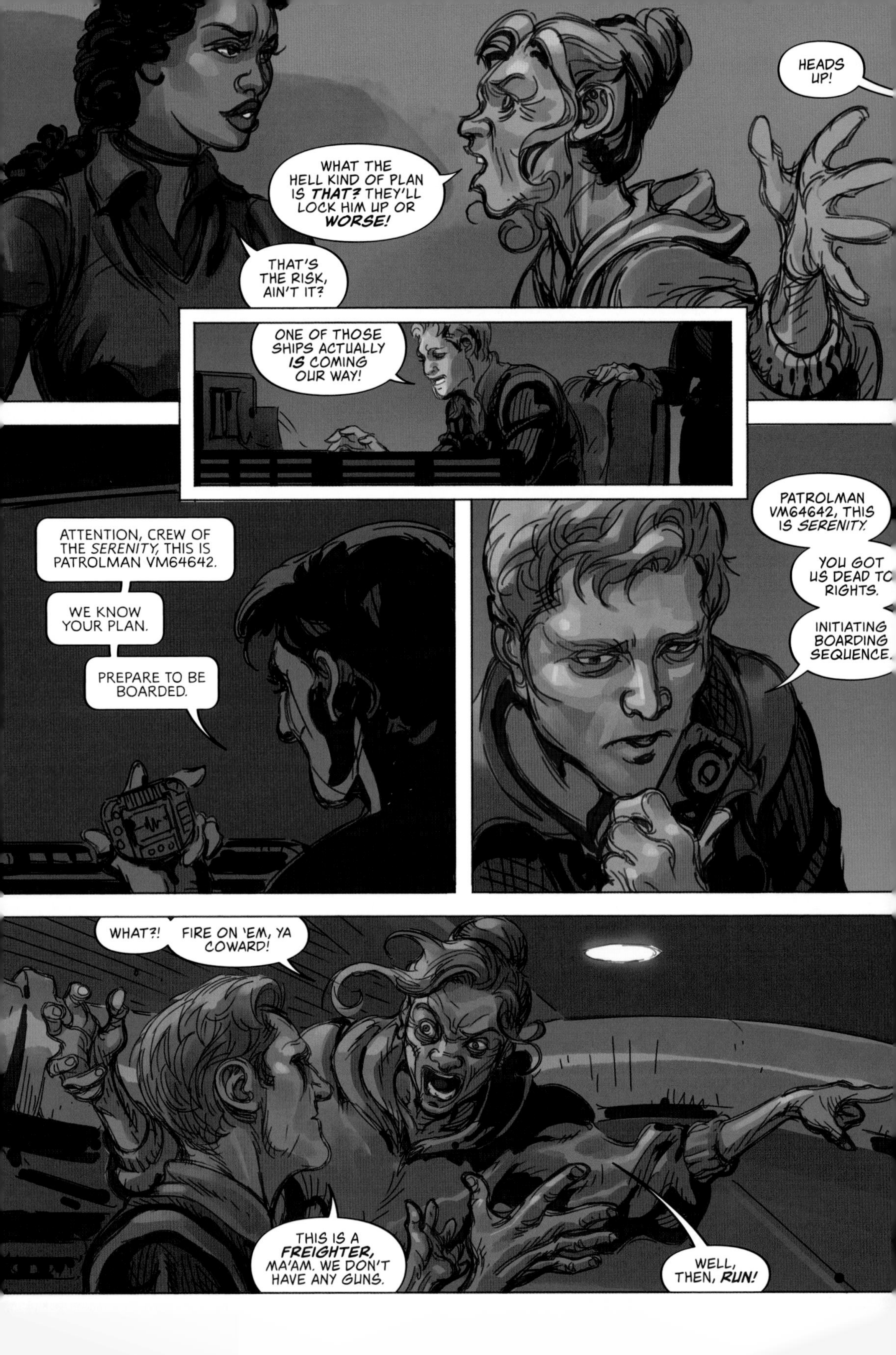
WHAT THE HELL KIND OF PLAN IS *THAT?* THEY'LL LOCK HIM UP OR *WORSE!*
THAT'S THE RISK, AIN'T IT?
HEADS UP!
ONE OF THOSE SHIPS ACTUALLY *IS* COMING OUR WAY!
ATTENTION, CREW OF THE *SERENITY,* THIS IS PATROLMAN VM64642.
WE KNOW YOUR PLAN.
PREPARE TO BE BOARDED.
PATROLMAN VM64642, THIS IS *SERENITY.*
YOU GOT US DEAD TO RIGHTS.
INITIATING BOARDING SEQUENCE.
WHAT?!
FIRE ON 'EM, YA COWARD!
THIS IS A *FREIGHTER,* MA'AM. WE DON'T HAVE ANY GUNS.
WELL, THEN, *RUN!*

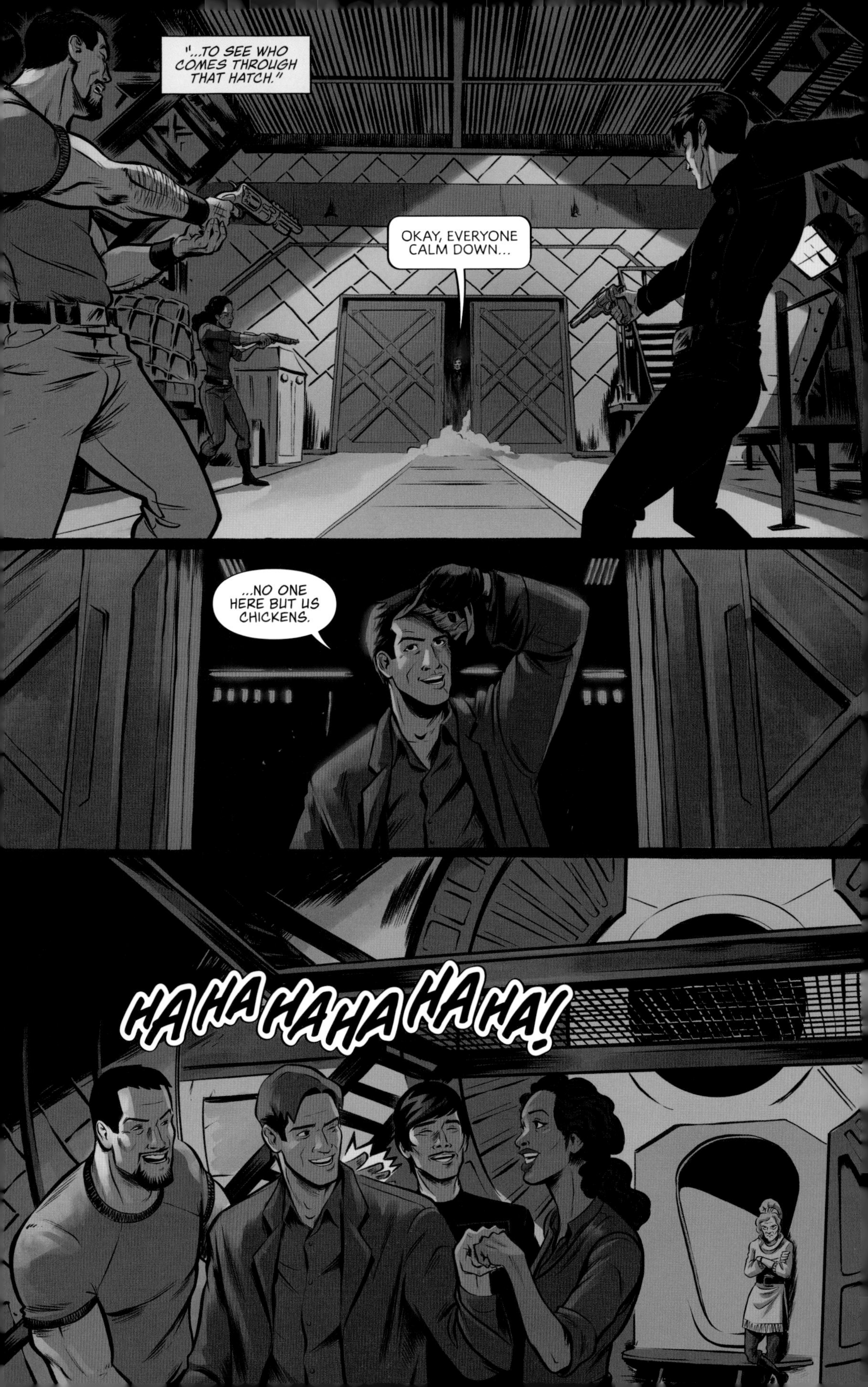
"...TO SEE WHO COMES THROUGH THAT HATCH."
OKAY, EVERYONE CALM DOWN...
...NO ONE HERE BUT US CHICKENS.
HA HA HA HA HA HA!

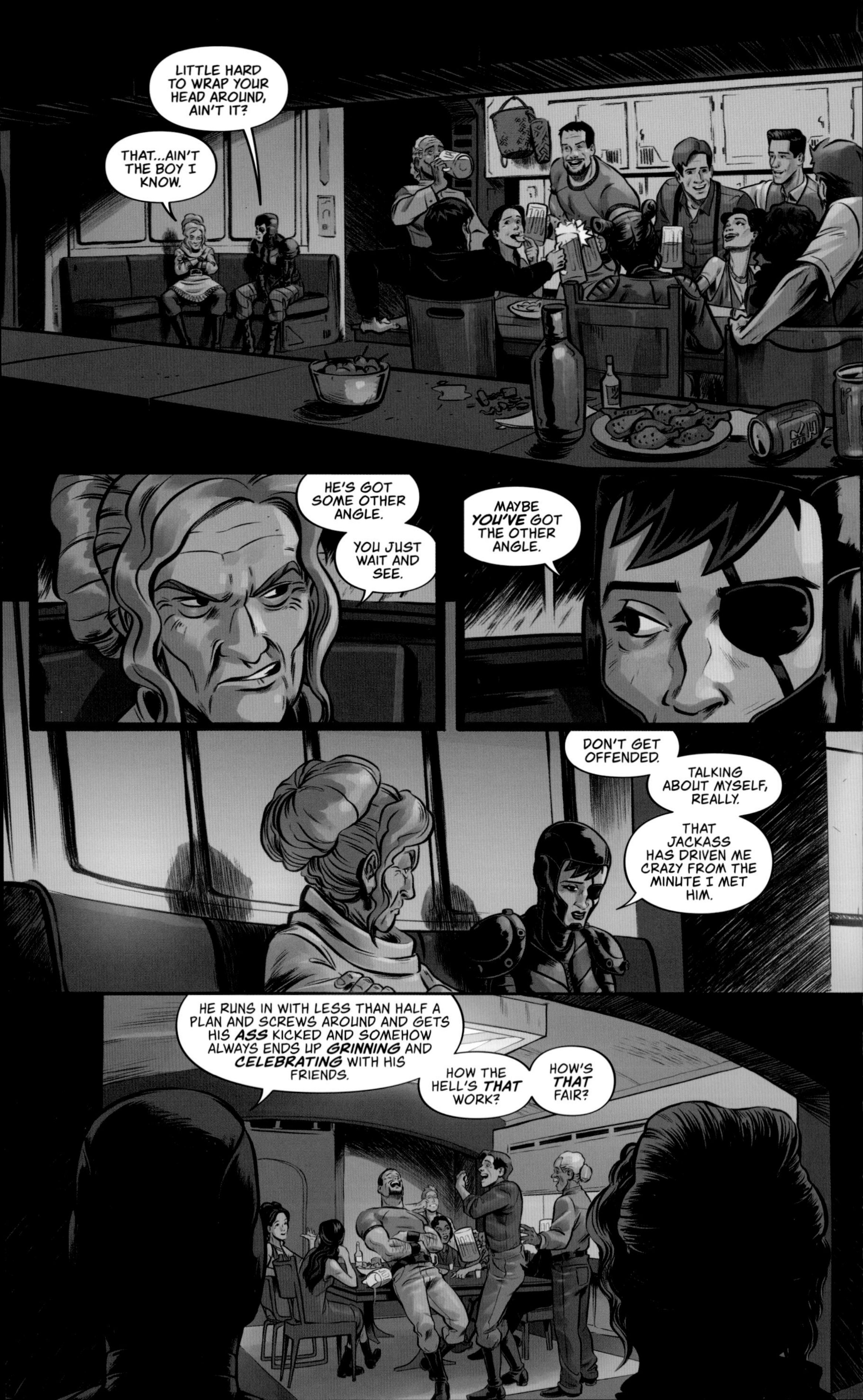

LITTLE HARD TO WRAP YOUR HEAD AROUND, AIN'T IT?
THAT...AIN'T THE BOY I KNOW.
HE'S GOT SOME OTHER ANGLE.
YOU JUST WAIT AND SEE.
MAYBE *YOU'VE* GOT THE OTHER ANGLE.
DON'T GET OFFENDED.
TALKING ABOUT MYSELF, REALLY.
THAT JACKASS HAS DRIVEN ME CRAZY FROM THE MINUTE I MET HIM.
HE RUNS IN WITH LESS THAN HALF A PLAN AND SCREWS AROUND AND GETS HIS ***ASS*** KICKED AND SOMEHOW ALWAYS ENDS UP ***GRINNING*** AND ***CELEBRATING*** WITH HIS FRIENDS.
HOW THE HELL'S ***THAT*** WORK?
HOW'S ***THAT*** FAIR?

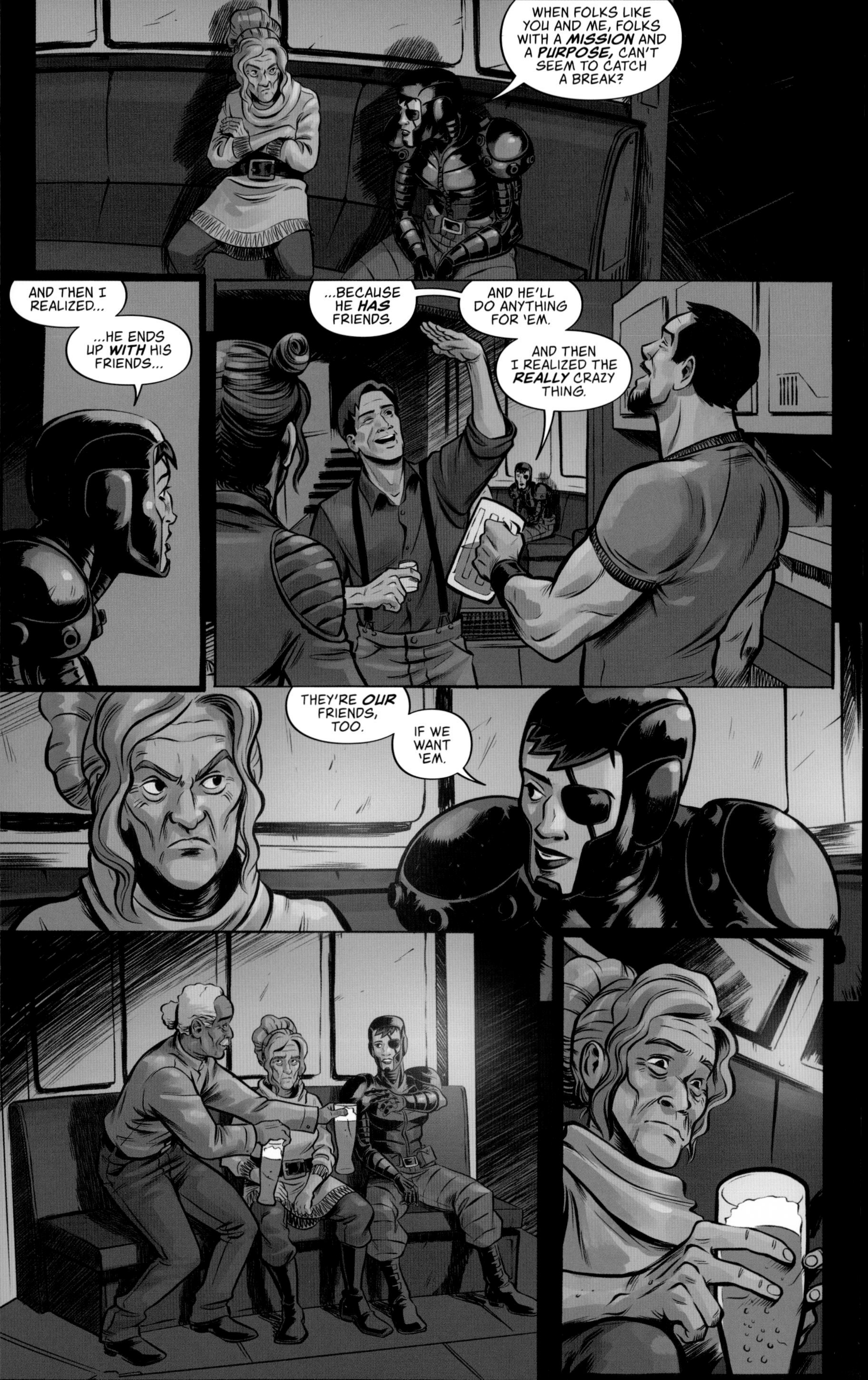
WHEN FOLKS LIKE YOU AND ME, FOLKS WITH A MISSION AND A PURPOSE, CAN'T SEEM TO CATCH A BREAK?
AND THEN I REALIZED...
...HE ENDS UP WITH HIS FRIENDS...
...BECAUSE HE HAS FRIENDS.
AND HE'LL DO ANYTHING FOR 'EM.
AND THEN I REALIZED THE REALLY CRAZY THING.
THEY'RE OUR FRIENDS, TOO.
IF WE WANT 'EM.

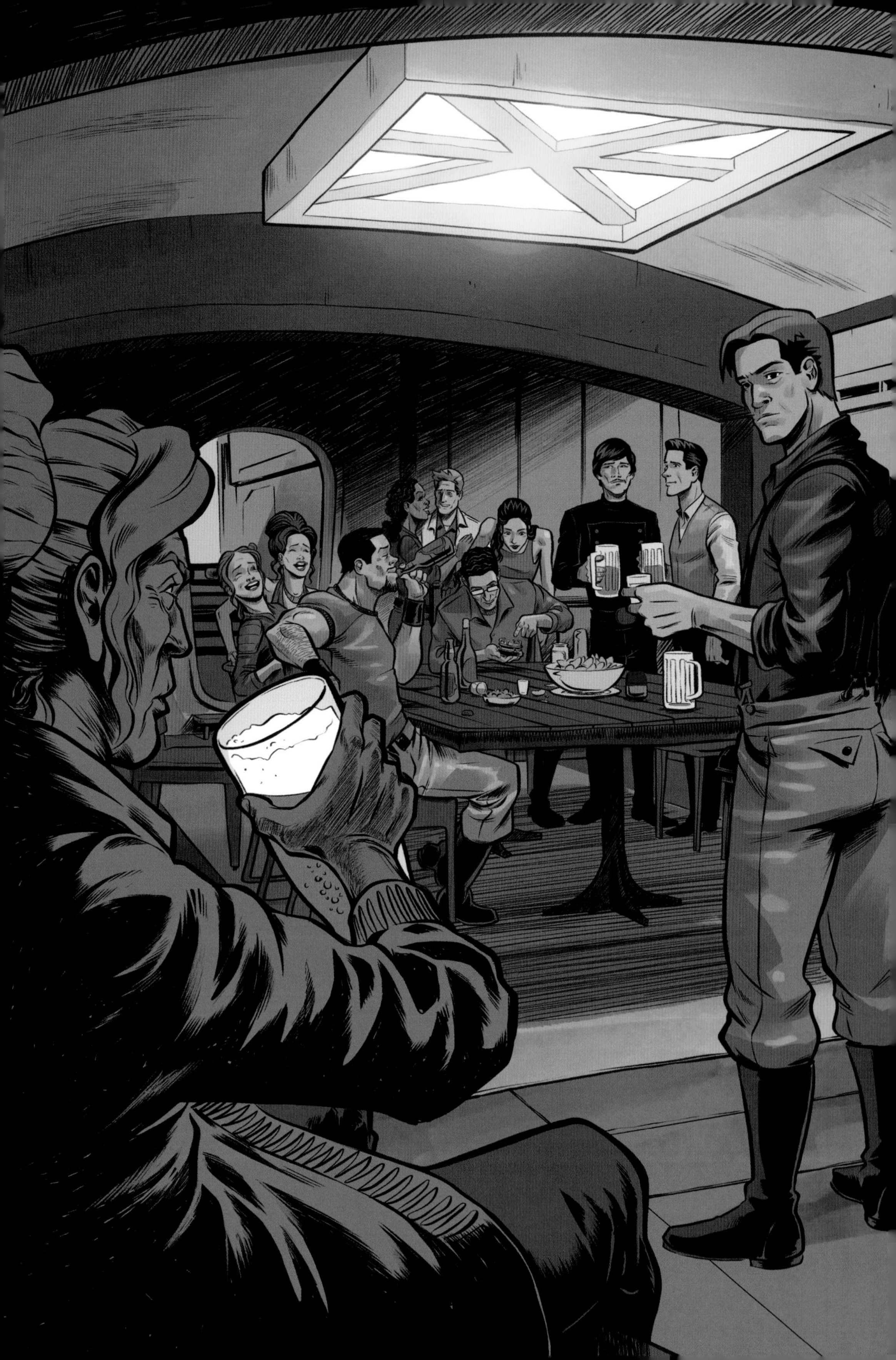

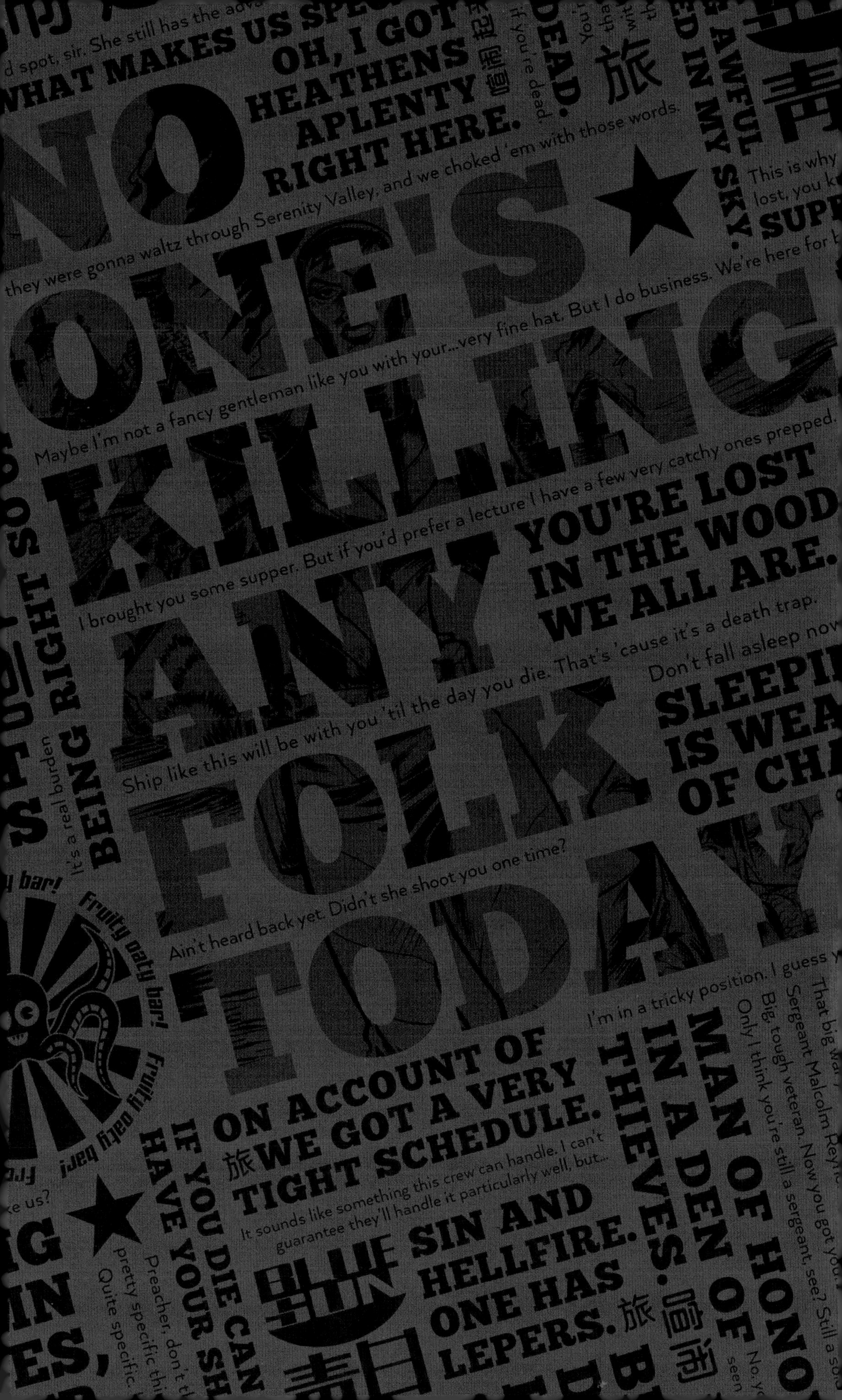
NO ONE'S KILLING ANY FOLK TODAY
WHAT MAKES US SPEC
OH, I GOT HEATHENS APLENTY RIGHT HERE.
DEAD.
If you're dead.
AWFUL
ED IN MY SKY.
This is why
lost, you k
SUPP
d spot, sir. She still has the adv
they were gonna waltz through Serenity Valley, and we choked 'em with those words.
We're here for
Maybe I'm not a fancy gentleman like you with your...very fine hat. But I do business.
I brought you some supper. But if you'd prefer a lecture I have a few very catchy ones prepped.
YOU'RE LOST IN THE WOOD WE ALL ARE.
Ship like this will be with you 'til the day you die. That's 'cause it's a death trap.
Don't fall asleep nov
SLEEPI IS WEA OF CHA
Ain't heard back yet. Didn't she shoot you one time?
I'm in a tricky position. I guess y
It's a real burden
BEING RIGHT SO OFTEN
Fruity oaty bar!
ON ACCOUNT OF WE GOT A VERY TIGHT SCHEDULE.
It sounds like something this crew can handle. I can't guarantee they'll handle it particularly well, but...
IF YOU DIE CAN HAVE YOUR SH
Preacher, don't
pretty specific
Quite specific
BLUE SUN
SIN AND HELLFIRE. ONE HAS LEPERS.
THIEVES.
IN A DEN OF
MAN OF HONO
That big w
Sergeant Malcolm Rey
Big, tough veteran. Now you got you
Only I think you're still a sergeant, see? Still a s

CHAPTER FIVE

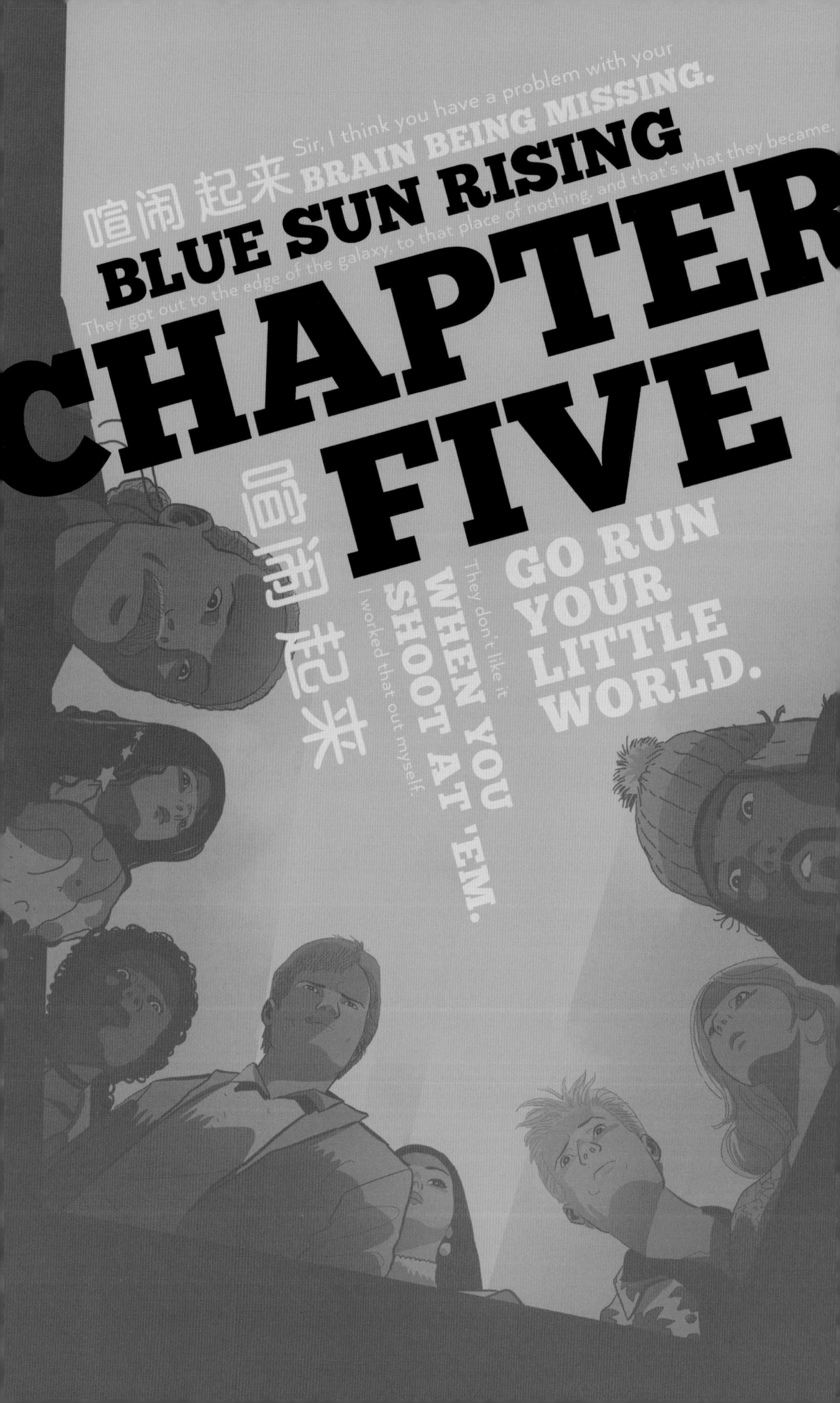

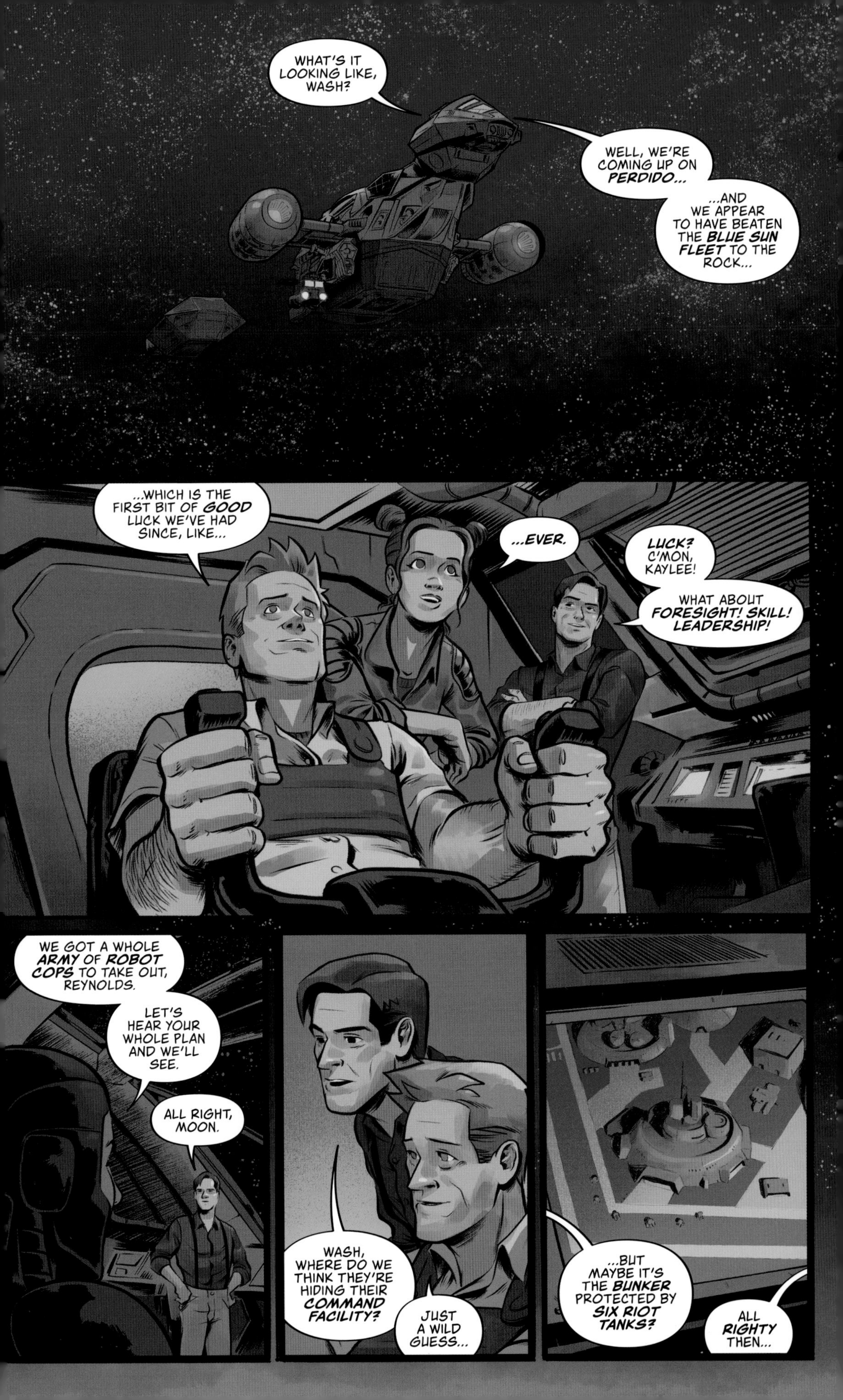

WHAT'S IT LOOKING LIKE, WASH?
WELL, WE'RE COMING UP ON PERDIDO...
...AND WE APPEAR TO HAVE BEATEN THE BLUE SUN FLEET TO THE ROCK...
...WHICH IS THE FIRST BIT OF GOOD LUCK WE'VE HAD SINCE, LIKE...
...EVER.
LUCK? C'MON, KAYLEE!
WHAT ABOUT FORESIGHT! SKILL! LEADERSHIP!
WE GOT A WHOLE ARMY OF ROBOT COPS TO TAKE OUT, REYNOLDS.
LET'S HEAR YOUR WHOLE PLAN AND WE'LL SEE.
ALL RIGHT, MOON.
WASH, WHERE DO WE THINK THEY'RE HIDING THEIR COMMAND FACILITY?
JUST A WILD GUESS...
...BUT MAYBE IT'S THE BUNKER PROTECTED BY SIX RIOT TANKS?
ALL RIGHTY THEN...

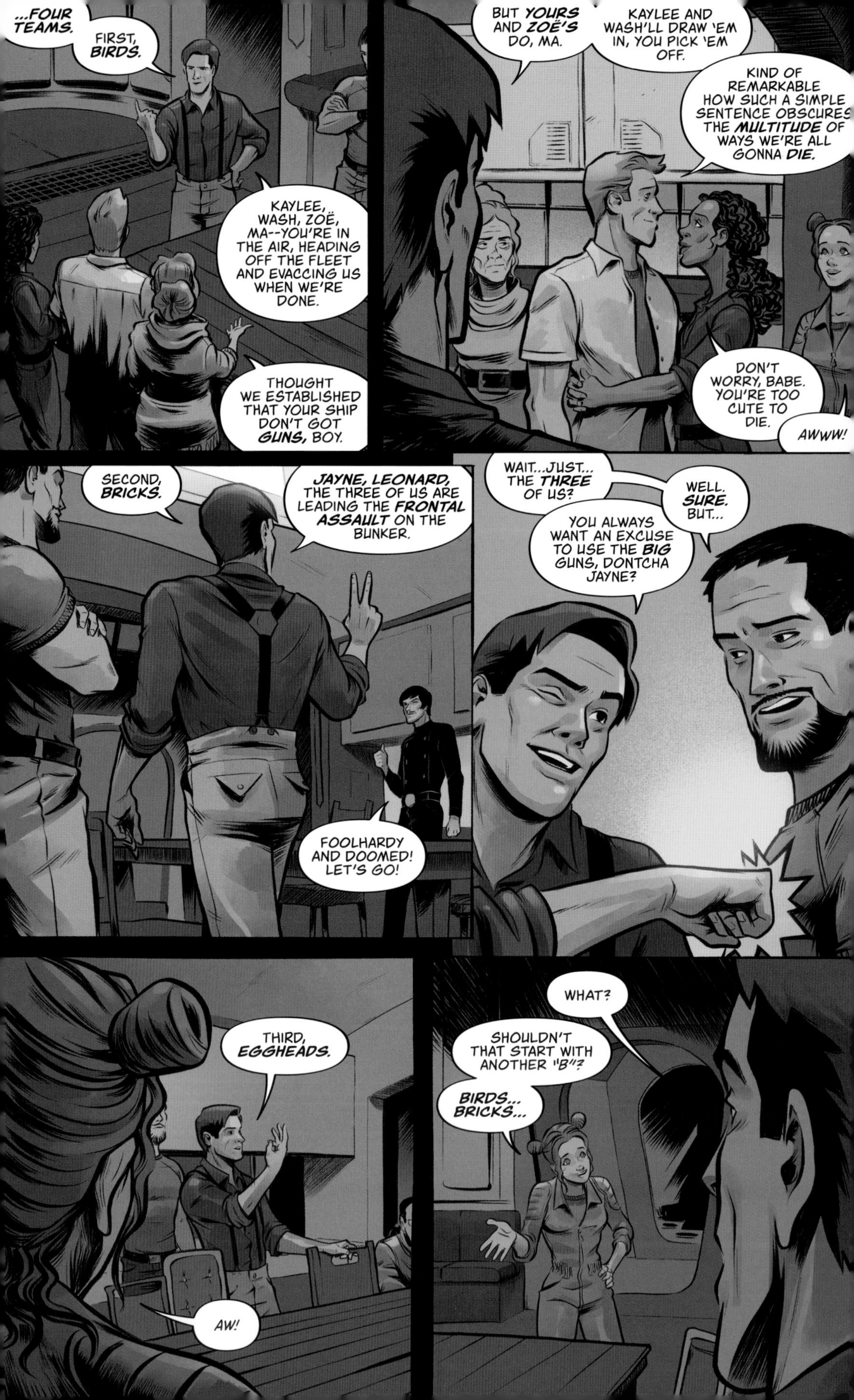

...FOUR TEAMS.
FIRST, BIRDS.
KAYLEE, WASH, ZOË, MA--YOU'RE IN THE AIR, HEADING OFF THE FLEET AND EVACCING US WHEN WE'RE DONE.
THOUGHT WE ESTABLISHED THAT YOUR SHIP DON'T GOT GUNS, BOY.
BUT YOURS AND ZOË'S DO, MA.
KAYLEE AND WASH'LL DRAW 'EM IN, YOU PICK 'EM OFF.
KIND OF REMARKABLE HOW SUCH A SIMPLE SENTENCE OBSCURES THE MULTITUDE OF WAYS WE'RE ALL GONNA DIE.
DON'T WORRY, BABE. YOU'RE TOO CUTE TO DIE.
AWWW!
SECOND, BRICKS.
JAYNE, LEONARD, THE THREE OF US ARE LEADING THE FRONTAL ASSAULT ON THE BUNKER.
FOOLHARDY AND DOOMED! LET'S GO!
WAIT...JUST... THE THREE OF US?
WELL. SURE. BUT...
YOU ALWAYS WANT AN EXCUSE TO USE THE BIG GUNS, DONTCHA JAYNE?
THIRD, EGGHEADS.
AW!
WHAT?
SHOULDN'T THAT START WITH ANOTHER "B"?
BIRDS... BRICKS...

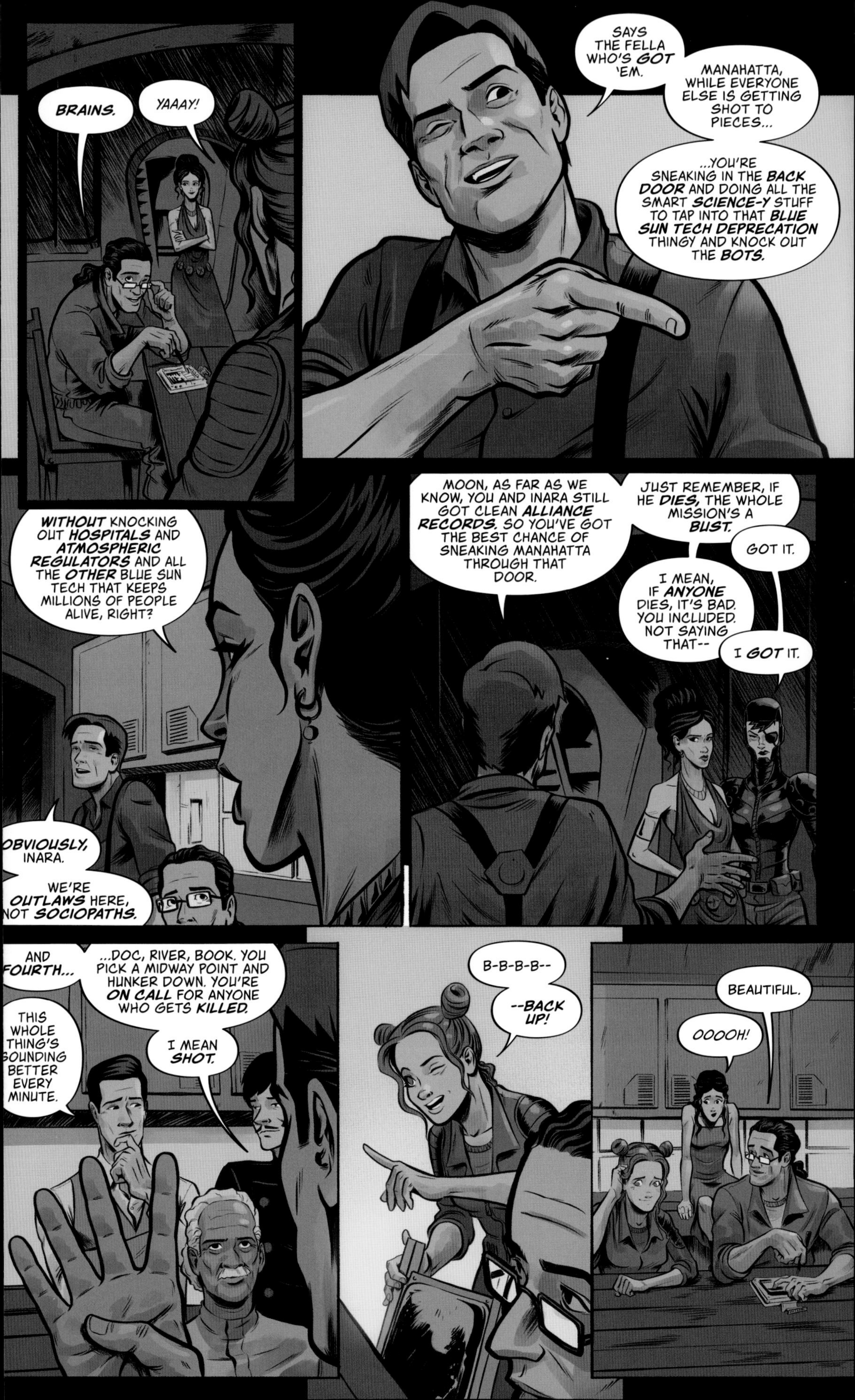
BRAINS.
YAAAY!
SAYS THE FELLA WHO'S GOT 'EM.
MANAHATTA, WHILE EVERYONE ELSE IS GETTING SHOT TO PIECES...
...YOU'RE SNEAKING IN THE BACK DOOR AND DOING ALL THE SMART SCIENCE-Y STUFF TO TAP INTO THAT BLUE SUN TECH DEPRECATION THINGY AND KNOCK OUT THE BOTS.
WITHOUT KNOCKING OUT HOSPITALS AND ATMOSPHERIC REGULATORS AND ALL THE OTHER BLUE SUN TECH THAT KEEPS MILLIONS OF PEOPLE ALIVE, RIGHT?
OBVIOUSLY, INARA.
WE'RE OUTLAWS HERE, NOT SOCIOPATHS.
MOON, AS FAR AS WE KNOW, YOU AND INARA STILL GOT CLEAN ALLIANCE RECORDS. SO YOU'VE GOT THE BEST CHANCE OF SNEAKING MANAHATTA THROUGH THAT DOOR.
JUST REMEMBER, IF HE DIES, THE WHOLE MISSION'S A BUST.
GOT IT.
I MEAN, IF ANYONE DIES, IT'S BAD. YOU INCLUDED. NOT SAYING THAT--
I GOT IT.
AND FOURTH...
...DOC, RIVER, BOOK. YOU PICK A MIDWAY POINT AND HUNKER DOWN. YOU'RE ON CALL FOR ANYONE WHO GETS KILLED.
THIS WHOLE THING'S SOUNDING BETTER EVERY MINUTE.
I MEAN SHOT.
B-B-B-B--
--BACK UP!
BEAUTIFUL.
OOOOH!

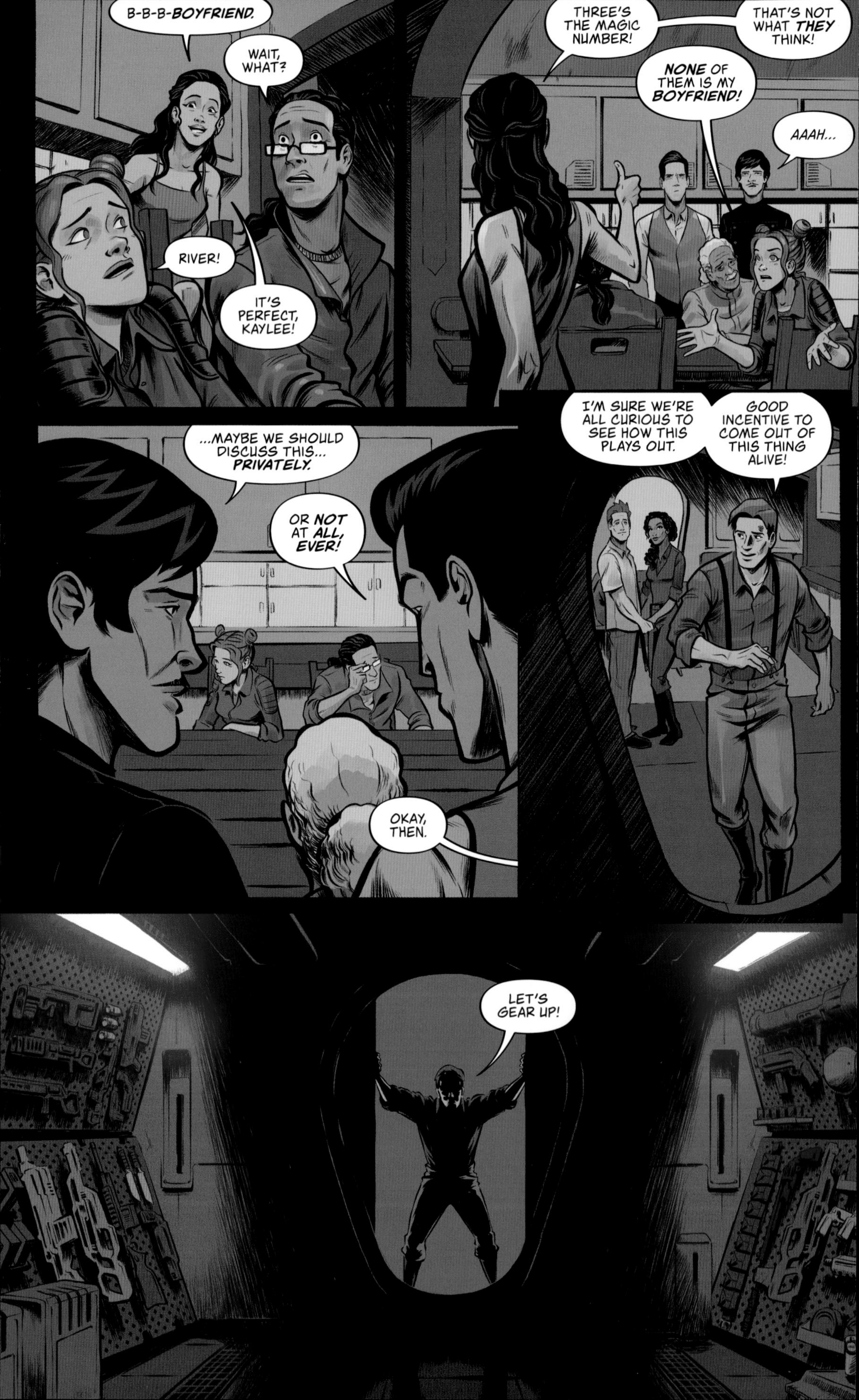
B-B-B-BOYFRIEND.
WAIT, WHAT?
RIVER!
IT'S PERFECT, KAYLEE!
THREE'S THE MAGIC NUMBER!
THAT'S NOT WHAT THEY THINK!
NONE OF THEM IS MY BOYFRIEND!
AAAH...
...MAYBE WE SHOULD DISCUSS THIS... PRIVATELY.
OR NOT AT ALL, EVER!
OKAY, THEN.
I'M SURE WE'RE ALL CURIOUS TO SEE HOW THIS PLAYS OUT.
GOOD INCENTIVE TO COME OUT OF THIS THING ALIVE!
LET'S GEAR UP!

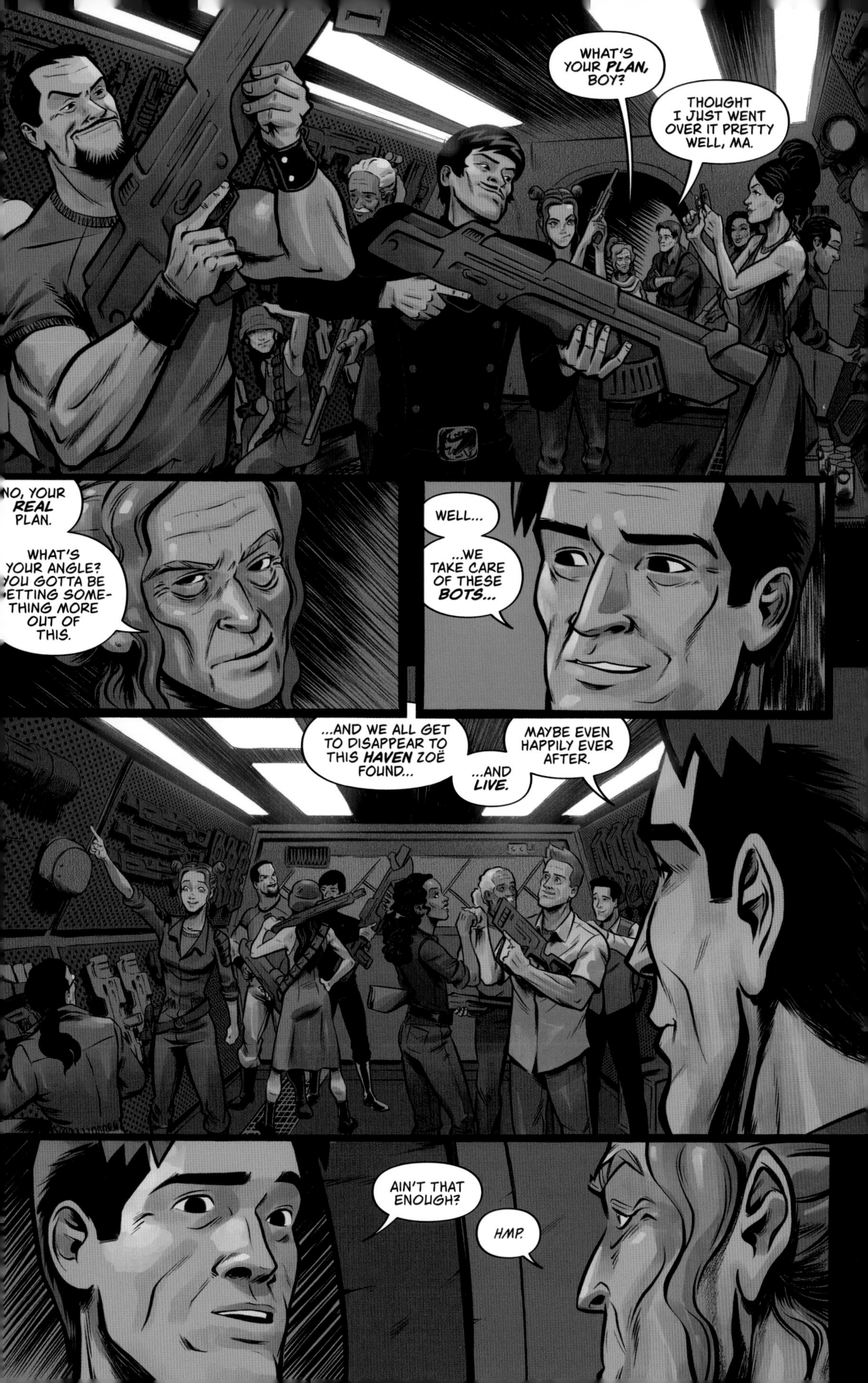
WHAT'S YOUR **PLAN,** BOY?
THOUGHT I JUST WENT OVER IT PRETTY WELL, MA.
NO, YOUR **REAL** PLAN.
WHAT'S YOUR ANGLE? YOU GOTTA BE GETTING SOMETHING MORE OUT OF THIS.
WELL...
...WE TAKE CARE OF THESE **BOTS...**
...AND WE ALL GET TO DISAPPEAR TO THIS **HAVEN** ZOË FOUND...
...AND **LIVE.**
MAYBE EVEN HAPPILY EVER AFTER.
AIN'T THAT ENOUGH?
HMP.

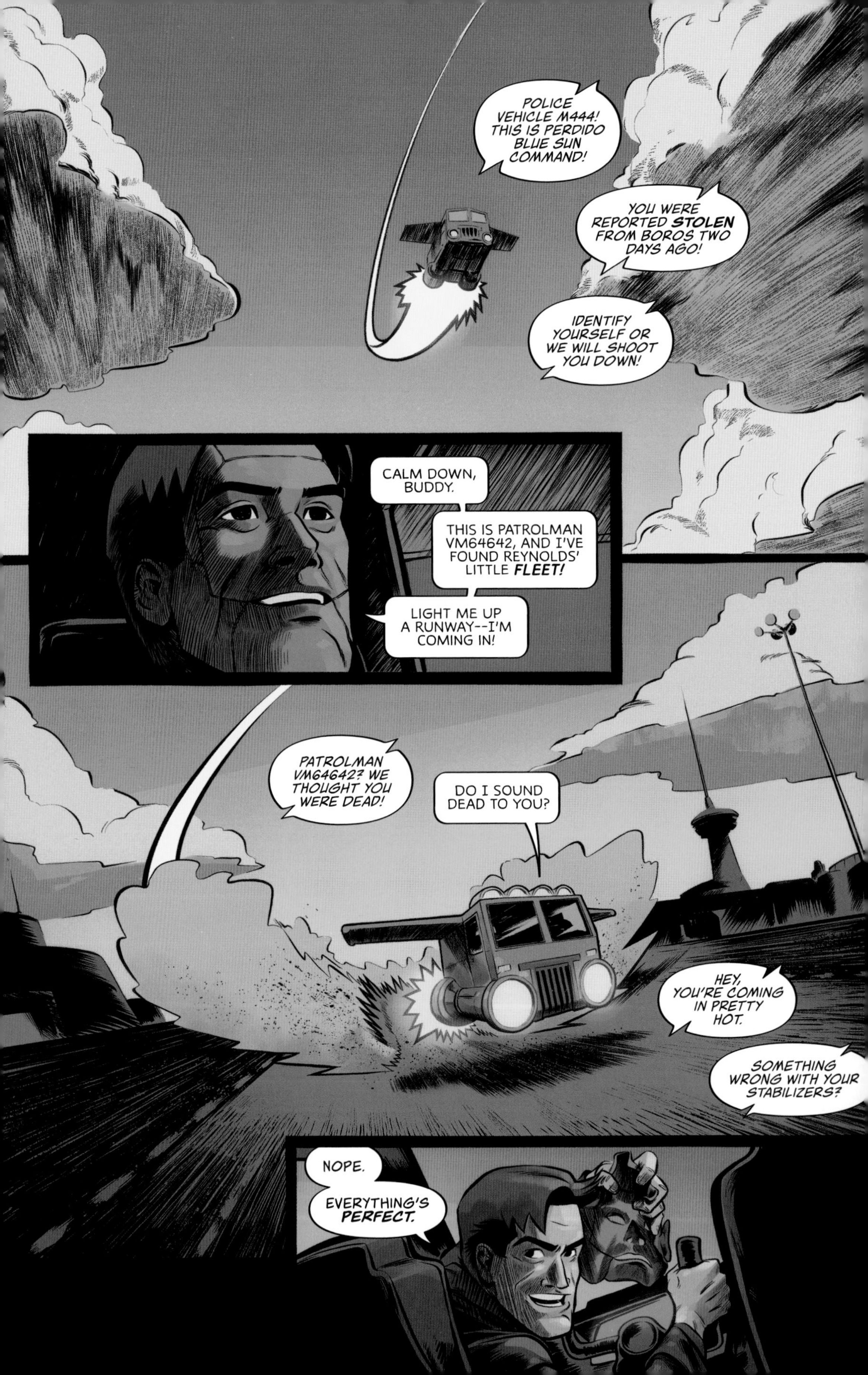
POLICE VEHICLE M444! THIS IS PERDIDO BLUE SUN COMMAND!
YOU WERE REPORTED **STOLEN** FROM BOROS TWO DAYS AGO!
IDENTIFY YOURSELF OR WE WILL SHOOT YOU DOWN!
CALM DOWN, BUDDY.
THIS IS PATROLMAN VM64642, AND I'VE FOUND REYNOLDS' LITTLE ***FLEET!***
LIGHT ME UP A RUNWAY--I'M COMING IN!
PATROLMAN VM64642? WE THOUGHT YOU WERE DEAD!
DO I SOUND DEAD TO YOU?
HEY, YOU'RE COMING IN PRETTY HOT.
SOMETHING WRONG WITH YOUR STABILIZERS?
NOPE.
EVERYTHING'S ***PERFECT.***

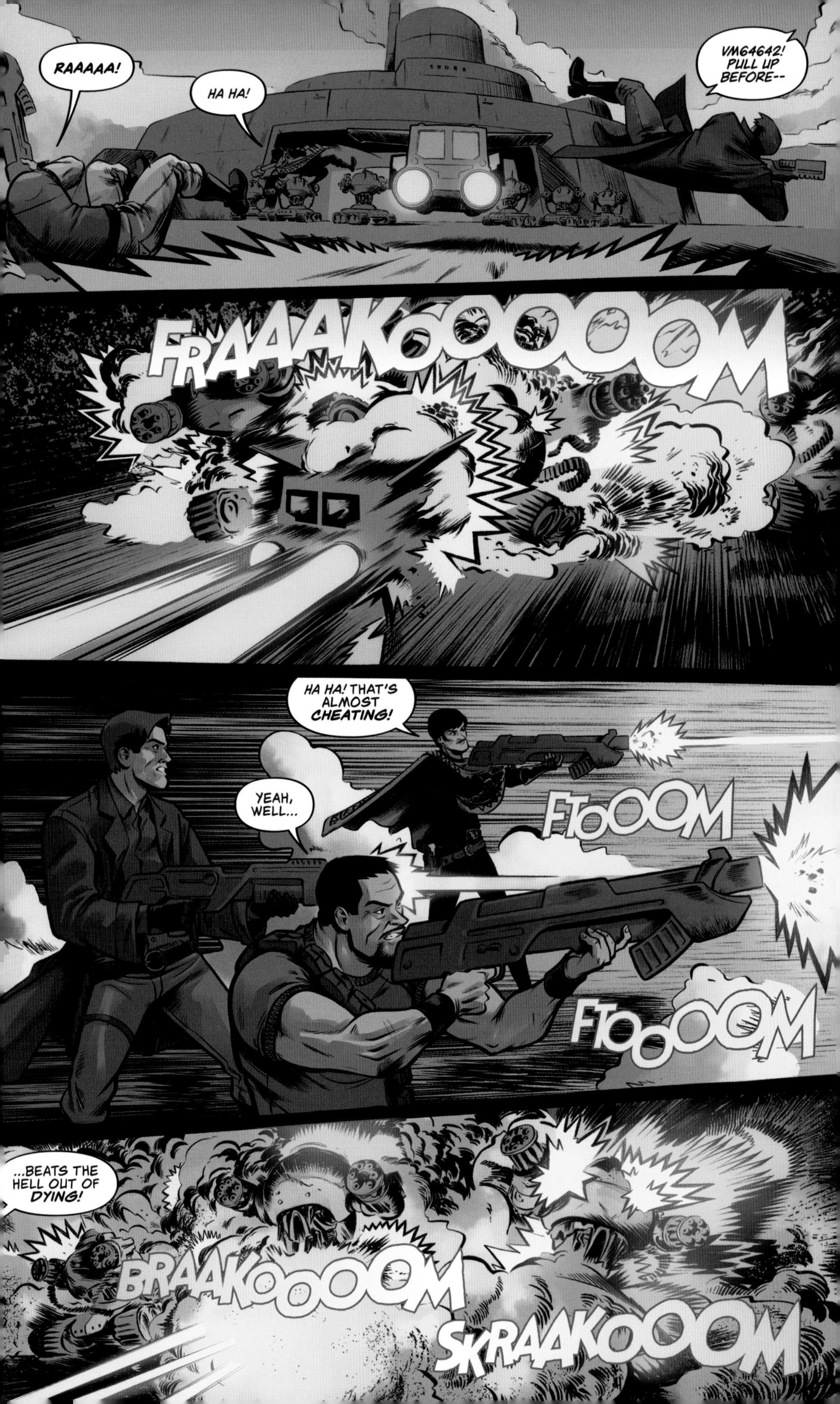
RAAAAA!
HA HA!
VM64642! PULL UP BEFORE--
FRAAAKOOOOOOM
HA HA! THAT'S ALMOST CHEATING!
YEAH, WELL...
FTOOOM
FTOOOOM
...BEATS THE HELL OUT OF DYING!
BRAAKOOOOOM
SKRAAKOOOM

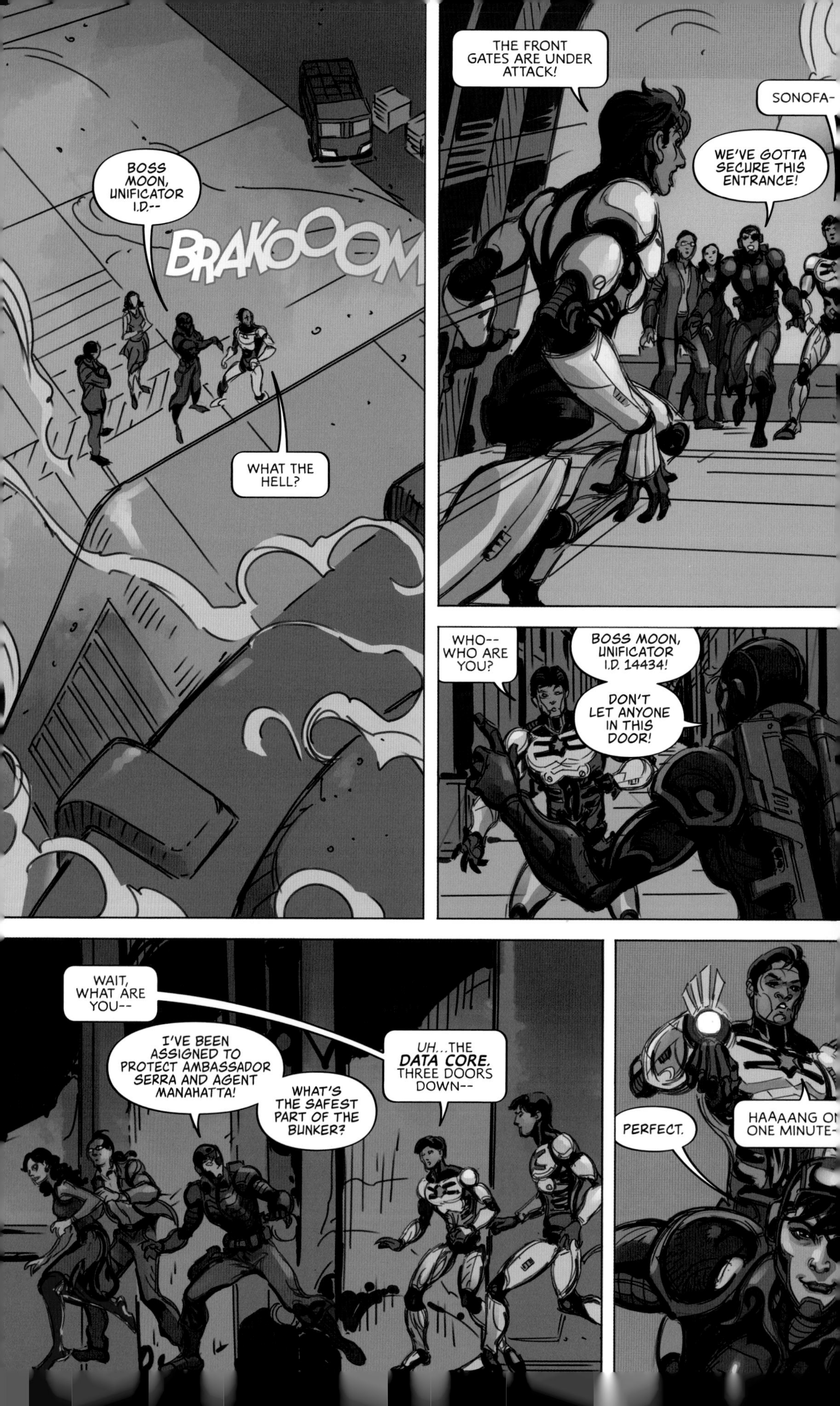
BOSS MOON, UNIFICATOR I.D.--
BRAKOOOM
WHAT THE HELL?
THE FRONT GATES ARE UNDER ATTACK!
SONOFA-
WE'VE GOTTA SECURE THIS ENTRANCE!
WHO-- WHO ARE YOU?
BOSS MOON, UNIFICATOR I.D. 14434!
DON'T LET ANYONE IN THIS DOOR!
WAIT, WHAT ARE YOU--
I'VE BEEN ASSIGNED TO PROTECT AMBASSADOR SERRA AND AGENT MANAHATTA!
WHAT'S THE SAFEST PART OF THE BUNKER?
UH...THE **DATA CORE.** THREE DOORS DOWN--
PERFECT.
HAAAANG O
ONE MINUTE-

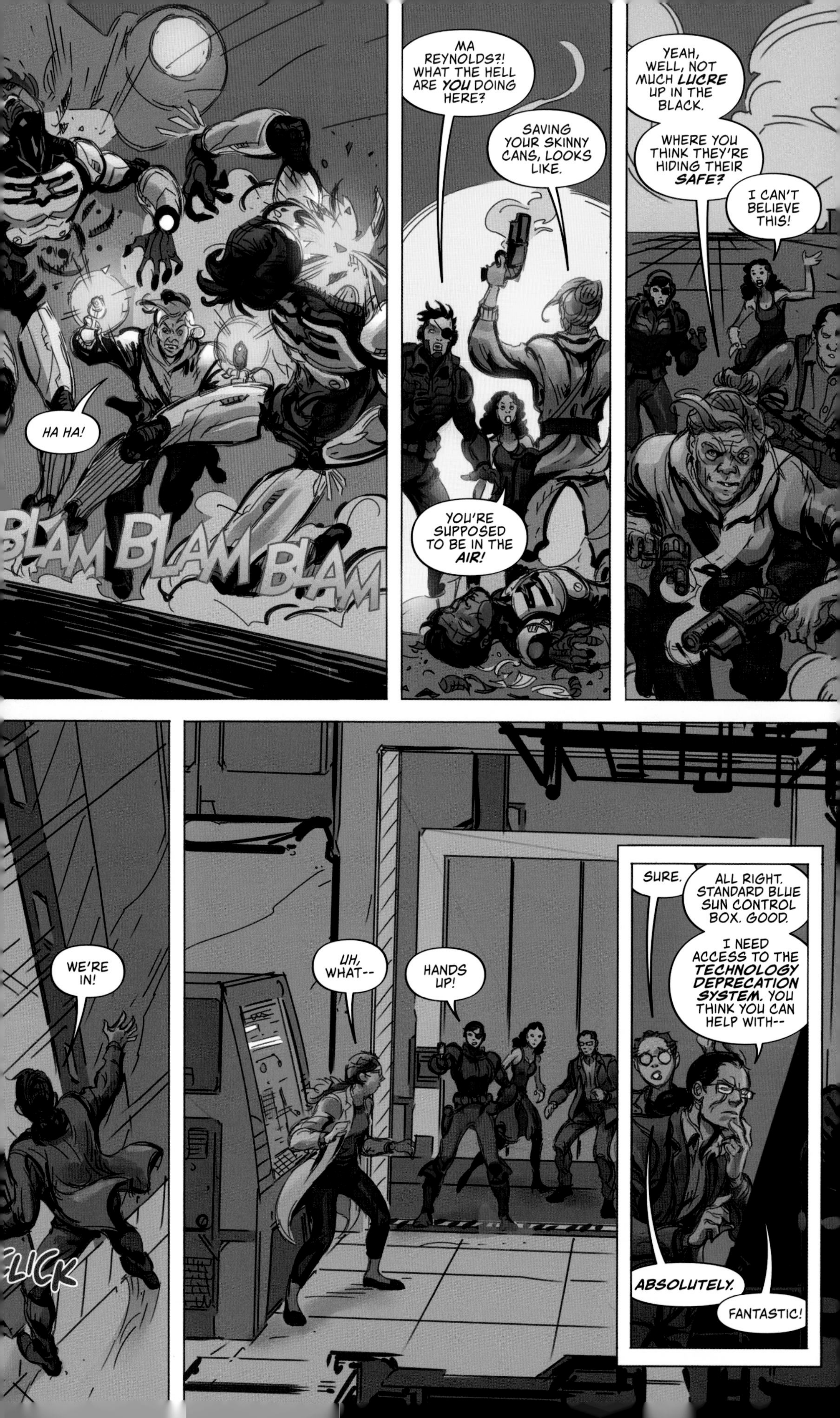
HA HA!
BLAM BLAM BLAM
MA REYNOLDS?! WHAT THE HELL ARE YOU DOING HERE?
SAVING YOUR SKINNY CANS, LOOKS LIKE.
YOU'RE SUPPOSED TO BE IN THE AIR!
YEAH, WELL, NOT MUCH LUCRE UP IN THE BLACK.
WHERE YOU THINK THEY'RE HIDING THEIR SAFE?
I CAN'T BELIEVE THIS!
WE'RE IN!
CLICK
UH, WHAT--
HANDS UP!
SURE.
ALL RIGHT. STANDARD BLUE SUN CONTROL BOX. GOOD.
I NEED ACCESS TO THE TECHNOLOGY DEPRECATION SYSTEM. YOU THINK YOU CAN HELP WITH--
ABSOLUTELY.
FANTASTIC!

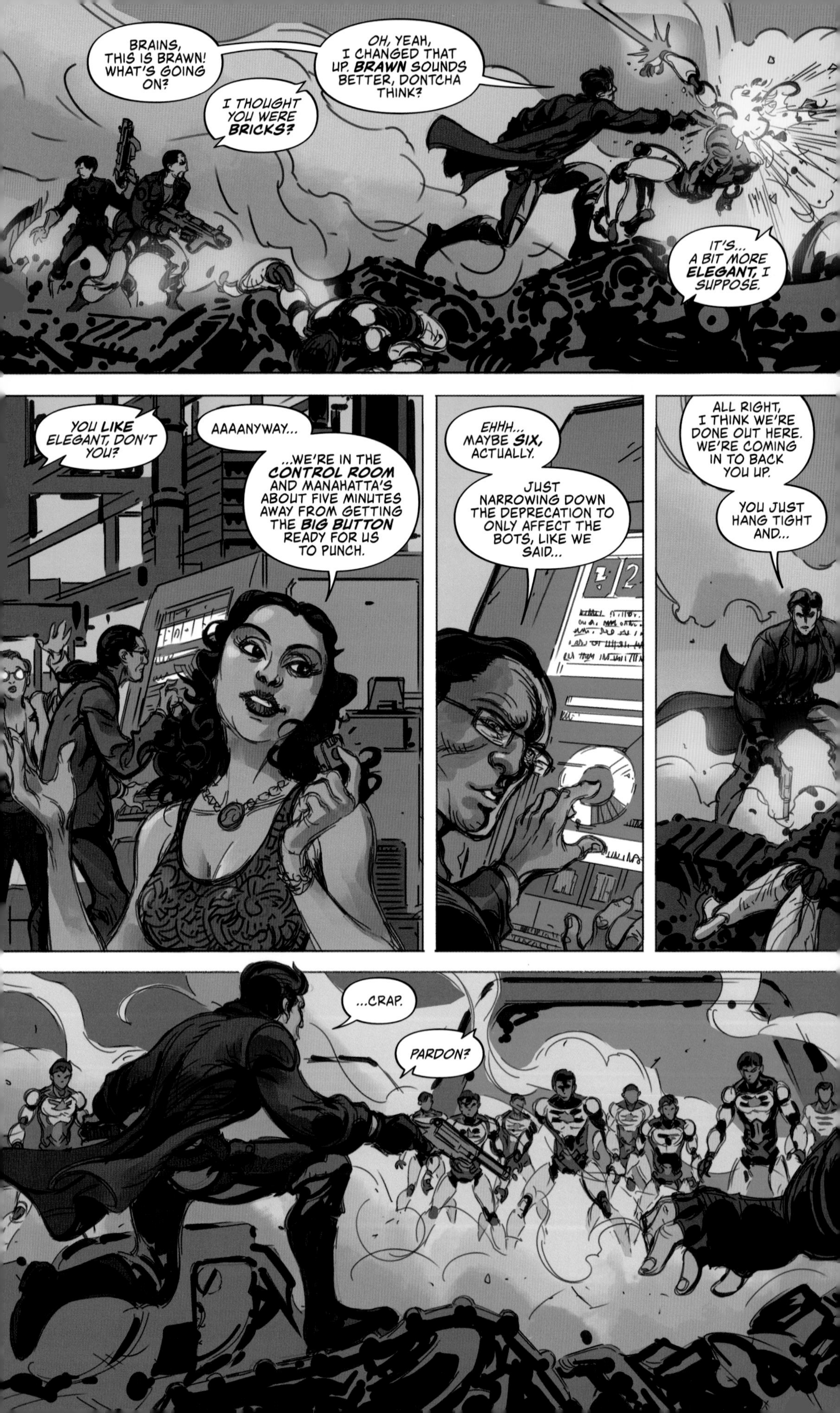
BRAINS, THIS IS BRAWN! WHAT'S GOING ON?
I THOUGHT YOU WERE BRICKS?
OH, YEAH, I CHANGED THAT UP. BRAWN SOUNDS BETTER, DONTCHA THINK?
IT'S... A BIT MORE ELEGANT, I SUPPOSE.
YOU LIKE ELEGANT, DON'T YOU?
AAAANYWAY...
...WE'RE IN THE CONTROL ROOM AND MANAHATTA'S ABOUT FIVE MINUTES AWAY FROM GETTING THE BIG BUTTON READY FOR US TO PUNCH.
EHHH... MAYBE SIX, ACTUALLY.
JUST NARROWING DOWN THE DEPRECATION TO ONLY AFFECT THE BOTS, LIKE WE SAID...
ALL RIGHT, I THINK WE'RE DONE OUT HERE. WE'RE COMING IN TO BACK YOU UP.
YOU JUST HANG TIGHT AND...
...CRAP.
PARDON?

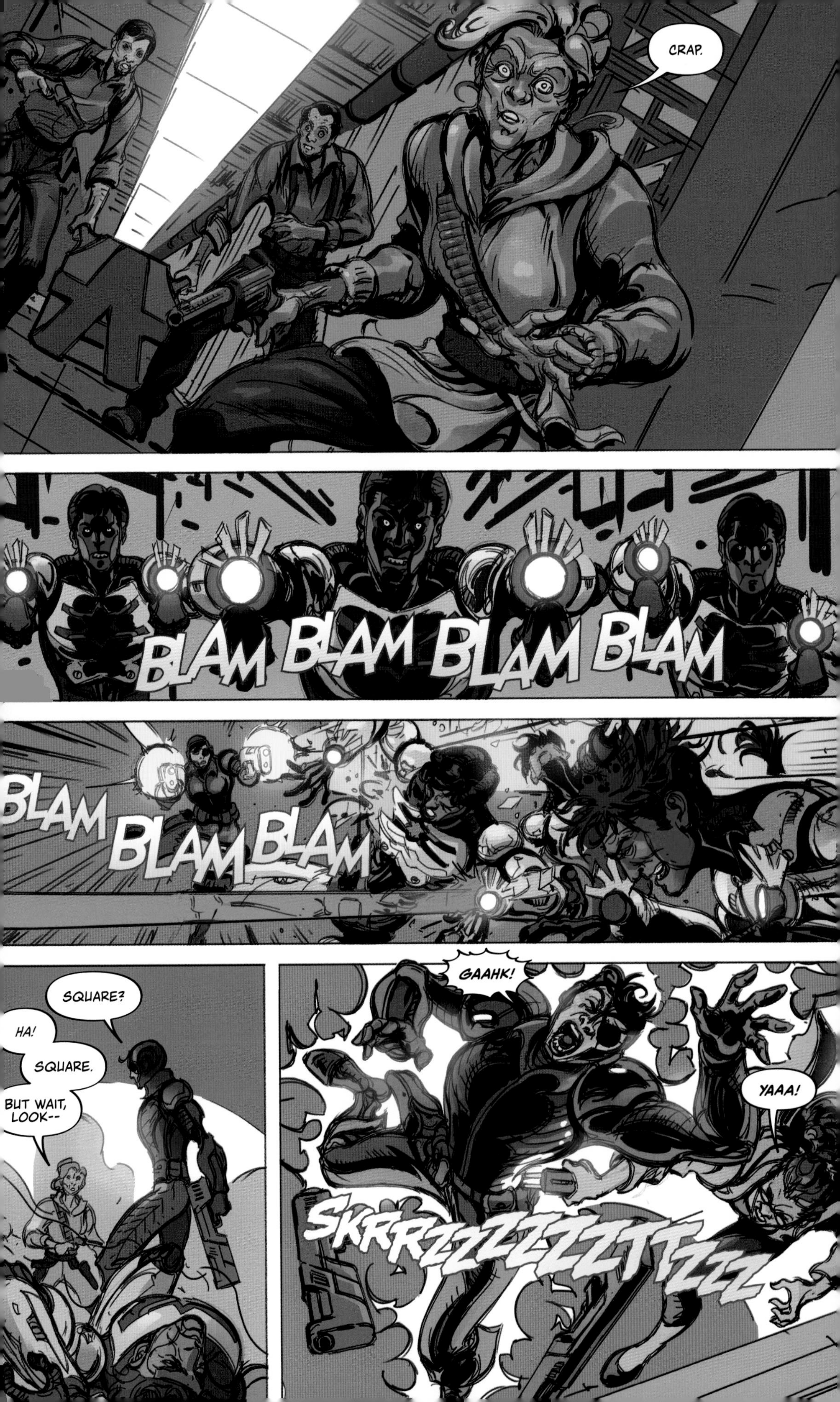
CRAP.
BLAM BLAM BLAM BLAM
BLAM
BLAM BLAM
SQUARE?
HA!
SQUARE.
BUT WAIT, LOOK--
GAAHK!
YAAA!
SKRRZZZZZZZTTZZZ

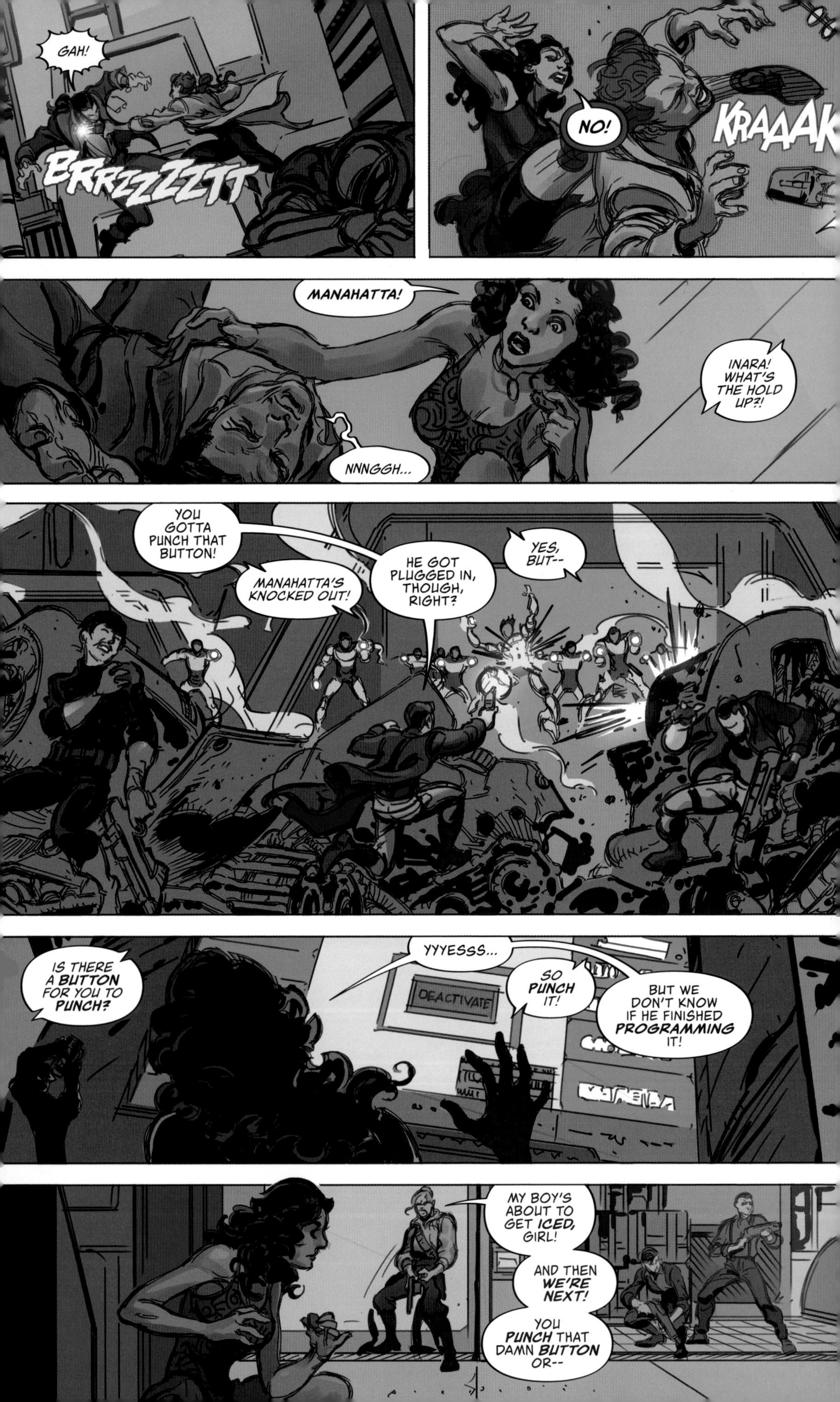
GAH!
BRRZZZZZTT
NO!
KRAAAK
MANAHATTA!
NNNGGH...
INARA! WHAT'S THE HOLD UP?!
YOU GOTTA PUNCH THAT BUTTON!
MANAHATTA'S KNOCKED OUT!
HE GOT PLUGGED IN, THOUGH, RIGHT?
YES, BUT--
IS THERE A BUTTON FOR YOU TO PUNCH?
YYYESSS...
DEACTIVATE
SO PUNCH IT!
BUT WE DON'T KNOW IF HE FINISHED PROGRAMMING IT!
MY BOY'S ABOUT TO GET ICED, GIRL!
AND THEN WE'RE NEXT!
YOU PUNCH THAT DAMN BUTTON OR--

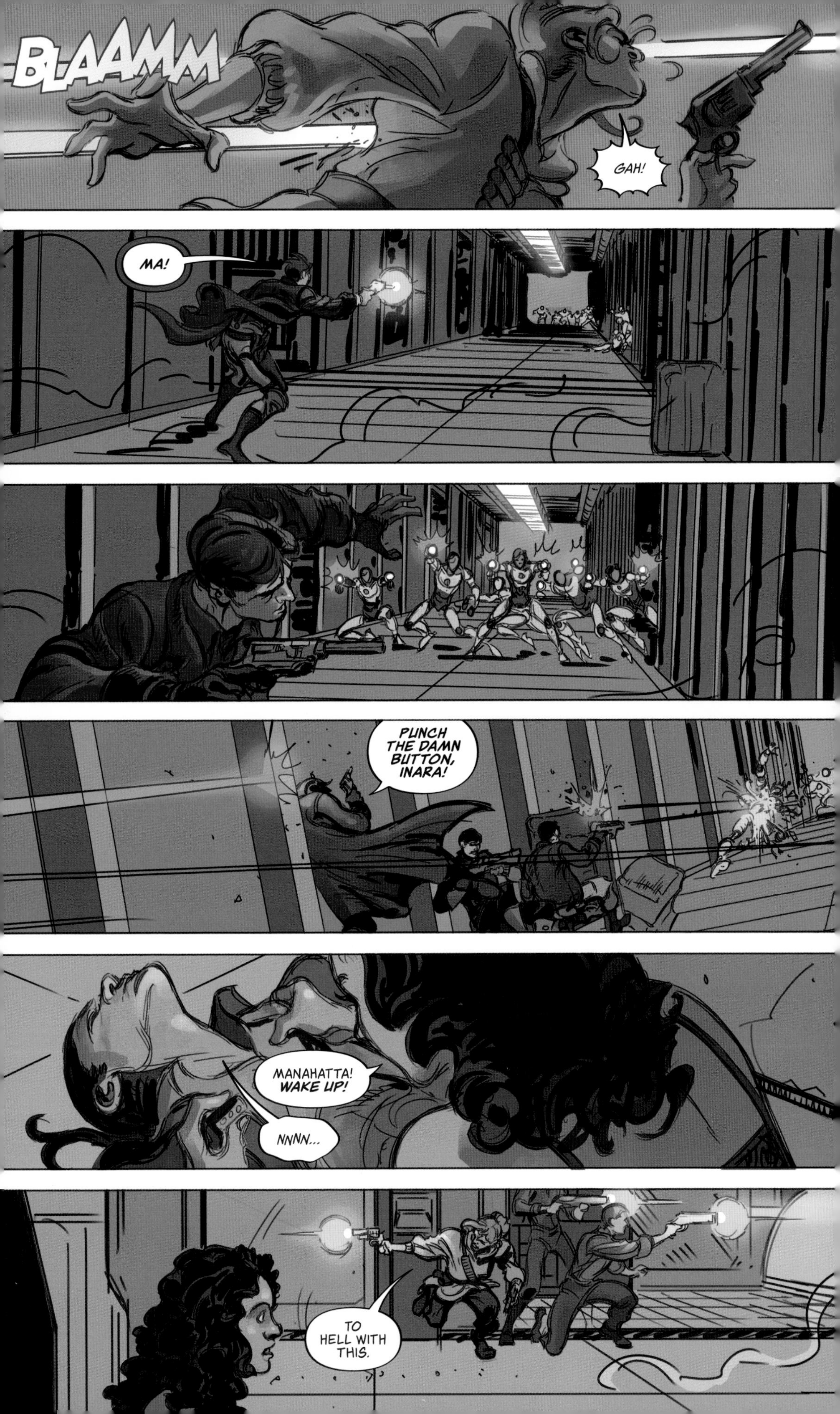
BLAAMM
GAH!
MA!
PUNCH THE DAMN BUTTON, INARA!
MANAHATTA! WAKE UP!
NNNN...
TO HELL WITH THIS.

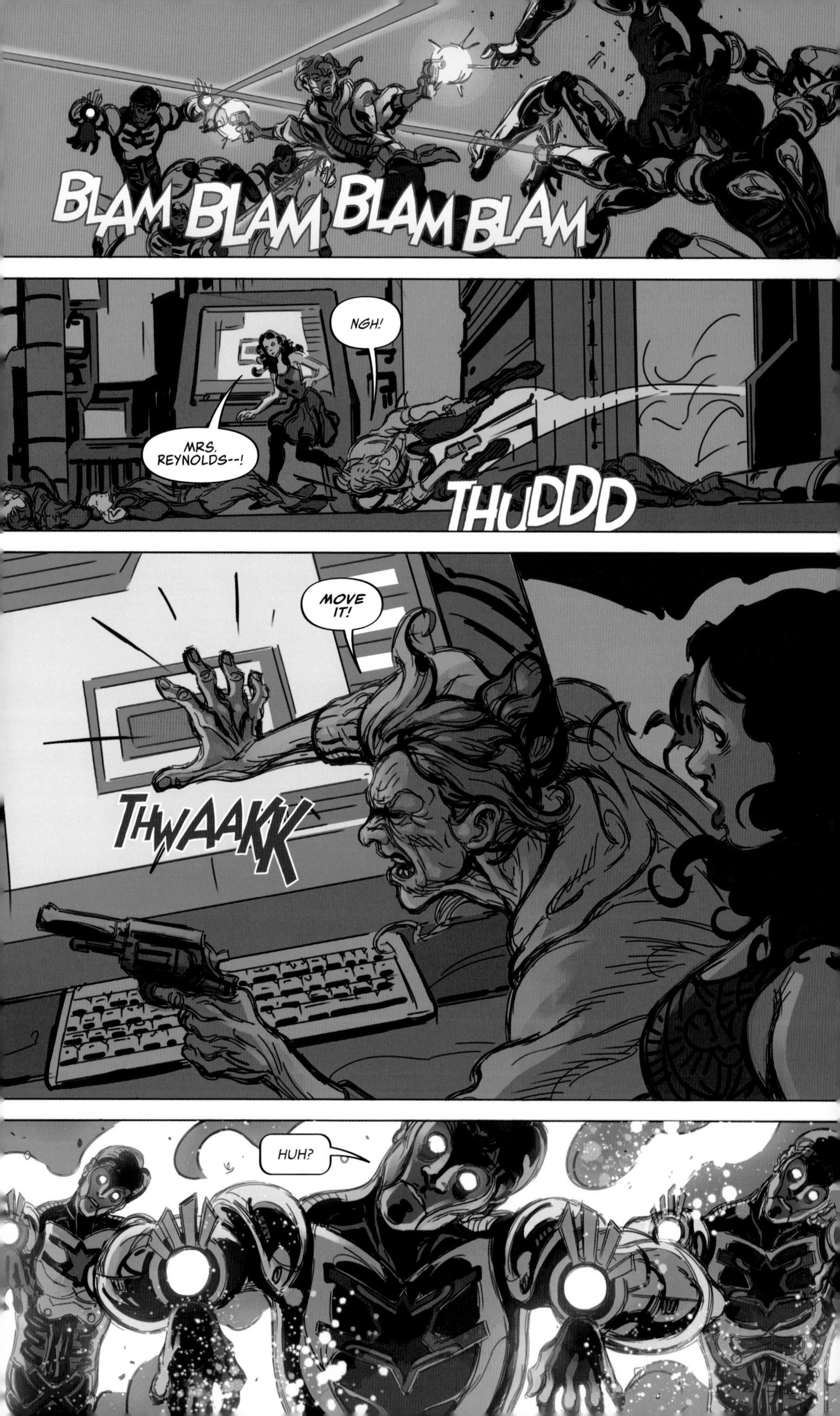
BLAM BLAM BLAM BLAM
NGH!
MRS. REYNOLDS--!
THUDDD
MOVE IT!
THWAAKK
HUH?

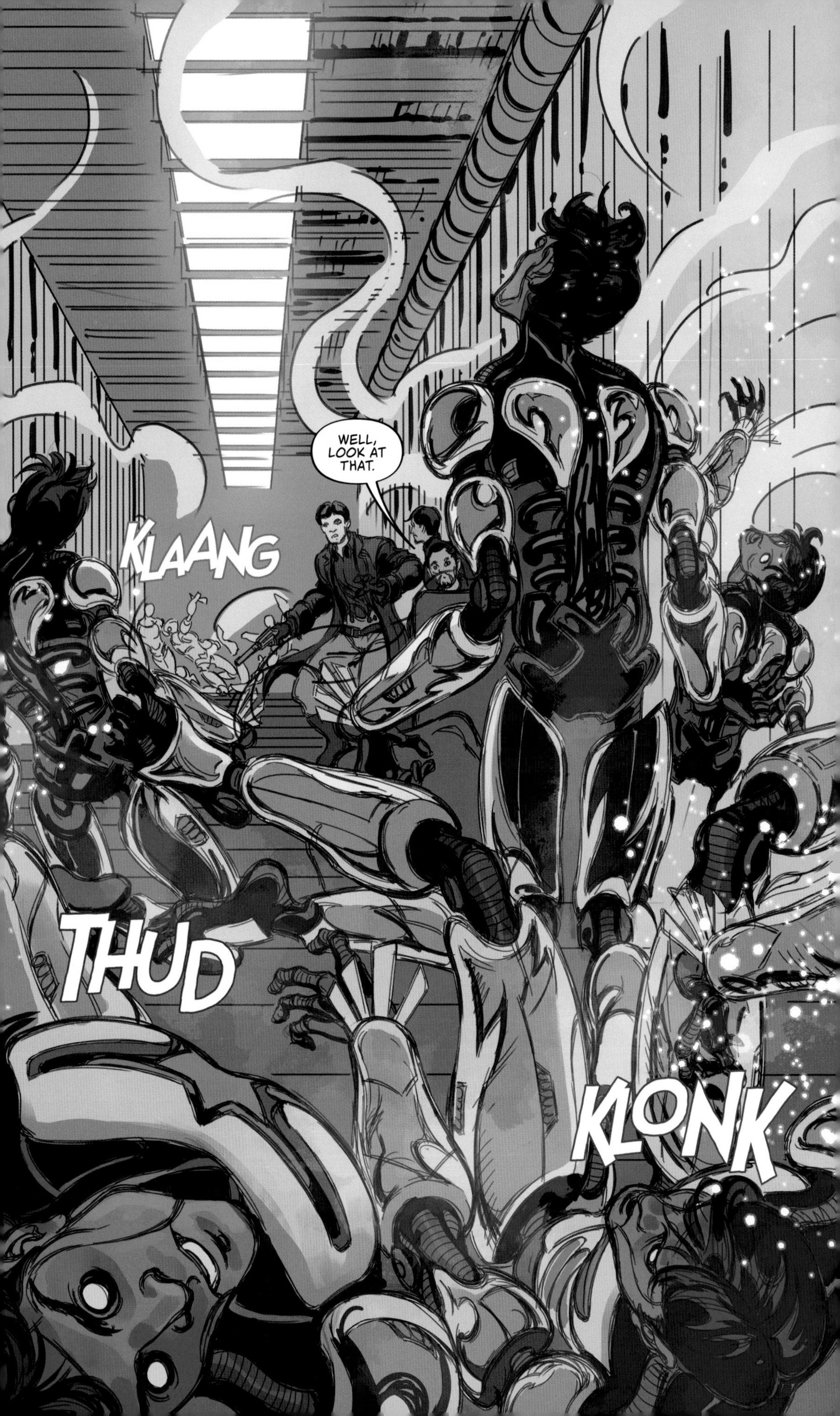
WELL, LOOK AT THAT.
KLAANG
THUD
KLONK

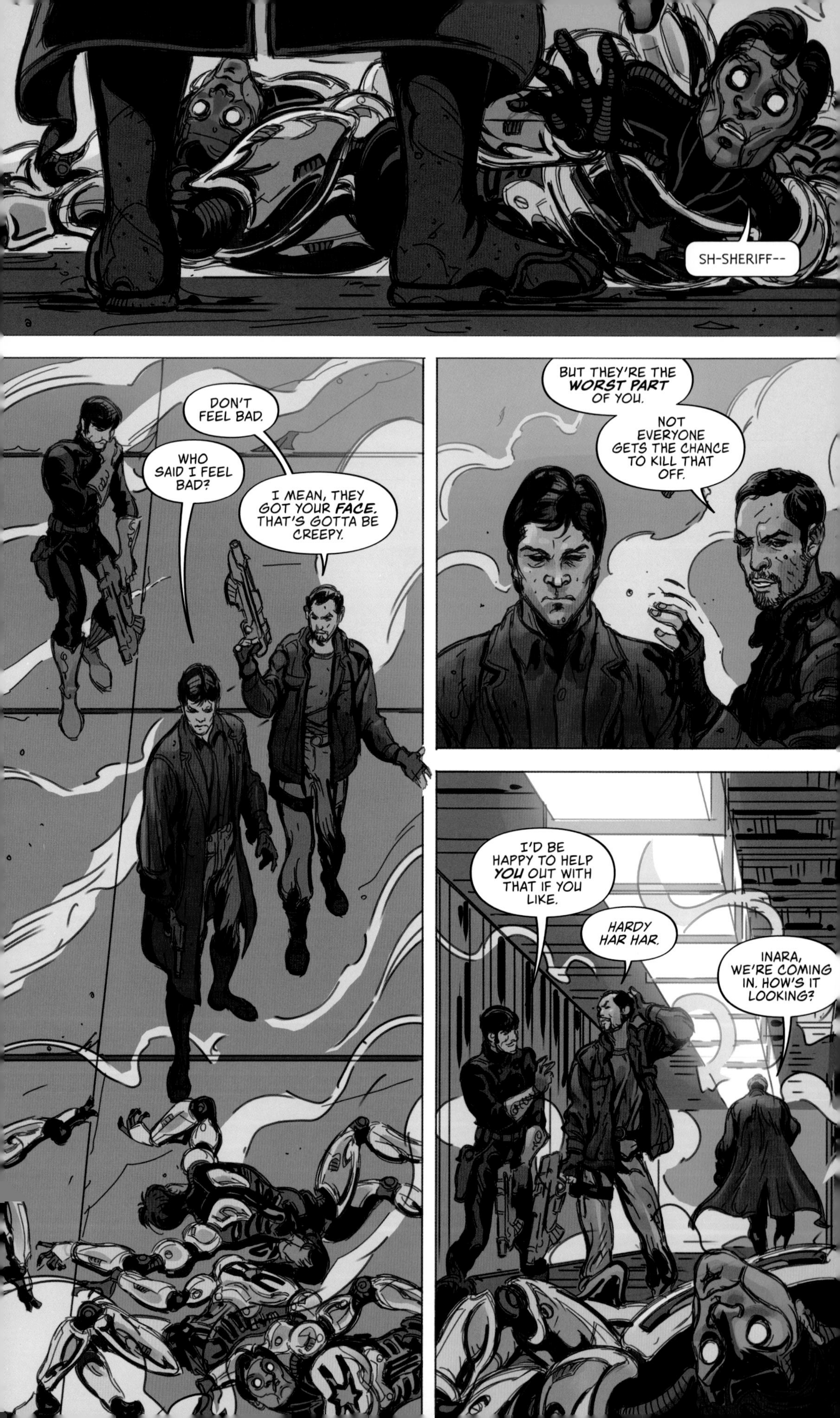
SH-SHERIFF--
DON'T FEEL BAD.
WHO SAID I FEEL BAD?
I MEAN, THEY GOT YOUR FACE. THAT'S GOTTA BE CREEPY.
BUT THEY'RE THE WORST PART OF YOU.
NOT EVERYONE GETS THE CHANCE TO KILL THAT OFF.
I'D BE HAPPY TO HELP YOU OUT WITH THAT IF YOU LIKE.
HARDY HAR HAR.
INARA, WE'RE COMING IN. HOW'S IT LOOKING?

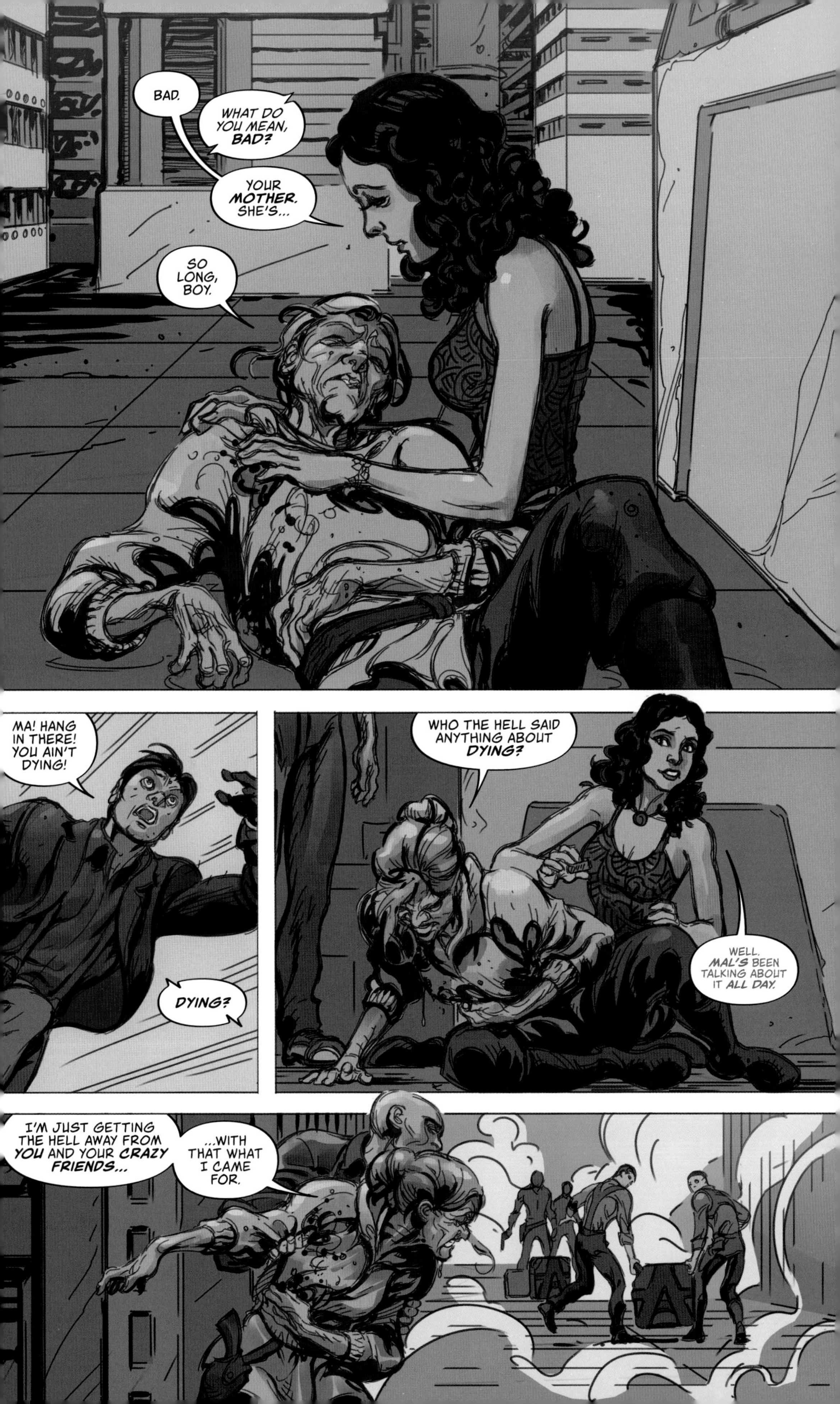
BAD.
WHAT DO YOU MEAN, BAD?
YOUR MOTHER. SHE'S...
SO LONG, BOY.
MA! HANG IN THERE! YOU AIN'T DYING!
DYING?
WHO THE HELL SAID ANYTHING ABOUT DYING?
WELL. MAL'S BEEN TALKING ABOUT IT ALL DAY.
I'M JUST GETTING THE HELL AWAY FROM YOU AND YOUR CRAZY FRIENDS...
...WITH THAT WHAT I CAME FOR.

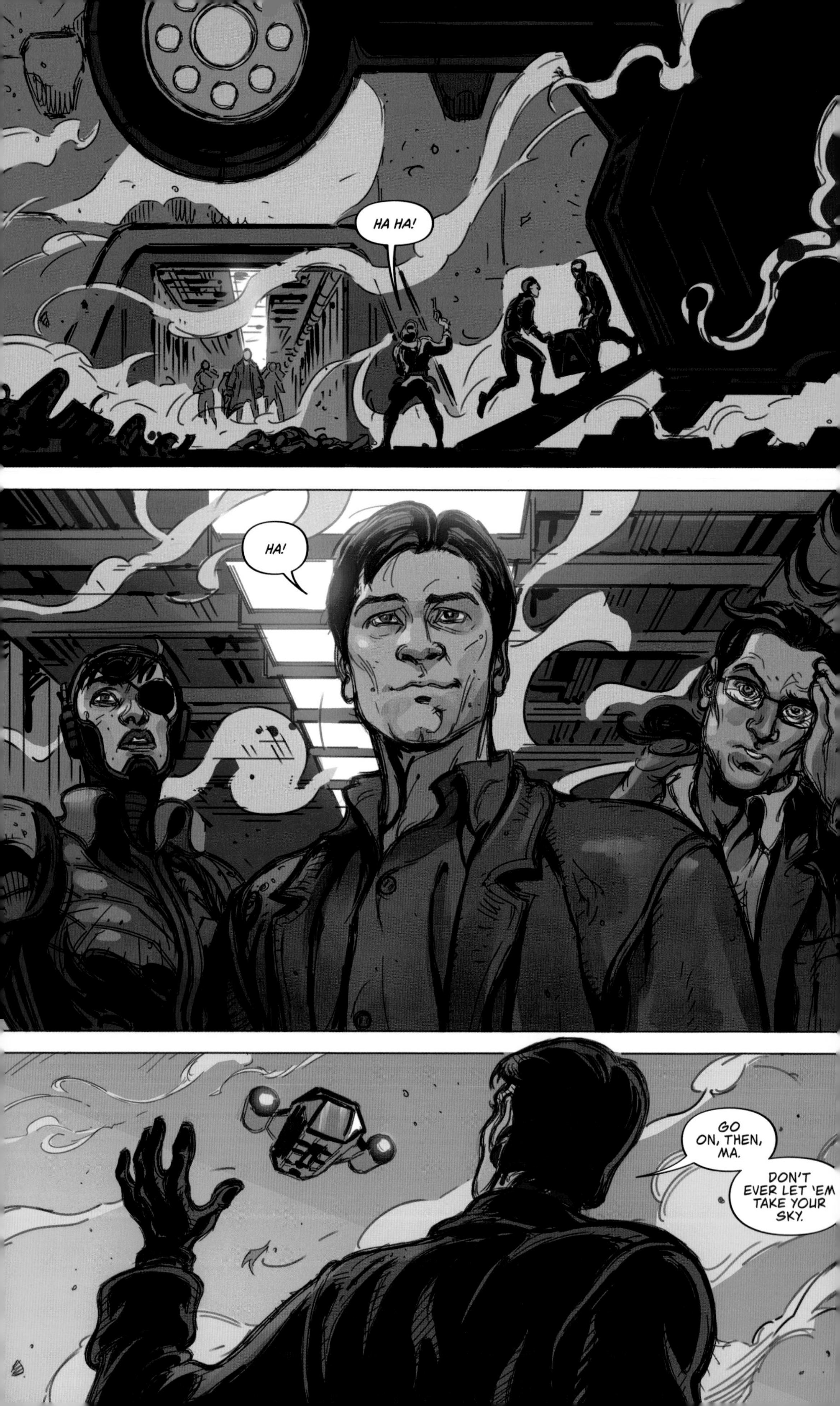
HA HA!
HA!
GO ON, THEN, MA.
DON'T EVER LET 'EM TAKE YOUR SKY.

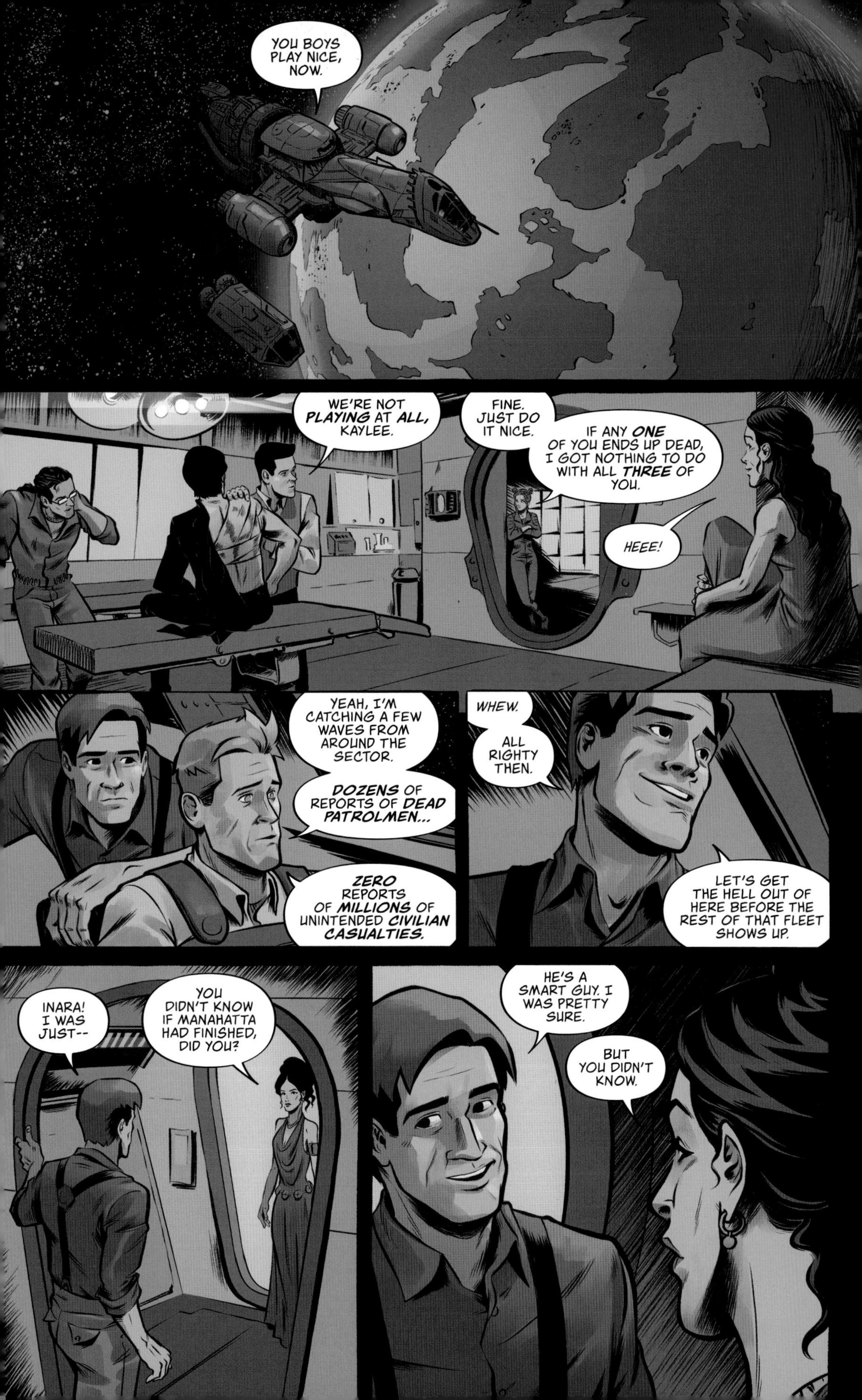
YOU BOYS PLAY NICE, NOW.
WE'RE NOT PLAYING AT ALL, KAYLEE.
FINE. JUST DO IT NICE.
IF ANY ONE OF YOU ENDS UP DEAD, I GOT NOTHING TO DO WITH ALL THREE OF YOU.
HEEE!
YEAH, I'M CATCHING A FEW WAVES FROM AROUND THE SECTOR.
DOZENS OF REPORTS OF DEAD PATROLMEN...
ZERO REPORTS OF MILLIONS OF UNINTENDED CIVILIAN CASUALTIES.
WHEW.
ALL RIGHTY THEN.
LET'S GET THE HELL OUT OF HERE BEFORE THE REST OF THAT FLEET SHOWS UP.
INARA! I WAS JUST--
YOU DIDN'T KNOW IF MANAHATTA HAD FINISHED, DID YOU?
HE'S A SMART GUY. I WAS PRETTY SURE.
BUT YOU DIDN'T KNOW.

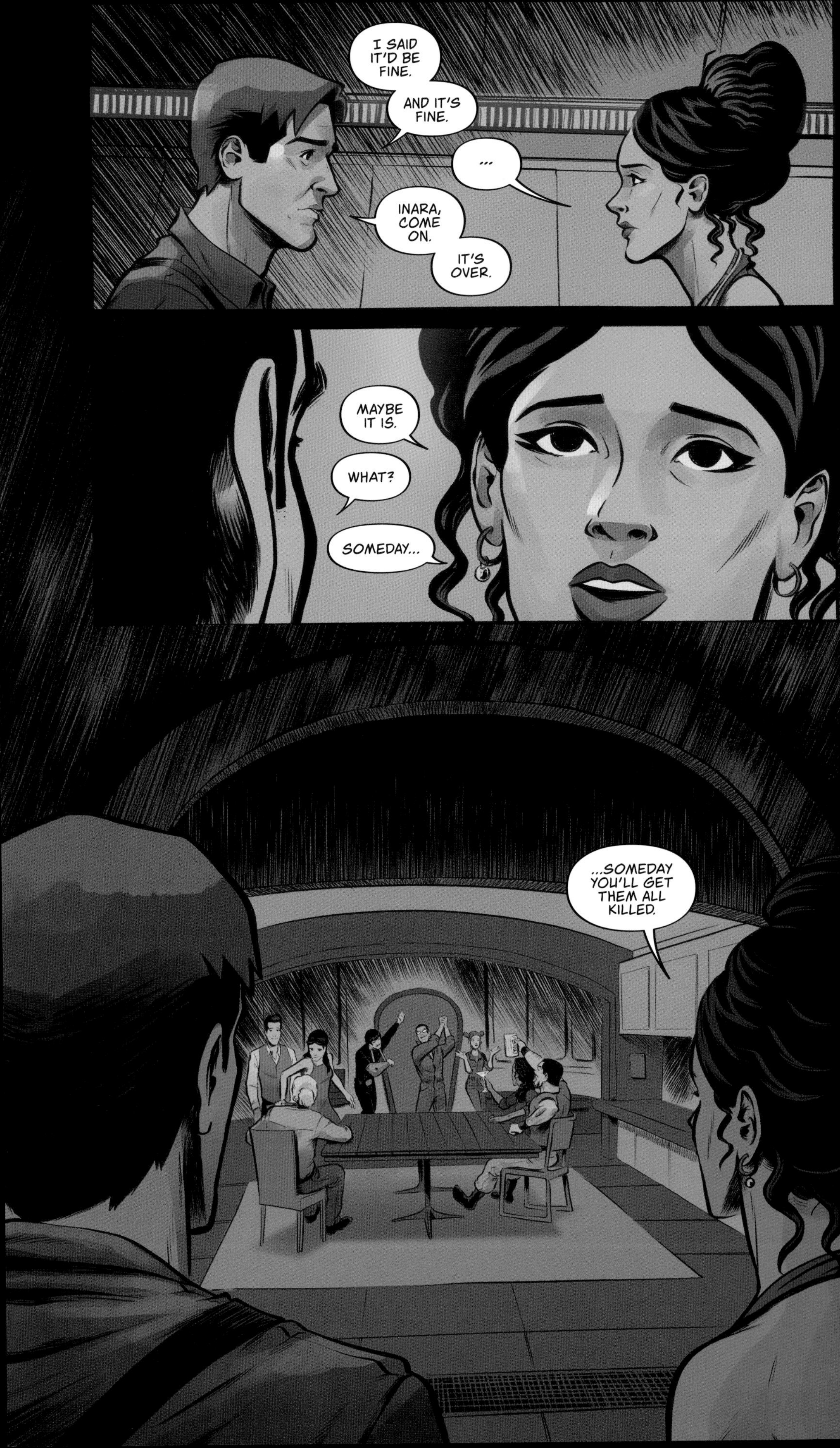
I SAID IT'D BE FINE.
AND IT'S FINE.
...
INARA, COME ON.
IT'S OVER.
MAYBE IT IS.
WHAT?
SOMEDAY...
...SOMEDAY YOU'LL GET THEM ALL KILLED.

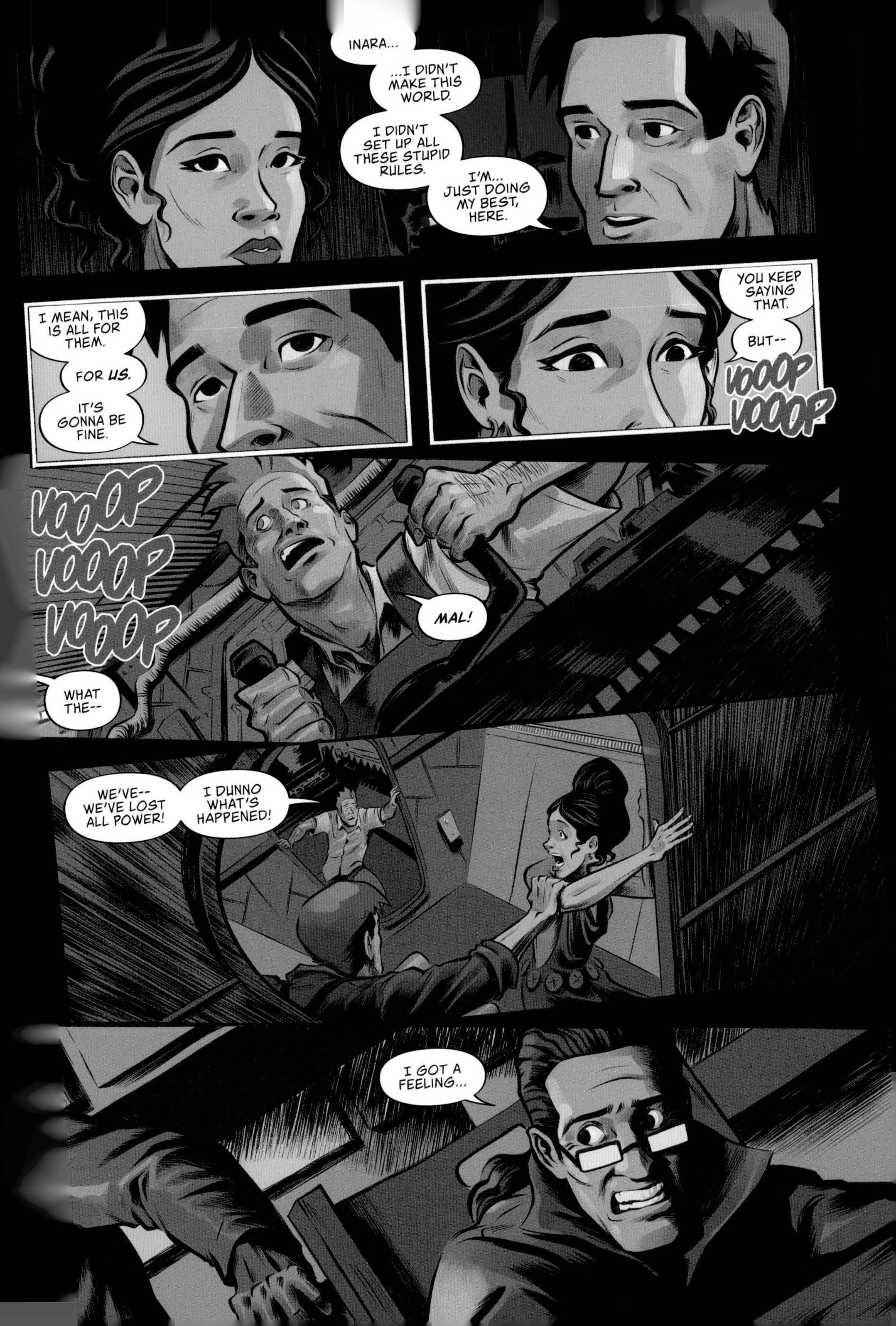
INARA...
...I DIDN'T MAKE THIS WORLD.
I DIDN'T SET UP ALL THESE STUPID RULES.
I'M... JUST DOING MY BEST, HERE.
I MEAN, THIS IS ALL FOR THEM.
FOR US.
IT'S GONNA BE FINE.
YOU KEEP SAYING THAT.
BUT--
VOOOP VOOOP
VOOOP VOOOP VOOOP
MAL!
WHAT THE--
WE'VE-- WE'VE LOST ALL POWER!
I DUNNO WHAT'S HAPPENED!
I GOT A FEELING...

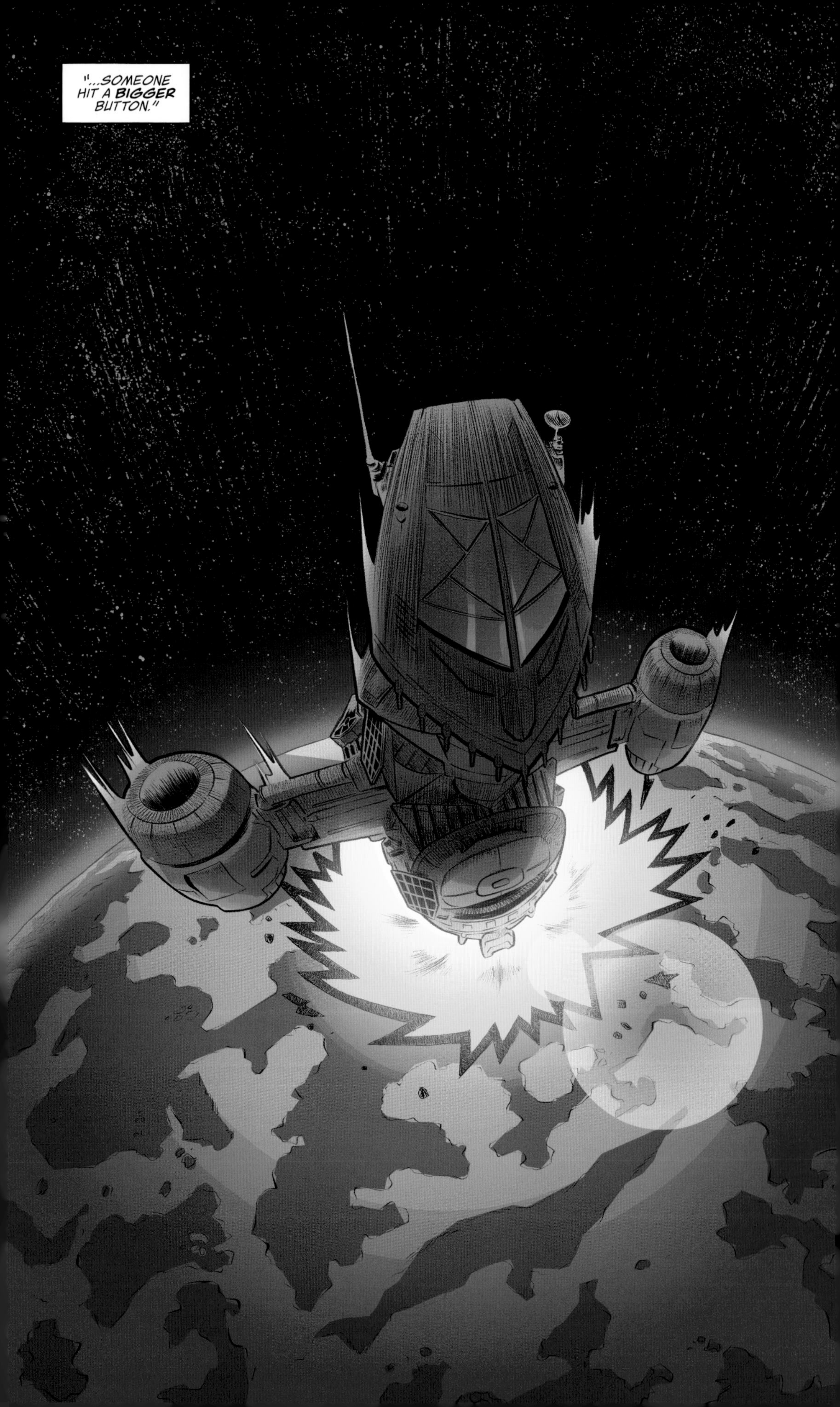
"...SOMEONE HIT A BIGGER BUTTON."

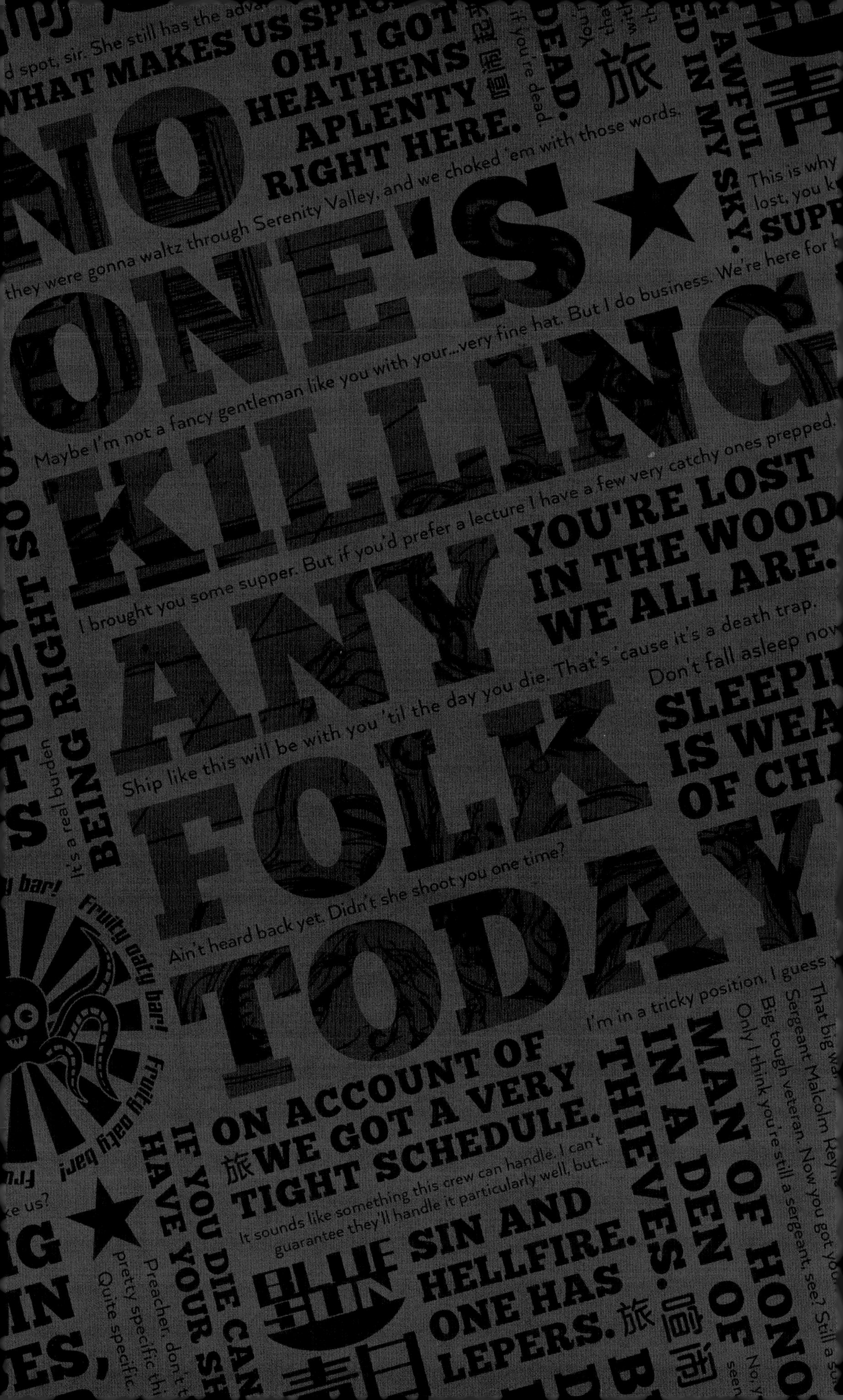

WHAT MAKES US SPEC
OH, I GOT HEATHENS APLENTY RIGHT HERE.
If you're dead
DEAD.
AWFUL IN MY SKY.
This is why
lost, you k
SUPP
they were gonna waltz through Serenity Valley, and we choked 'em with those words.
NO ONE'S ★ KILLING ANY FOLK TODAY
Maybe I'm not a fancy gentleman like you with your...very fine hat. But I do business. We're here for
I brought you some supper. But if you'd prefer a lecture I have a few very catchy ones prepped.
YOU'RE LOST IN THE WOOD WE ALL ARE.
Ship like this will be with you 'til the day you die. That's 'cause it's a death trap.
Don't fall asleep now
SLEEPI IS WEA OF CHA
It's a real burden
BEING RIGHT SO OF
Ain't heard back yet. Didn't she shoot you one time?
Fruity oaty bar!
I'm in a tricky position, I guess
That big wa
Sergeant Malcolm Reyn
Big, tough veteran. Now you got you
Only I think you're still a sergeant, see? Still a
ON ACCOUNT OF WE GOT A VERY TIGHT SCHEDULE.
It sounds like something this crew can handle. I can't guarantee they'll handle it particularly well, but...
IF YOU DIE CAN
HAVE YOUR SH
Preacher, don't
pretty specific thi
Quite specific
BLUE SUN
SIN AND HELLFIRE. ONE HAS LEPERS.
THIEVES. IN A DEN OF
MAN OF HONO

CHAPTER SIX

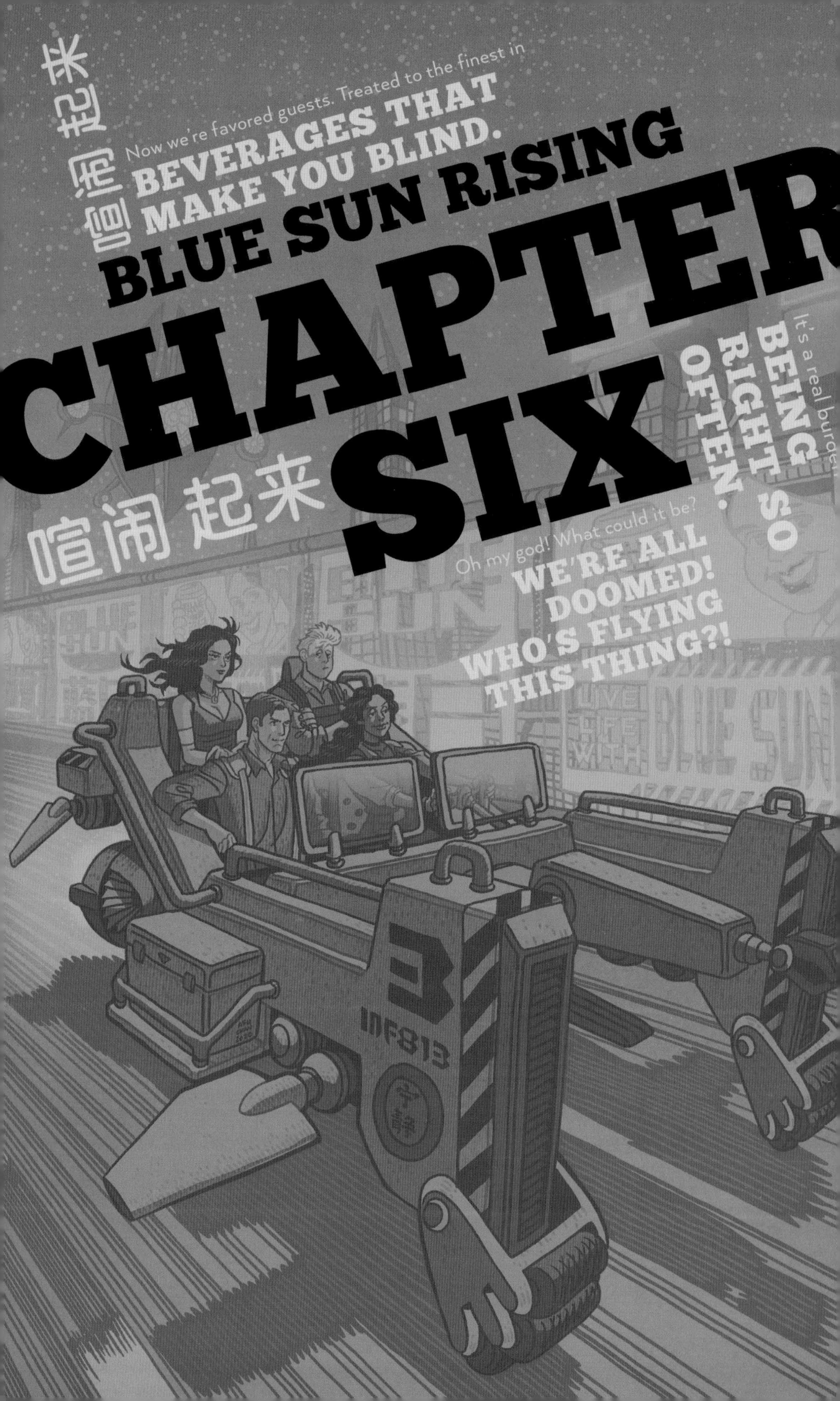
喧闹起来
Now we're favored guests. Treated to the finest in
BEVERAGES THAT
MAKE YOU BLIND.
BLUE SUN RISING
喧闹起来
It's a real burde
BEING
RIGHT SO
OFTEN.
Oh my god! What could it be?
WE'RE ALL
DOOMED!
WHO'S FLYING
THIS THING?!
LIVE
LIFE
WITH
BLUE SUN
3
MF813

PERDIDO.

MY GOD. THEY *DID* IT.

DID *WHAT*, MANAHATTA?

ALL OF MY *BLUE SUN* TECH IS *DEAD...*

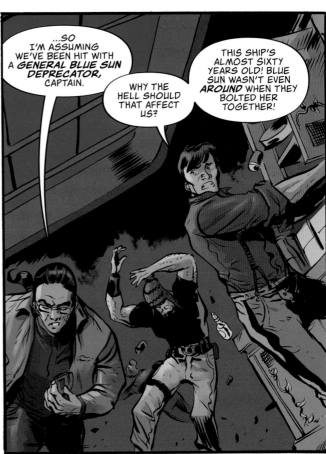

...SO I'M ASSUMING WE'VE BEEN HIT WITH A *GENERAL BLUE SUN DEPRECATOR,* CAPTAIN.

WHY THE HELL SHOULD THAT AFFECT US?

THIS SHIP'S ALMOST SIXTY YEARS OLD! BLUE SUN WASN'T EVEN *AROUND* WHEN THEY BOLTED HER TOGETHER!

BUT WE BEEN FIXING HER UP WITH ANY DAMN THING WE COULD FIND SINCE WE GOT HER!

AND I AIN'T BEEN *CHECKING PARTS* FOR *BLUE SUN LOGOS!*

SO GET TO THE *ENGINE ROOM* AND TELL ME WHAT'S GOING ON, KAYLEE!

WHADDAYA THINK I'M *DOING,* CAPTAIN?

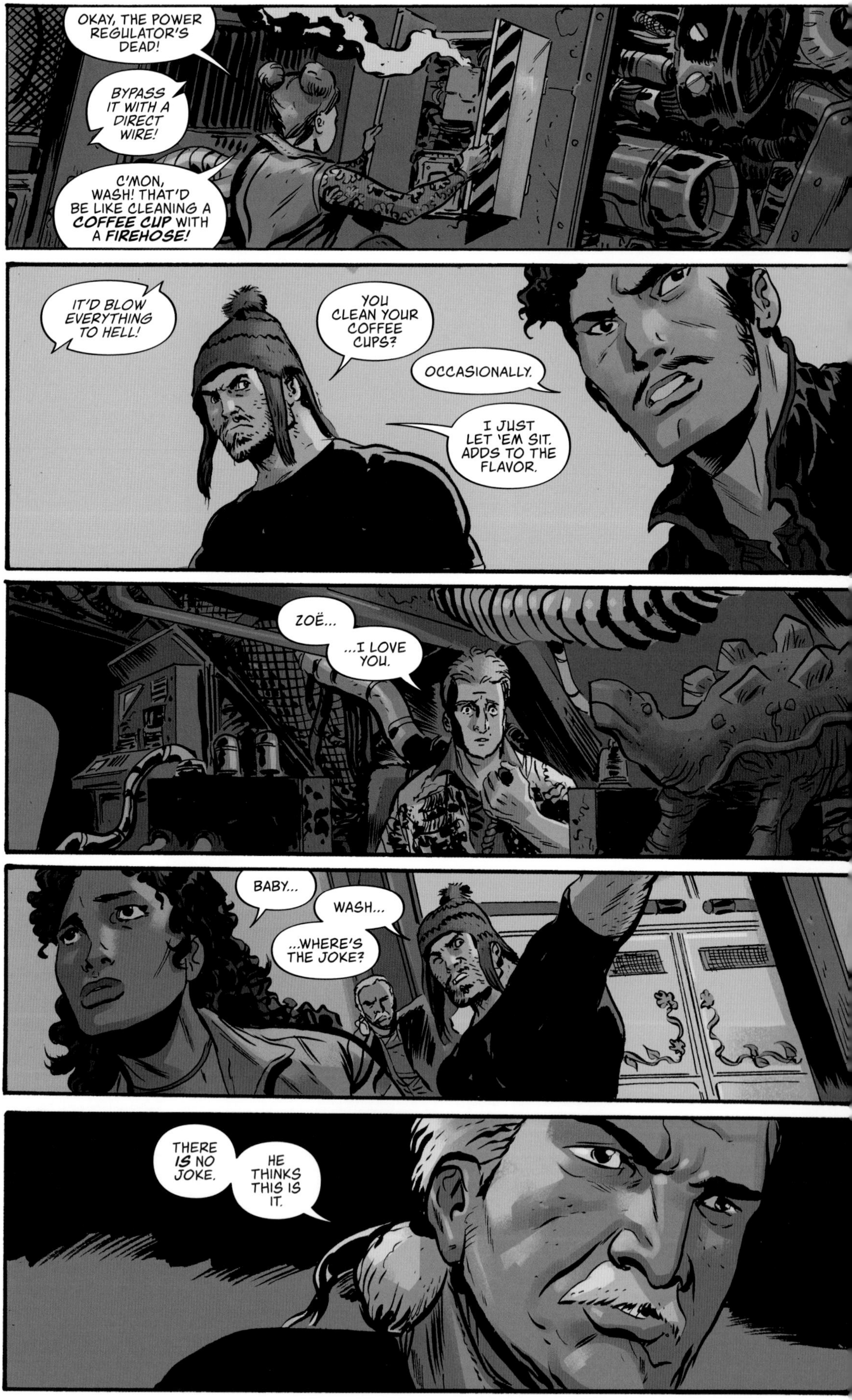

OKAY, THE POWER REGULATOR'S DEAD!
BYPASS IT WITH A DIRECT WIRE!
C'MON, WASH! THAT'D BE LIKE CLEANING A **COFFEE CUP** WITH A **FIREHOSE!**
IT'D BLOW EVERYTHING TO HELL!
YOU CLEAN YOUR COFFEE CUPS?
OCCASIONALLY.
I JUST LET 'EM SIT. ADDS TO THE FLAVOR.
ZOË...
...I LOVE YOU.
BABY...
WASH...
...WHERE'S THE JOKE?
THERE **IS** NO JOKE.
HE THINKS THIS IS IT.

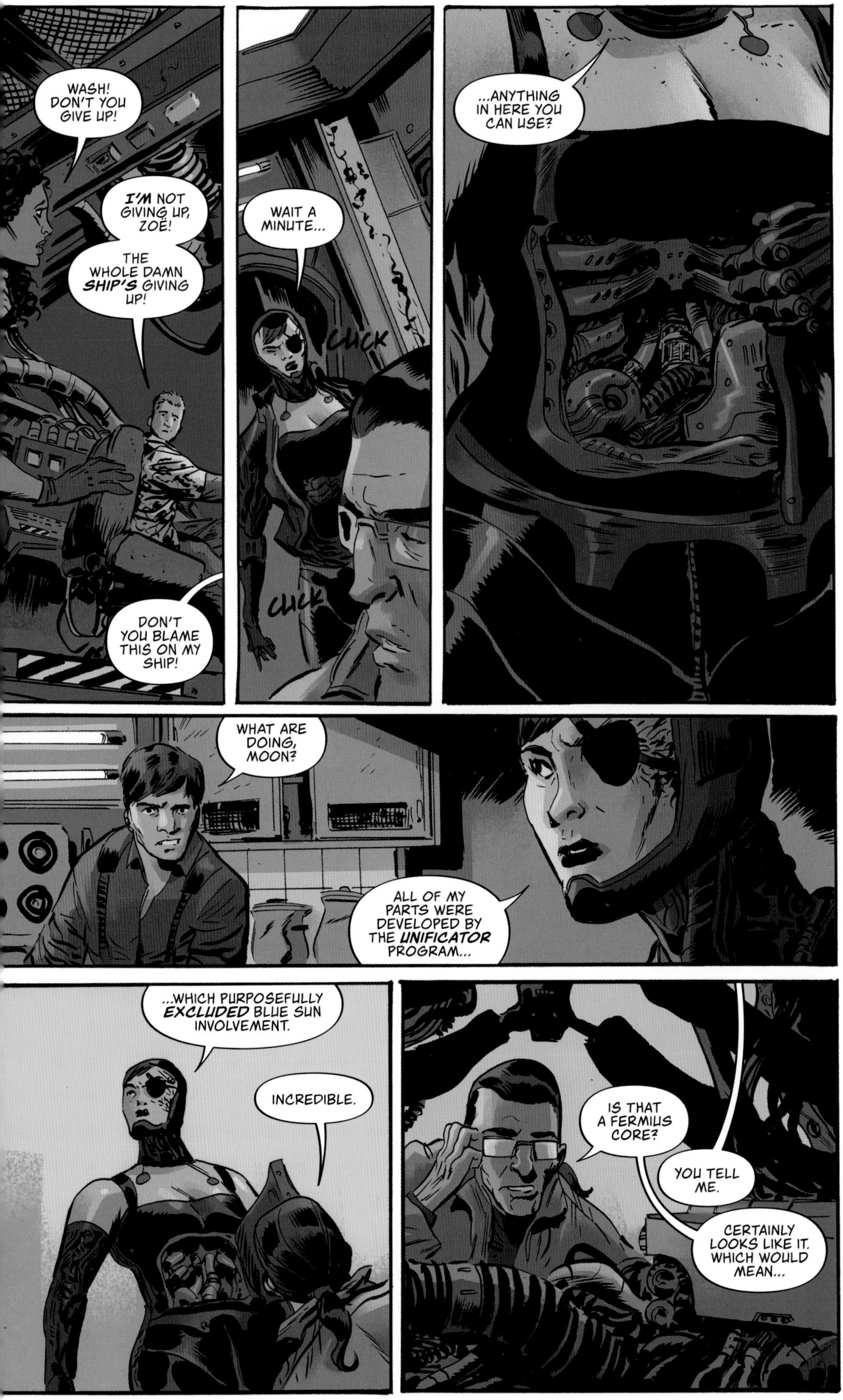
WASH! DON'T YOU GIVE UP!
I'M NOT GIVING UP, ZOË!
THE WHOLE DAMN SHIP'S GIVING UP!
DON'T YOU BLAME THIS ON MY SHIP!
WAIT A MINUTE...
CLICK
CLICK
...ANYTHING IN HERE YOU CAN USE?
WHAT ARE DOING, MOON?
ALL OF MY PARTS WERE DEVELOPED BY THE UNIFICATOR PROGRAM...
...WHICH PURPOSEFULLY EXCLUDED BLUE SUN INVOLVEMENT.
INCREDIBLE.
IS THAT A FERMIUS CORE?
YOU TELL ME.
CERTAINLY LOOKS LIKE IT. WHICH WOULD MEAN...

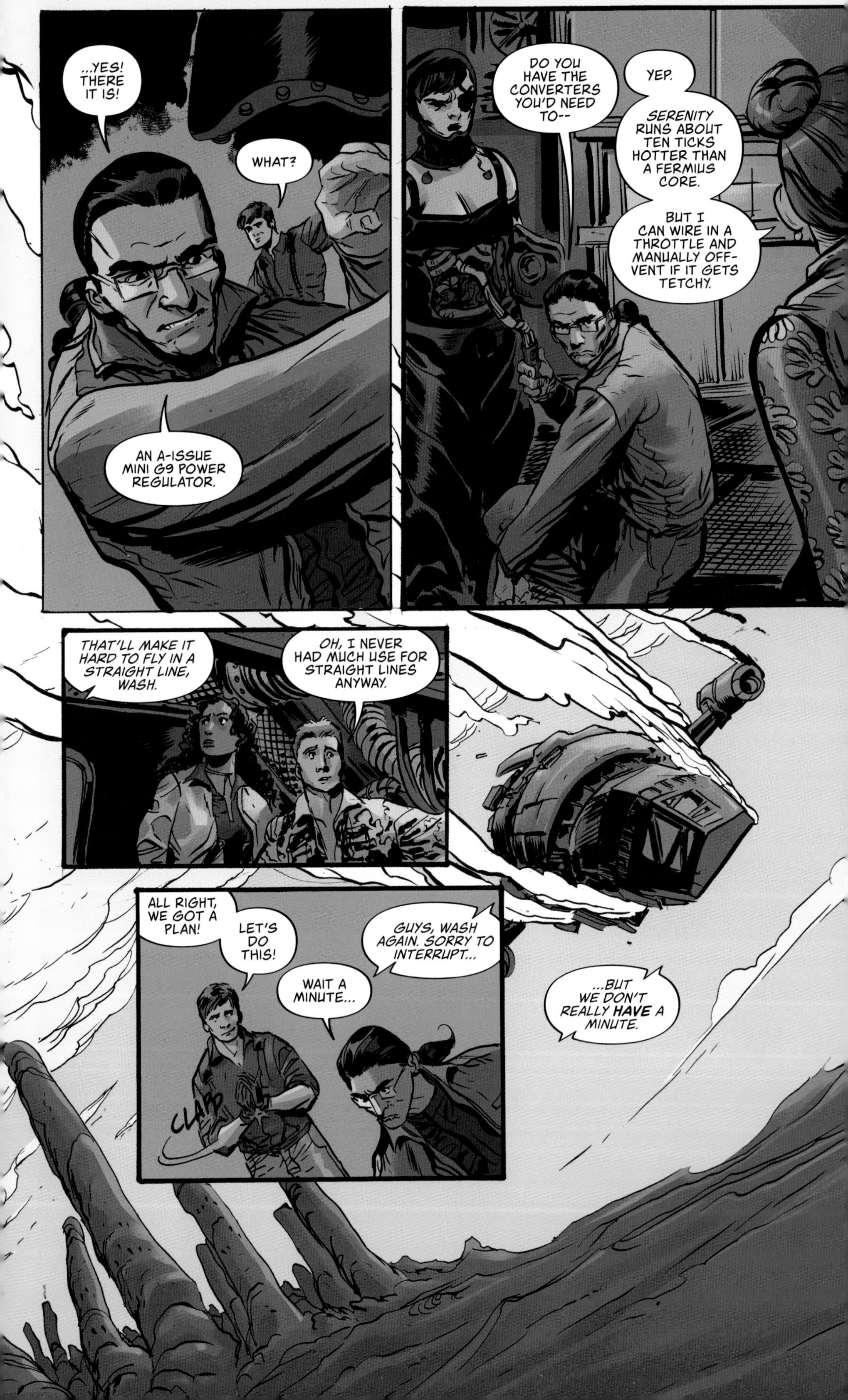
...YES! THERE IT IS!
WHAT?
AN A-ISSUE MINI G9 POWER REGULATOR.
DO YOU HAVE THE CONVERTERS YOU'D NEED TO--
YEP.
SERENITY RUNS ABOUT TEN TICKS HOTTER THAN A FERMIUS CORE.
BUT I CAN WIRE IN A THROTTLE AND MANUALLY OFF-VENT IF IT GETS TETCHY.
THAT'LL MAKE IT HARD TO FLY IN A STRAIGHT LINE, WASH.
OH, I NEVER HAD MUCH USE FOR STRAIGHT LINES ANYWAY.
ALL RIGHT, WE GOT A PLAN!
LET'S DO THIS!
WAIT A MINUTE...
GUYS, WASH AGAIN. SORRY TO INTERRUPT...
...BUT WE DON'T REALLY HAVE A MINUTE.
CLAP

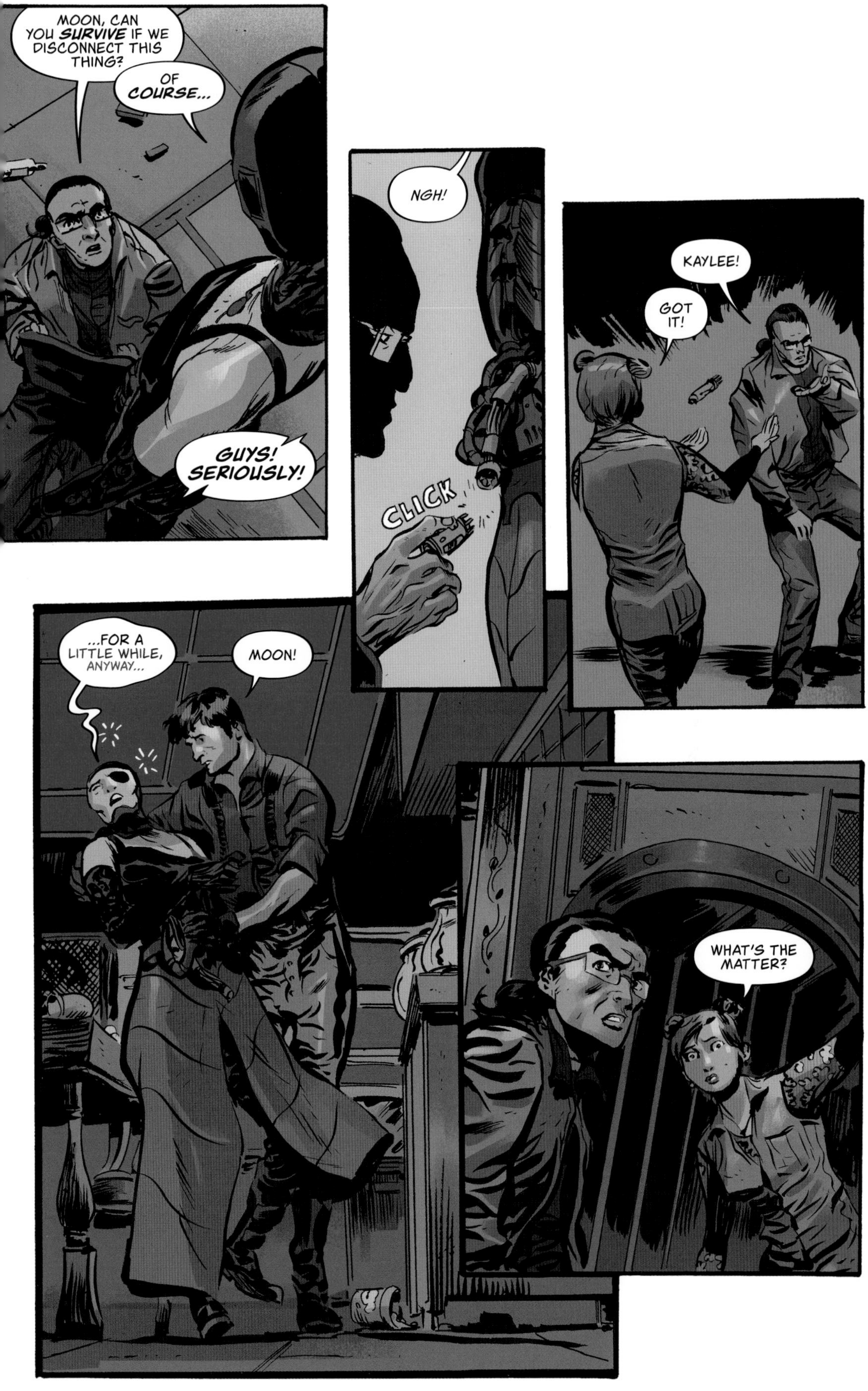
MOON, CAN YOU SURVIVE IF WE DISCONNECT THIS THING?
OF COURSE...
GUYS! SERIOUSLY!
NGH!
CLICK
KAYLEE!
GOT IT!
...FOR A LITTLE WHILE, ANYWAY...
MOON!
WHAT'S THE MATTER?

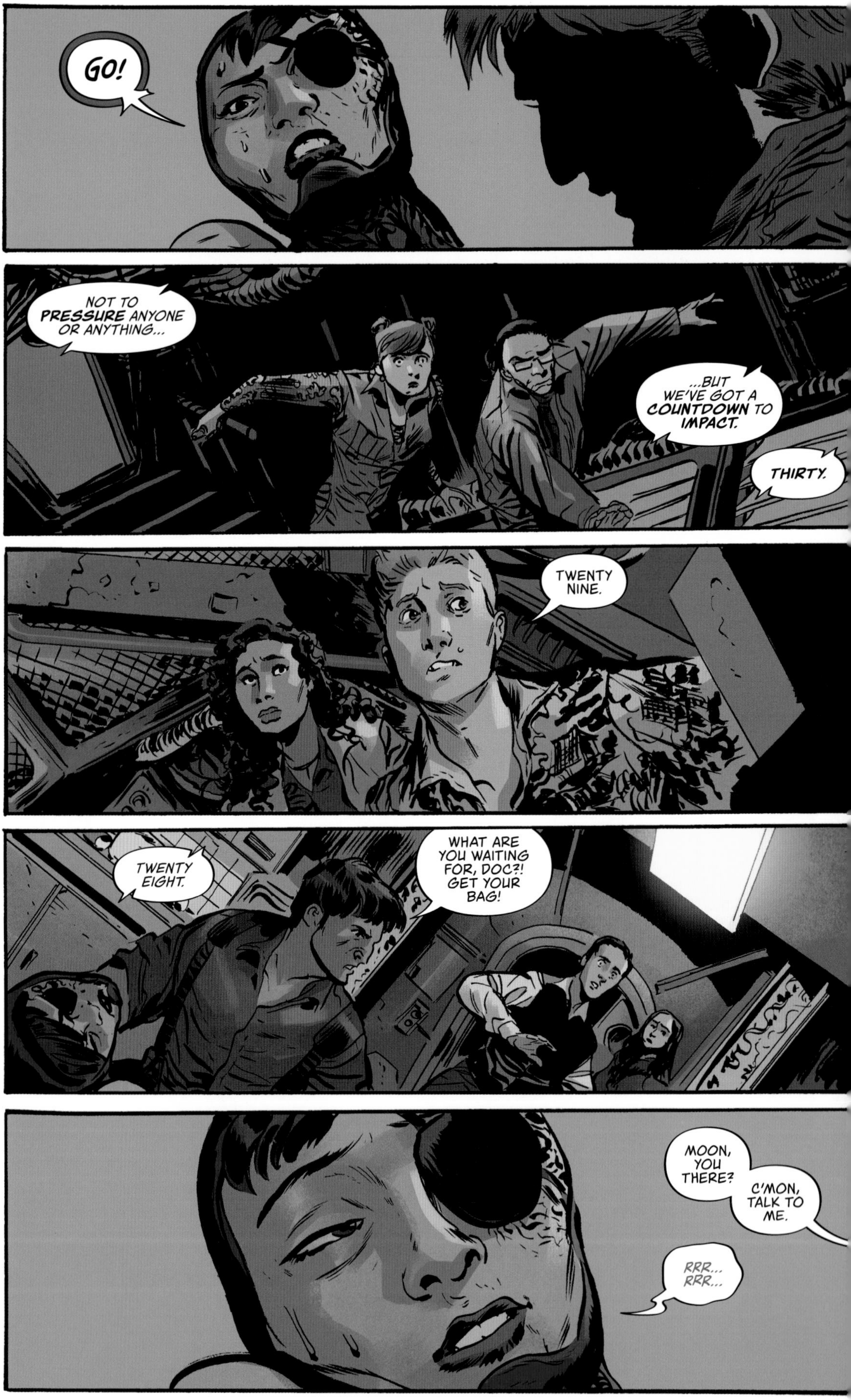
GO!
NOT TO PRESSURE ANYONE OR ANYTHING...
...BUT WE'VE GOT A COUNTDOWN TO IMPACT.
THIRTY.
TWENTY NINE.
TWENTY EIGHT.
WHAT ARE YOU WAITING FOR, DOC?! GET YOUR BAG!
MOON, YOU THERE?
C'MON, TALK TO ME.
RRR... RRR...

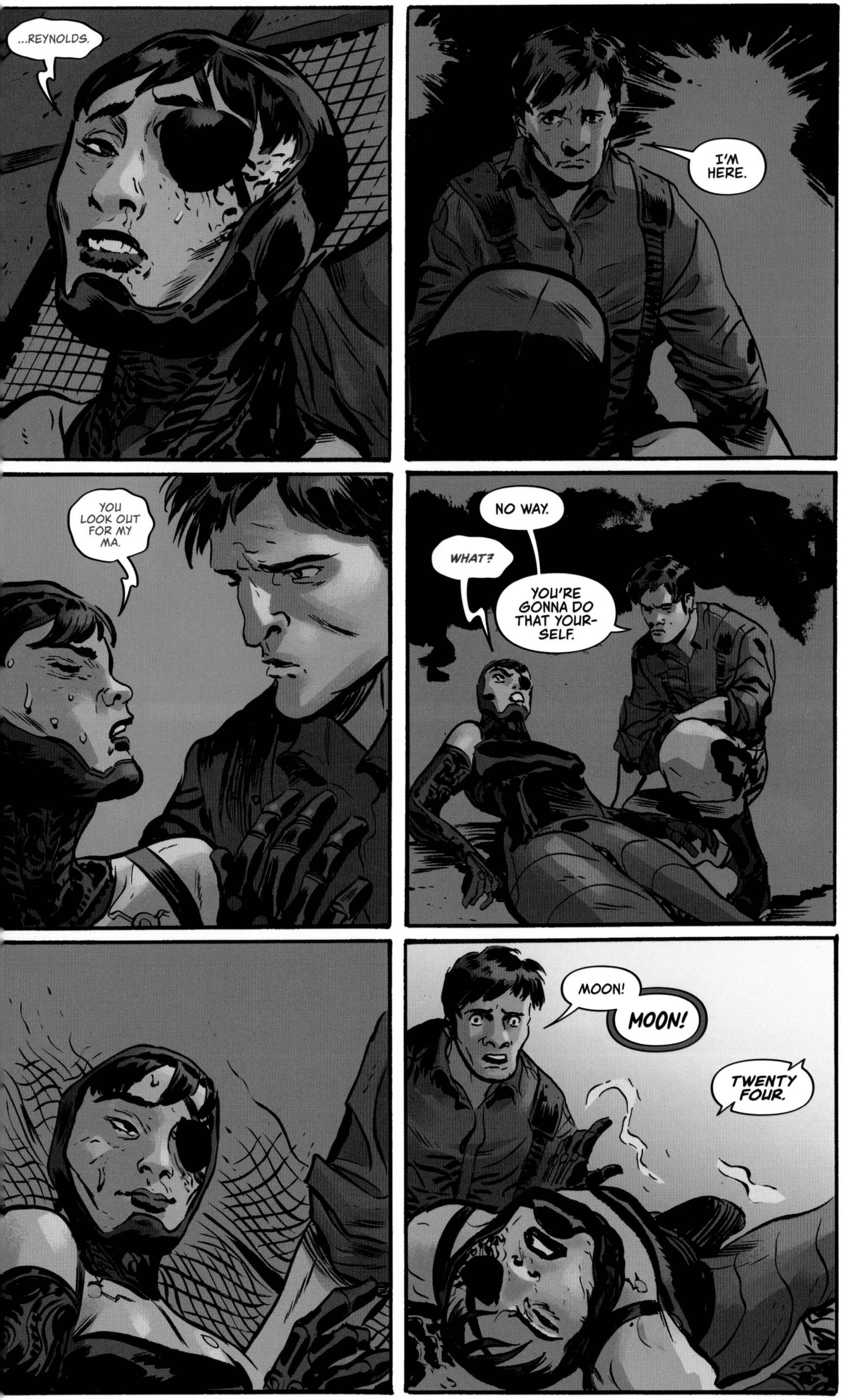
...REYNOLDS.
I'M HERE.
YOU LOOK OUT FOR MY MA.
WHAT?
NO WAY.
YOU'RE GONNA DO THAT YOUR-SELF.
MOON!
MOON!
TWENTY FOUR.

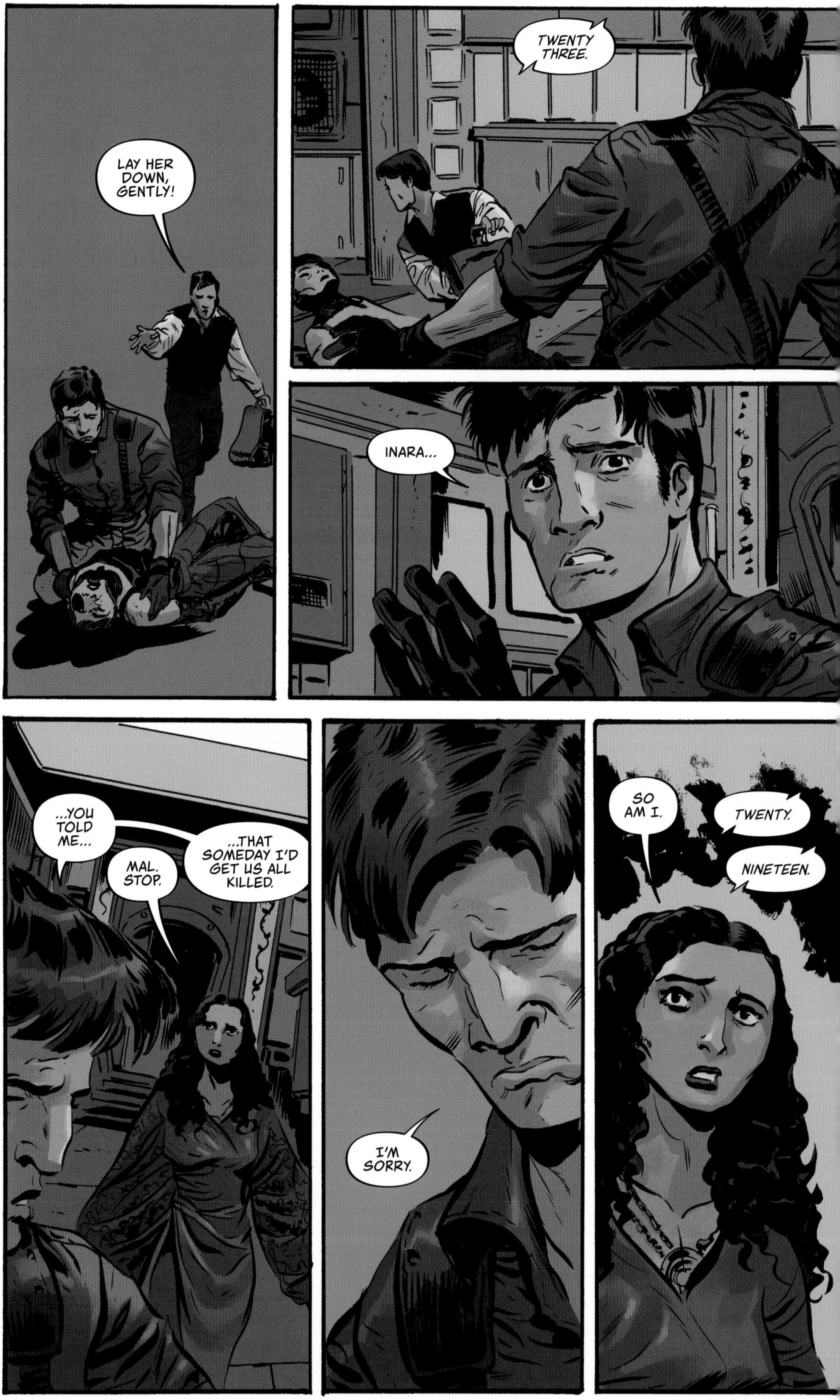
LAY HER DOWN, GENTLY!
TWENTY THREE.
INARA...
...YOU TOLD ME...
MAL. STOP.
...THAT SOMEDAY I'D GET US ALL KILLED.
I'M SORRY.
SO AM I.
TWENTY.
NINETEEN.

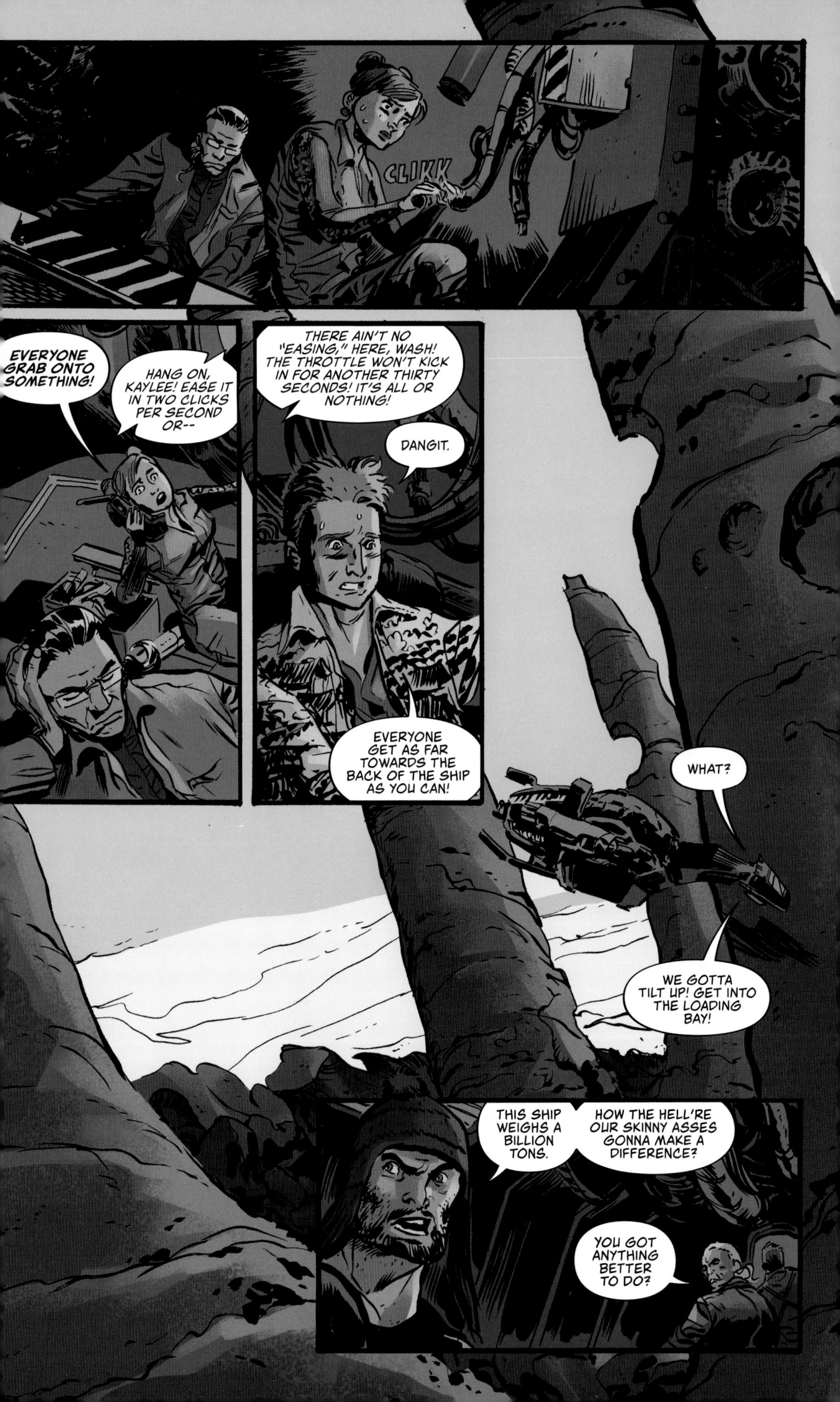
CLIKK
EVERYONE GRAB ONTO SOMETHING!
HANG ON, KAYLEE! EASE IT IN TWO CLICKS PER SECOND OR--
THERE AIN'T NO "EASING," HERE, WASH! THE THROTTLE WON'T KICK IN FOR ANOTHER THIRTY SECONDS! IT'S ALL OR NOTHING!
DANGIT.
EVERYONE GET AS FAR TOWARDS THE BACK OF THE SHIP AS YOU CAN!
WHAT?
WE GOTTA TILT UP! GET INTO THE LOADING BAY!
THIS SHIP WEIGHS A BILLION TONS.
HOW THE HELL'RE OUR SKINNY ASSES GONNA MAKE A DIFFERENCE?
YOU GOT ANYTHING BETTER TO DO?

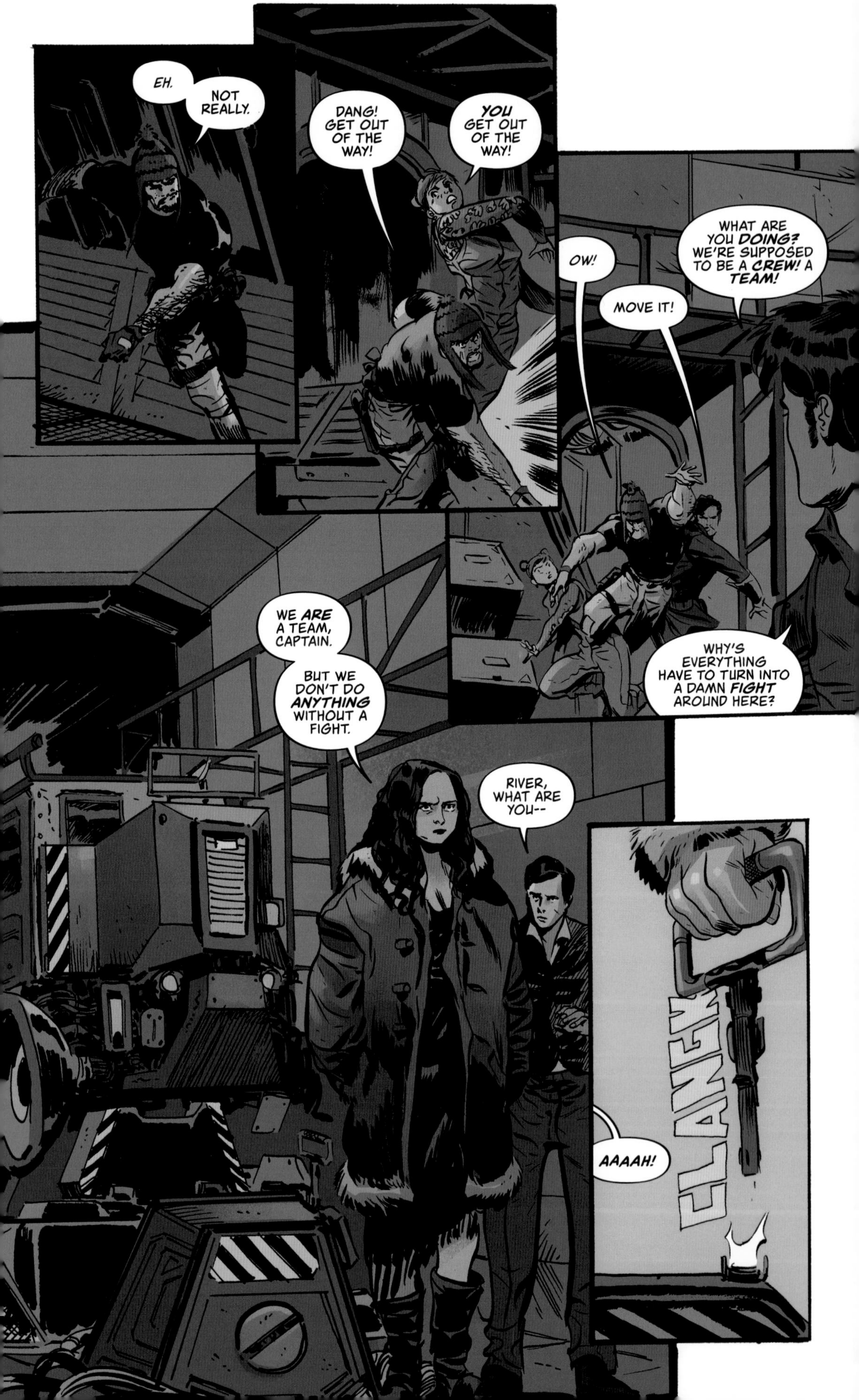
EH.
NOT REALLY.
DANG! GET OUT OF THE WAY!
YOU GET OUT OF THE WAY!
OW!
MOVE IT!
WHAT ARE YOU DOING? WE'RE SUPPOSED TO BE A CREW! A TEAM!
WHY'S EVERYTHING HAVE TO TURN INTO A DAMN FIGHT AROUND HERE?
WE ARE A TEAM, CAPTAIN.
BUT WE DON'T DO ANYTHING WITHOUT A FIGHT.
RIVER, WHAT ARE YOU--
AAAAH!
CLANK

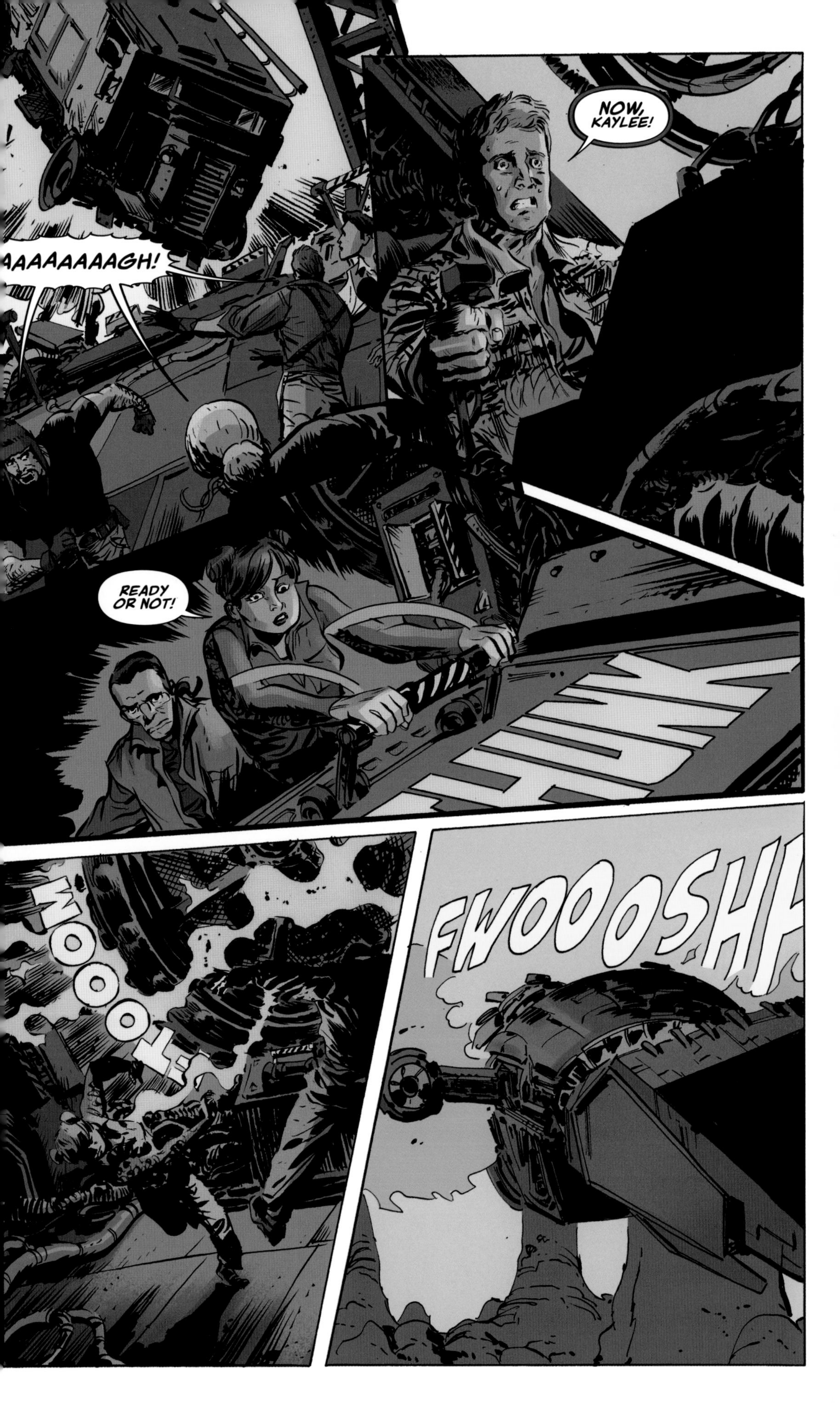
AAAAAAAAGH!
NOW, KAYLEE!
READY OR NOT!
WHUMP
FWOOOSH
WOOOOT

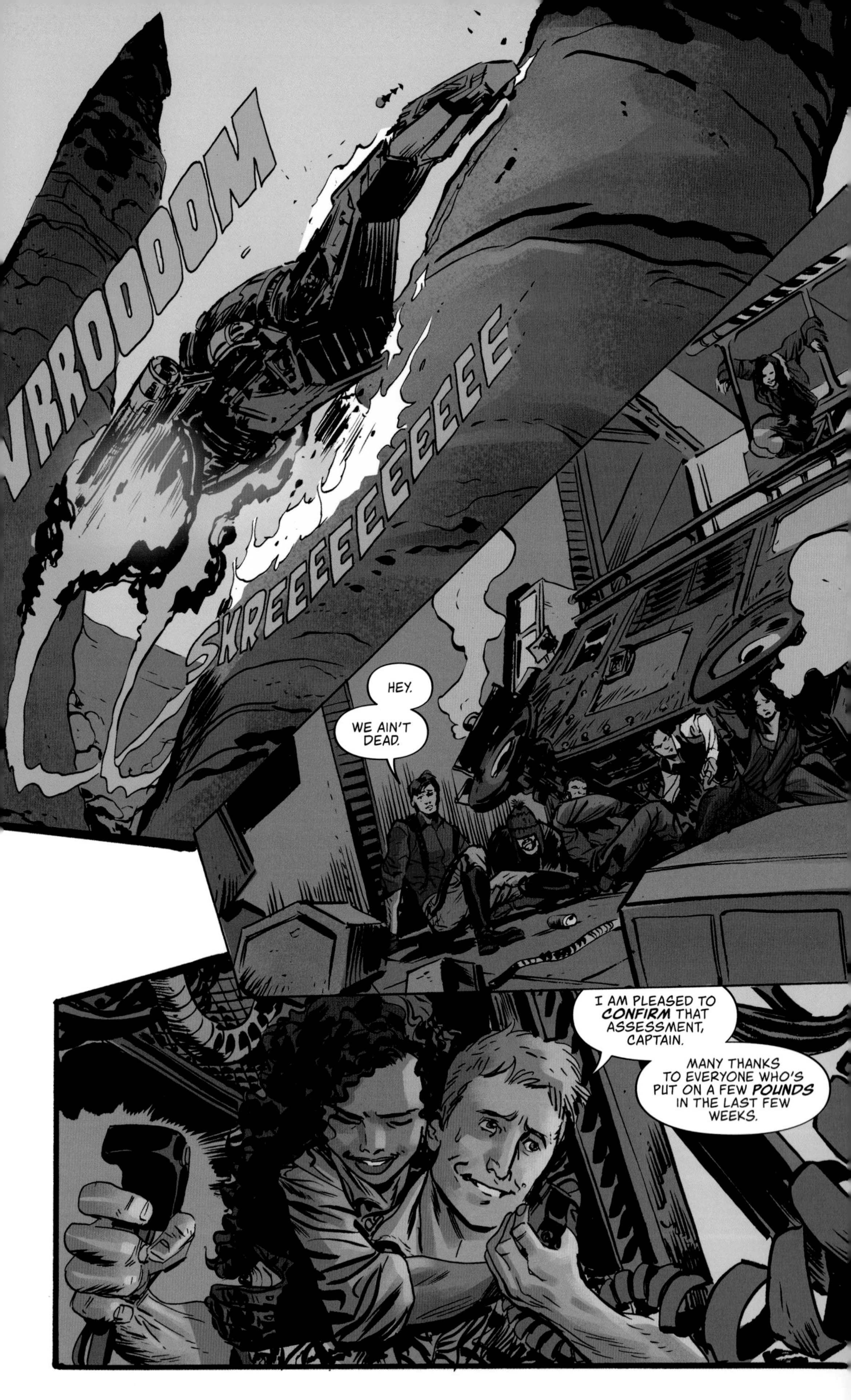
VRROOOOM
SKREEEEEEEEEE
HEY.
WE AIN'T DEAD.
I AM PLEASED TO **CONFIRM** THAT ASSESSMENT, CAPTAIN.
MANY THANKS TO EVERYONE WHO'S PUT ON A FEW **POUNDS** IN THE LAST FEW WEEKS.

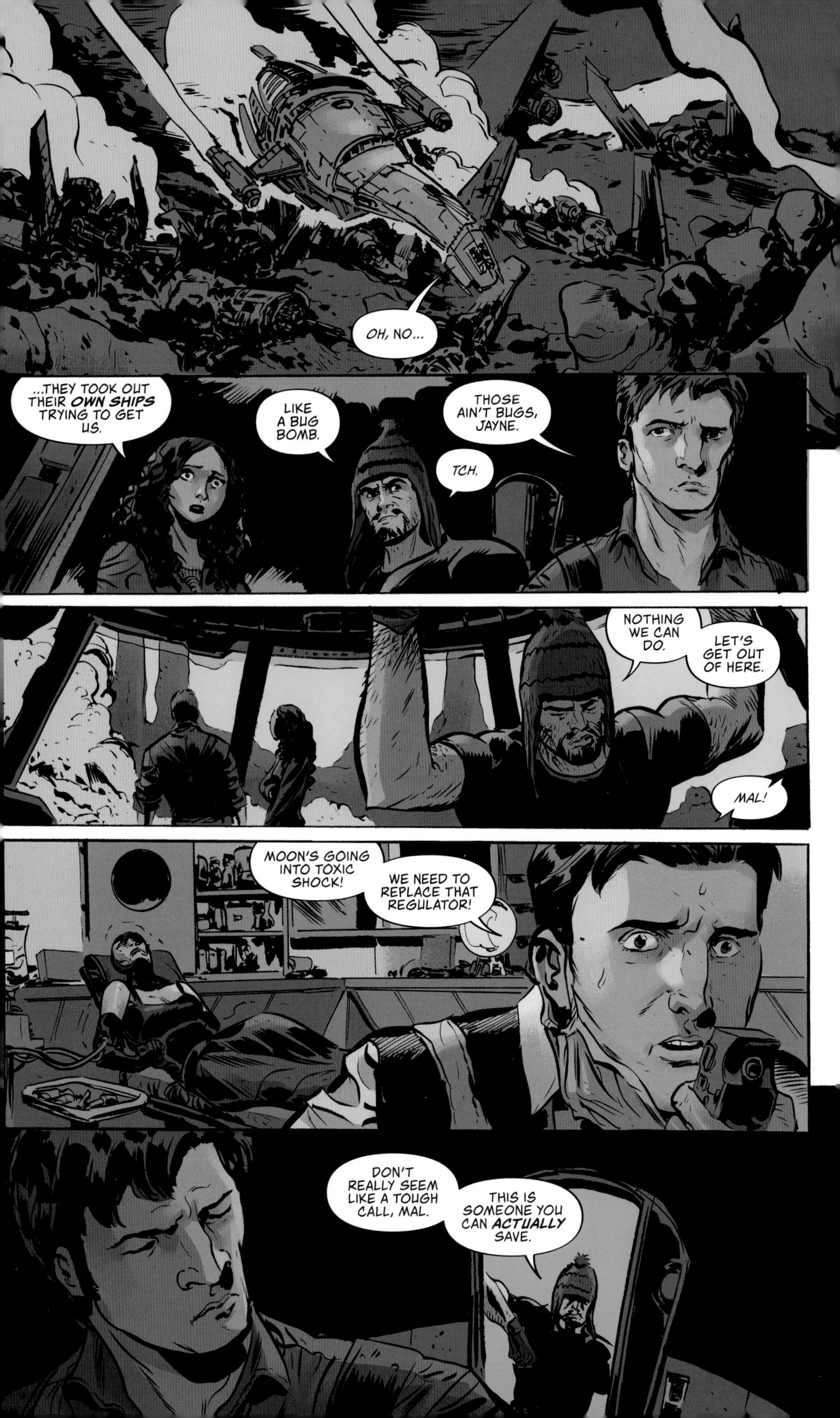
OH, NO...
...THEY TOOK OUT THEIR OWN SHIPS TRYING TO GET US.
LIKE A BUG BOMB.
THOSE AIN'T BUGS, JAYNE.
TCH.
NOTHING WE CAN DO.
LET'S GET OUT OF HERE.
MAL!
MOON'S GOING INTO TOXIC SHOCK!
WE NEED TO REPLACE THAT REGULATOR!
DON'T REALLY SEEM LIKE A TOUGH CALL, MAL.
THIS IS SOMEONE YOU CAN ACTUALLY SAVE.

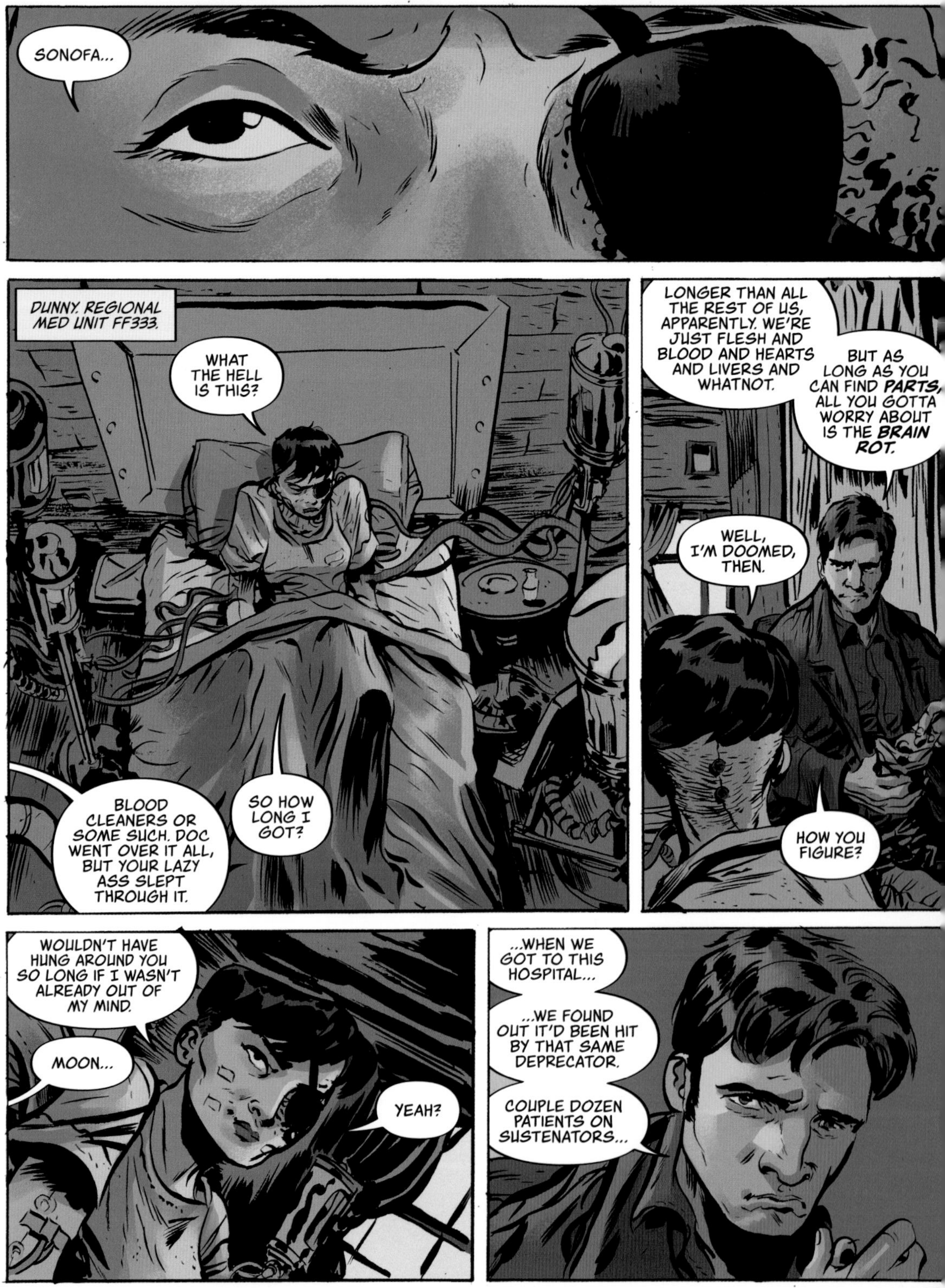
SONOFA...
DUNNY. REGIONAL MED UNIT FF333.
WHAT THE HELL IS THIS?
BLOOD CLEANERS OR SOME SUCH. DOC WENT OVER IT ALL, BUT YOUR LAZY ASS SLEPT THROUGH IT.
SO HOW LONG I GOT?
LONGER THAN ALL THE REST OF US, APPARENTLY. WE'RE JUST FLESH AND BLOOD AND HEARTS AND LIVERS AND WHATNOT.
BUT AS LONG AS YOU CAN FIND PARTS, ALL YOU GOTTA WORRY ABOUT IS THE BRAIN ROT.
WELL, I'M DOOMED, THEN.
HOW YOU FIGURE?
WOULDN'T HAVE HUNG AROUND YOU SO LONG IF I WASN'T ALREADY OUT OF MY MIND.
MOON...
YEAH?
...WHEN WE GOT TO THIS HOSPITAL...
...WE FOUND OUT IT'D BEEN HIT BY THAT SAME DEPRECATOR.
COUPLE DOZEN PATIENTS ON SUSTENATORS...

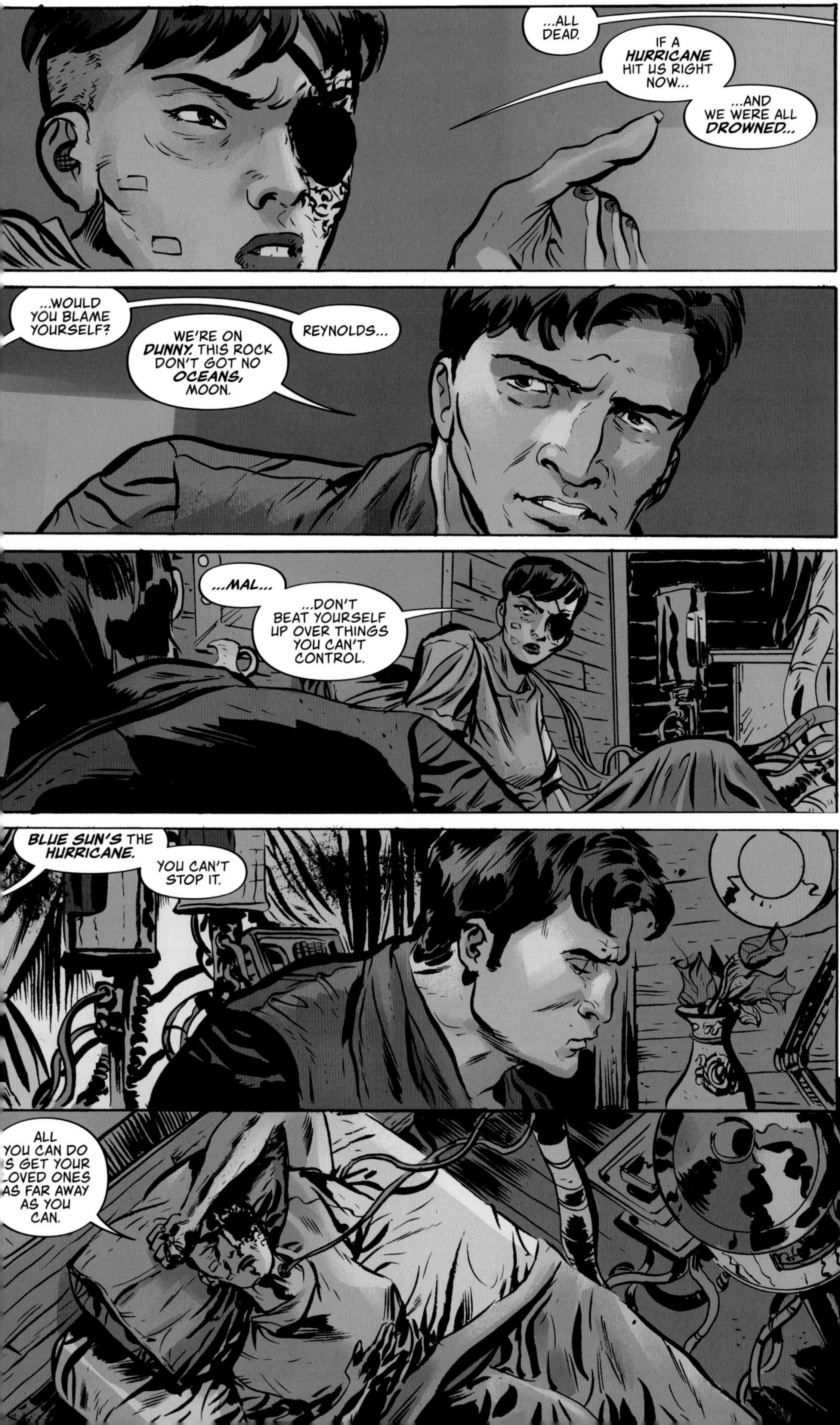
...ALL DEAD.
IF A HURRICANE HIT US RIGHT NOW...
...AND WE WERE ALL DROWNED...
...WOULD YOU BLAME YOURSELF?
REYNOLDS...
WE'RE ON DUNNY. THIS ROCK DON'T GOT NO OCEANS, MOON.
...MAL...
...DON'T BEAT YOURSELF UP OVER THINGS YOU CAN'T CONTROL.
BLUE SUN'S THE HURRICANE.
YOU CAN'T STOP IT.
ALL YOU CAN DO S GET YOUR LOVED ONES AS FAR AWAY AS YOU CAN.

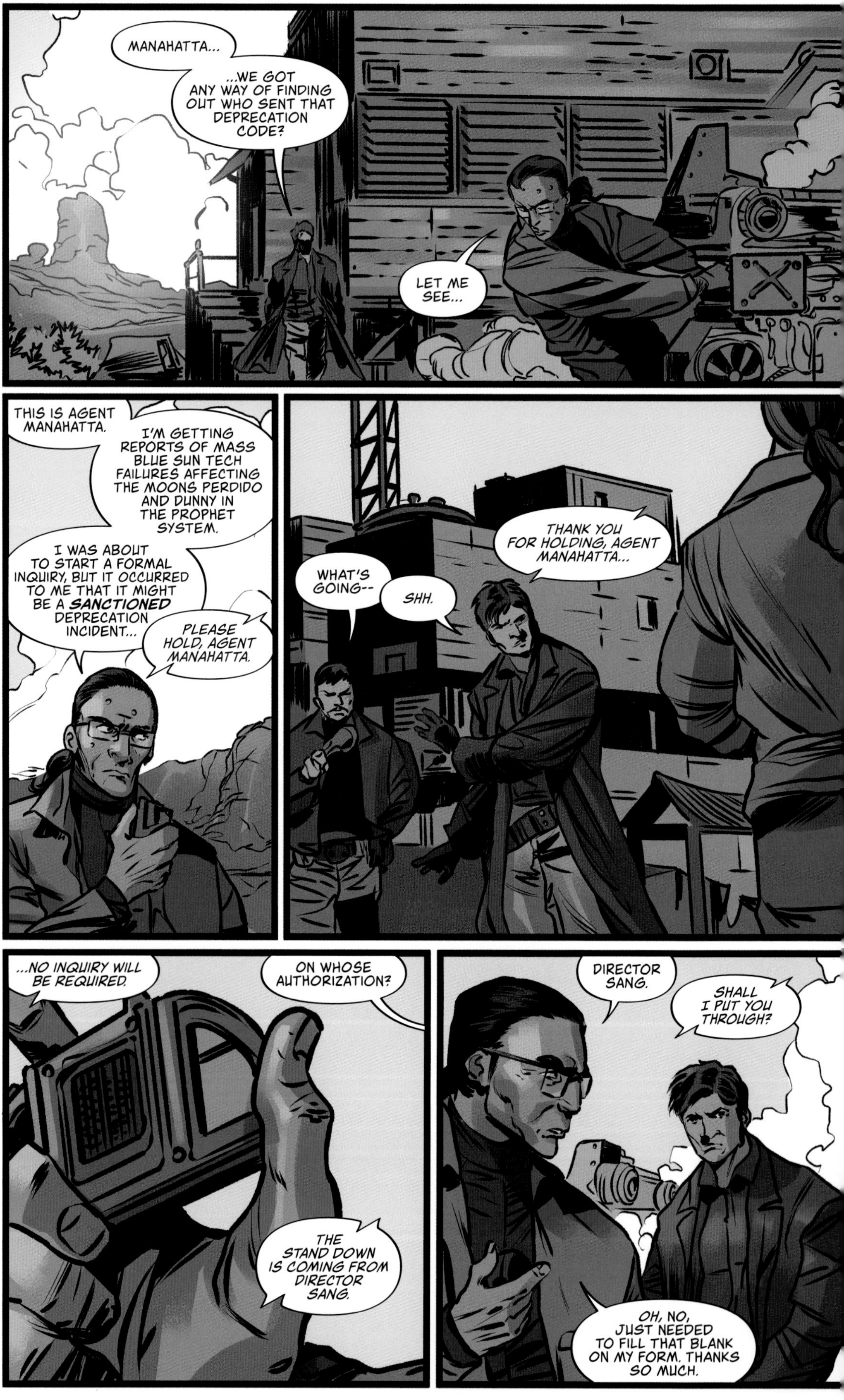
MANAHATTA...
...WE GOT ANY WAY OF FINDING OUT WHO SENT THAT DEPRECATION CODE?
LET ME SEE...
THIS IS AGENT MANAHATTA.
I'M GETTING REPORTS OF MASS BLUE SUN TECH FAILURES AFFECTING THE MOONS PERDIDO AND DUNNY IN THE PROPHET SYSTEM.
I WAS ABOUT TO START A FORMAL INQUIRY, BUT IT OCCURRED TO ME THAT IT MIGHT BE A SANCTIONED DEPRECATION INCIDENT...
PLEASE HOLD, AGENT MANAHATTA.
THANK YOU FOR HOLDING, AGENT MANAHATTA...
WHAT'S GOING--
SHH.
...NO INQUIRY WILL BE REQUIRED.
ON WHOSE AUTHORIZATION?
THE STAND DOWN IS COMING FROM DIRECTOR SANG.
DIRECTOR SANG.
SHALL I PUT YOU THROUGH?
OH, NO, JUST NEEDED TO FILL THAT BLANK ON MY FORM. THANKS SO MUCH.

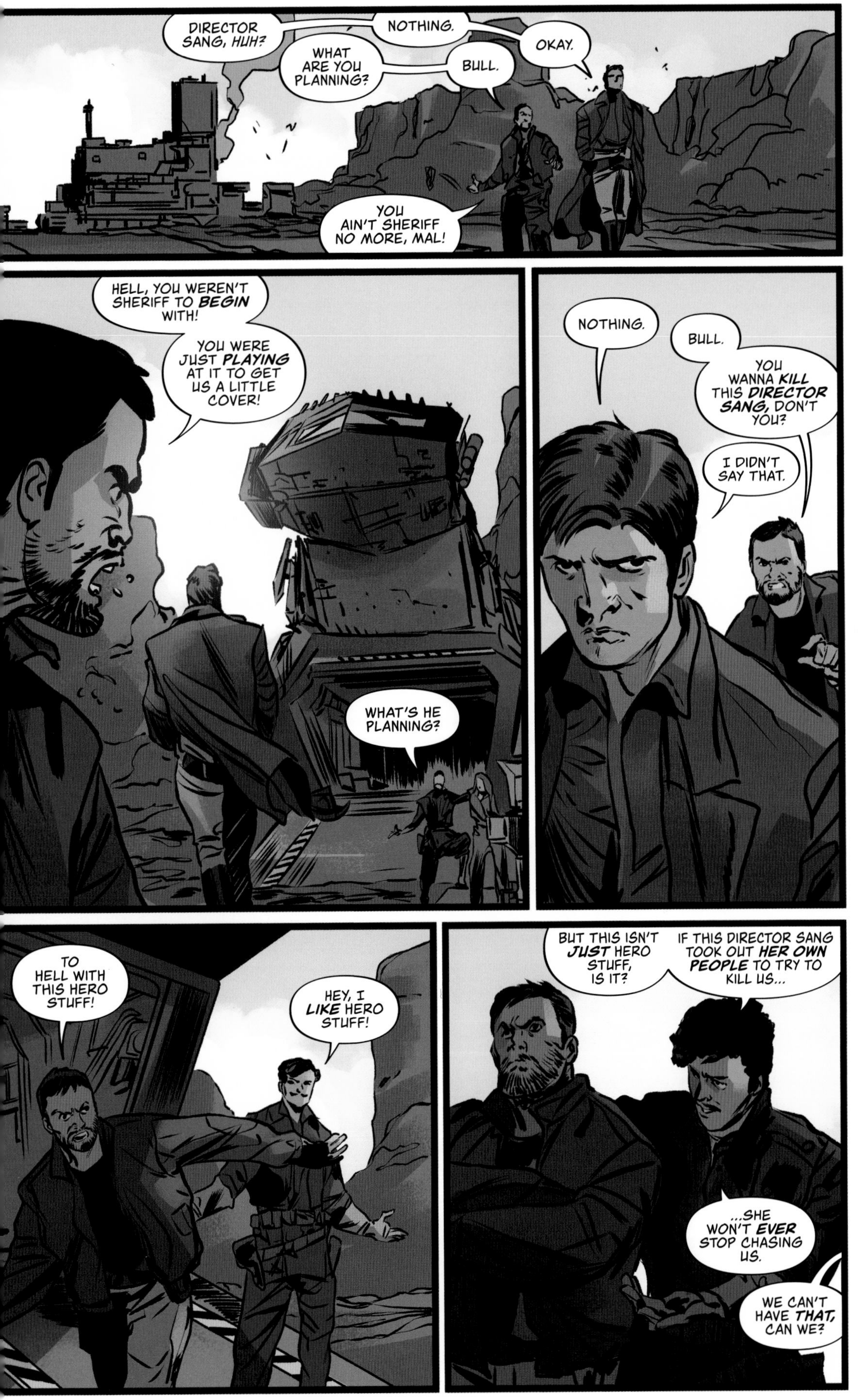
DIRECTOR SANG, HUH?
NOTHING.
WHAT ARE YOU PLANNING?
BULL.
OKAY.
YOU AIN'T SHERIFF NO MORE, MAL!
HELL, YOU WEREN'T SHERIFF TO BEGIN WITH!
YOU WERE JUST PLAYING AT IT TO GET US A LITTLE COVER!
WHAT'S HE PLANNING?
NOTHING.
BULL.
YOU WANNA KILL THIS DIRECTOR SANG, DON'T YOU?
I DIDN'T SAY THAT.
TO HELL WITH THIS HERO STUFF!
HEY, I LIKE HERO STUFF!
BUT THIS ISN'T JUST HERO STUFF, IS IT?
IF THIS DIRECTOR SANG TOOK OUT HER OWN PEOPLE TO TRY TO KILL US...
...SHE WON'T EVER STOP CHASING US.
WE CAN'T HAVE THAT, CAN WE?

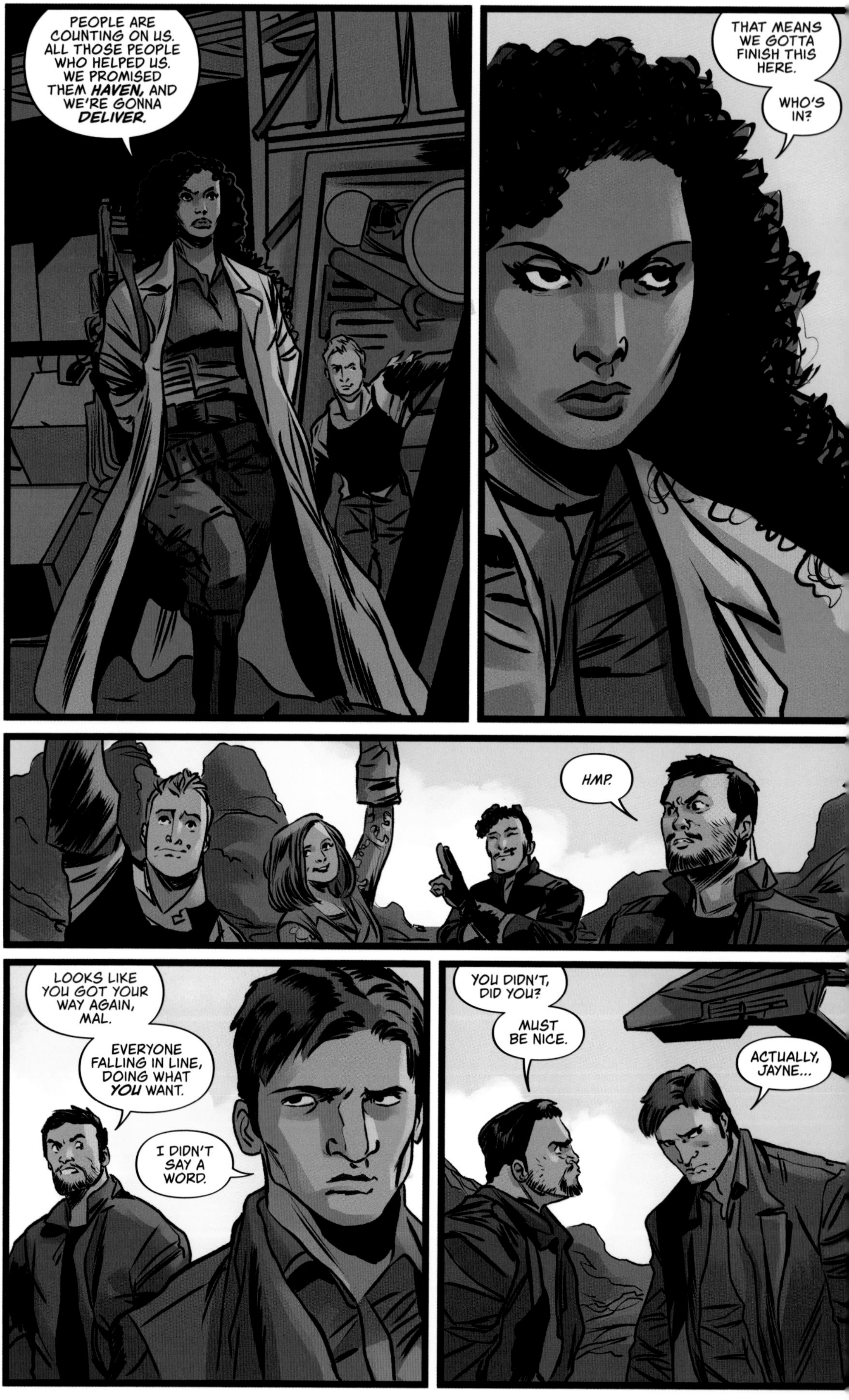
PEOPLE ARE COUNTING ON US. ALL THOSE PEOPLE WHO HELPED US. WE PROMISED THEM **HAVEN,** AND WE'RE GONNA **DELIVER.**
THAT MEANS WE GOTTA FINISH THIS HERE.
WHO'S IN?
HMP.
LOOKS LIKE YOU GOT YOUR WAY AGAIN, MAL.
EVERYONE FALLING IN LINE, DOING WHAT ***YOU*** WANT.
I DIDN'T SAY A WORD.
YOU DIDN'T, DID YOU?
MUST BE NICE.
ACTUALLY, JAYNE...

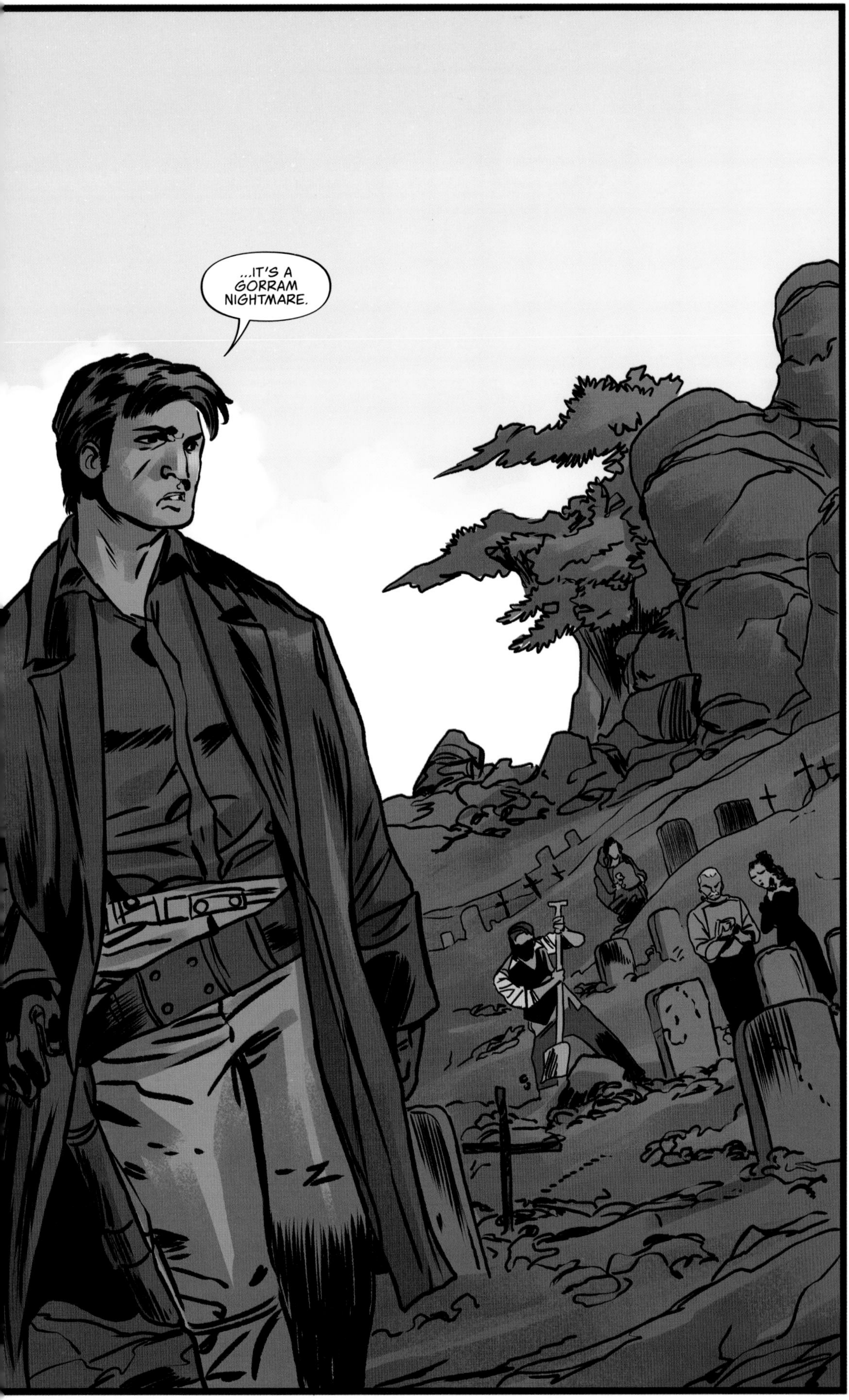
...IT'S A GORRAM NIGHTMARE.

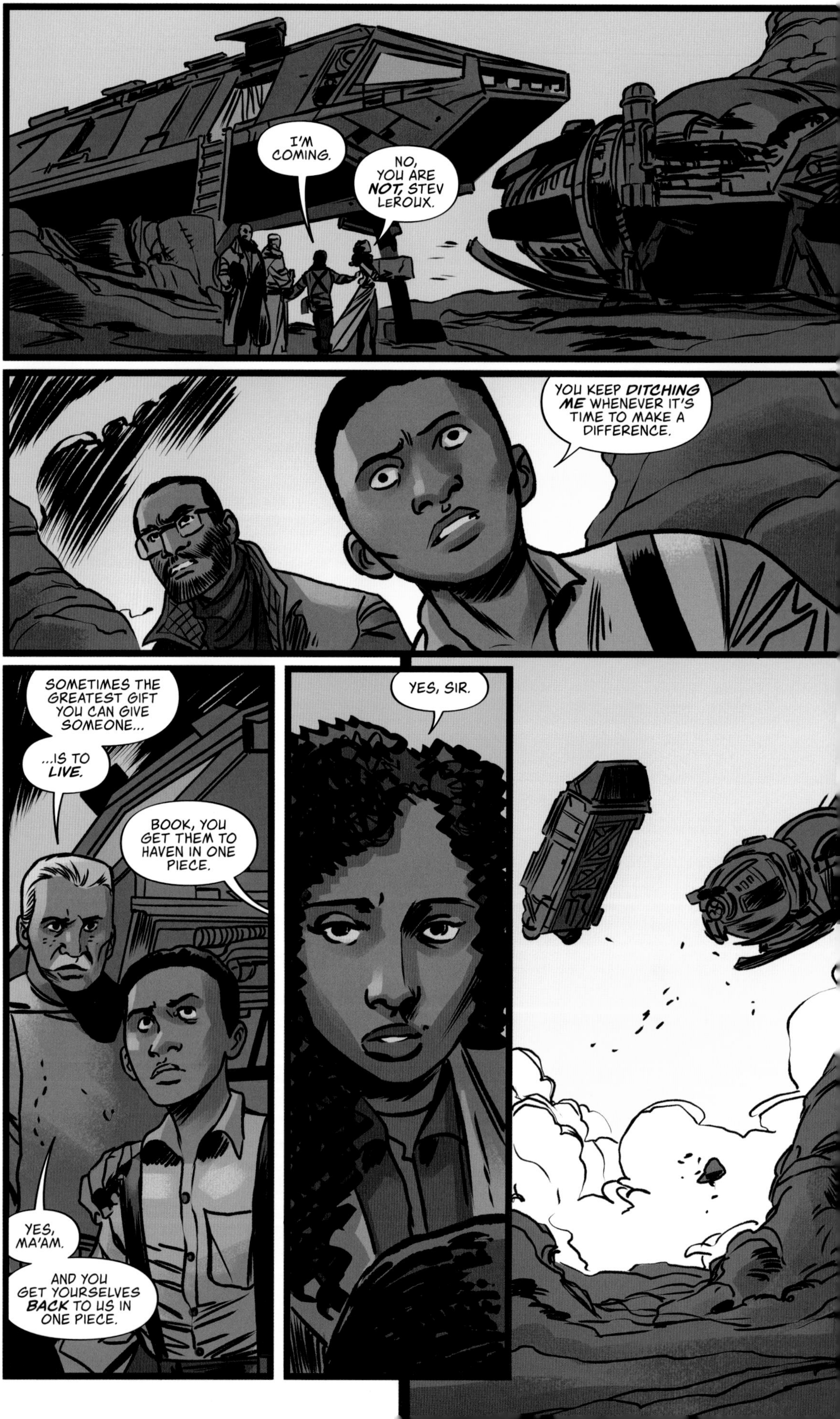
I'M COMING.
NO, YOU ARE NOT, STEV LEROUX.
YOU KEEP DITCHING ME WHENEVER IT'S TIME TO MAKE A DIFFERENCE.
SOMETIMES THE GREATEST GIFT YOU CAN GIVE SOMEONE...
...IS TO LIVE.
BOOK, YOU GET THEM TO HAVEN IN ONE PIECE.
YES, MA'AM.
AND YOU GET YOURSELVES BACK TO US IN ONE PIECE.
YES, SIR.

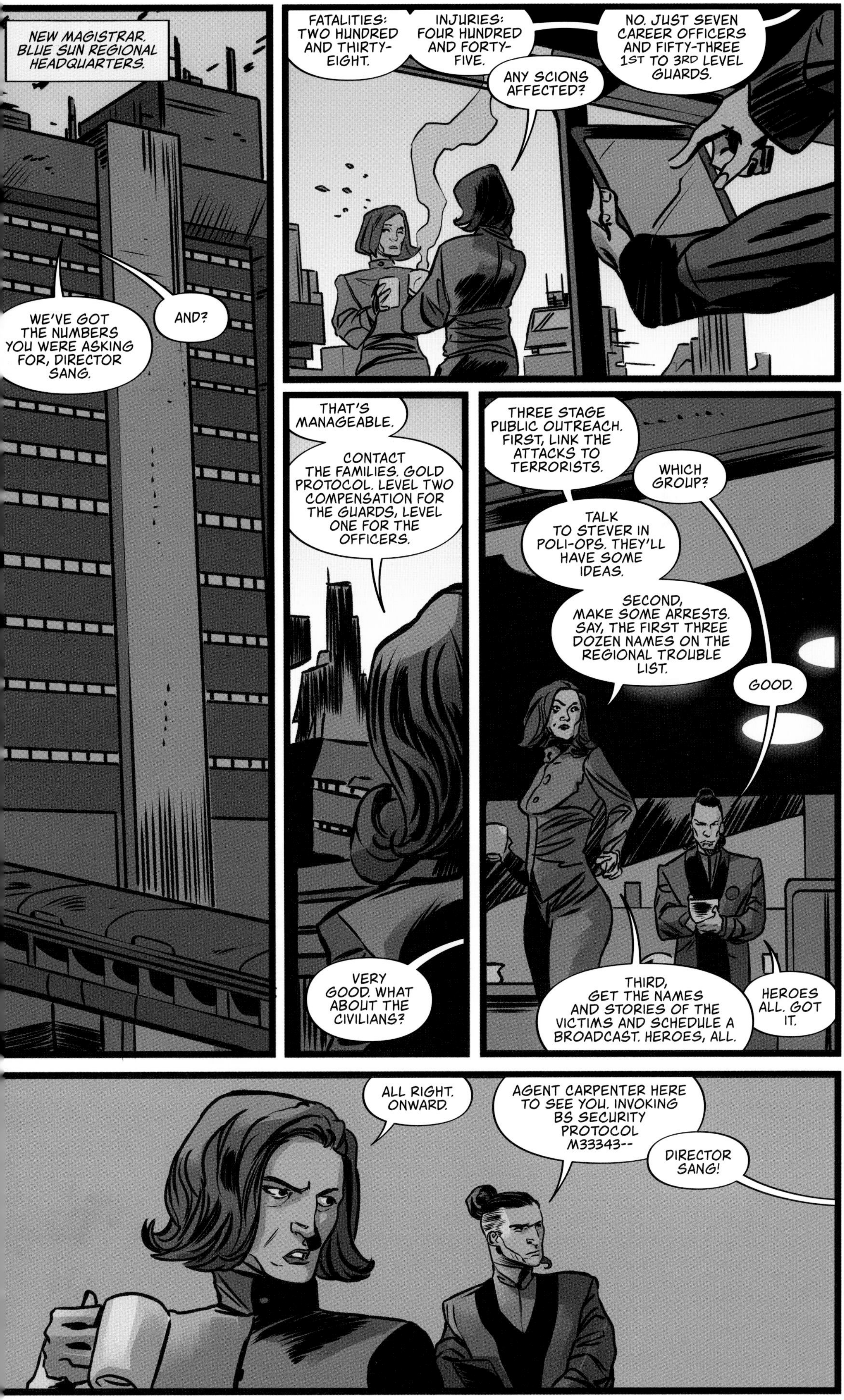
NEW MAGISTRAR. BLUE SUN REGIONAL HEADQUARTERS.
WE'VE GOT THE NUMBERS YOU WERE ASKING FOR, DIRECTOR SANG.
AND?
FATALITIES: TWO HUNDRED AND THIRTY-EIGHT.
INJURIES: FOUR HUNDRED AND FORTY-FIVE.
ANY SCIONS AFFECTED?
NO. JUST SEVEN CAREER OFFICERS AND FIFTY-THREE 1ST TO 3RD LEVEL GUARDS.
THAT'S MANAGEABLE.
CONTACT THE FAMILIES. GOLD PROTOCOL. LEVEL TWO COMPENSATION FOR THE GUARDS, LEVEL ONE FOR THE OFFICERS.
VERY GOOD. WHAT ABOUT THE CIVILIANS?
THREE STAGE PUBLIC OUTREACH. FIRST, LINK THE ATTACKS TO TERRORISTS.
WHICH GROUP?
TALK TO STEVER IN POLI-OPS. THEY'LL HAVE SOME IDEAS.
SECOND, MAKE SOME ARRESTS. SAY, THE FIRST THREE DOZEN NAMES ON THE REGIONAL TROUBLE LIST.
GOOD.
THIRD, GET THE NAMES AND STORIES OF THE VICTIMS AND SCHEDULE A BROADCAST. HEROES, ALL.
HEROES ALL. GOT IT.
ALL RIGHT. ONWARD.
AGENT CARPENTER HERE TO SEE YOU. INVOKING BS SECURITY PROTOCOL M33343--
DIRECTOR SANG!

AGENT, STAND DOWN OR--

DIRECTOR SANG, I'M AGENT CARPENTER! I INVOKED BS SECURITY PROTOCOL M33--

I KNOW. LET'S HEAR IT.

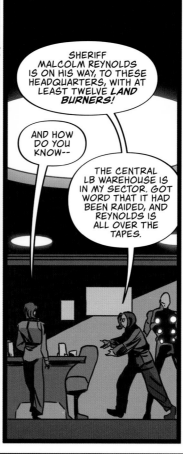

SHERIFF MALCOLM REYNOLDS IS ON HIS WAY, TO THESE HEADQUARTERS, WITH AT LEAST TWELVE *LAND BURNERS!*

AND HOW DO YOU KNOW--

THE CENTRAL LB WAREHOUSE IS IN MY SECTOR. GOT WORD THAT IT HAD BEEN RAIDED, AND REYNOLDS IS ALL OVER THE TAPES.

THE BURNERS ARE TAGGED--THEY SEND OUT PERIODIC LOCATION PINGS. WE'RE TRACKING THE TRAJECTORY, AND IT ENDS *RIGHT HERE...*

...IN LESS THAN AN HOUR.

YOU DIDN'T LEAVE ME MUCH TIME, AGENT CARPENTER.

DO YOU *KNOW* HOW MANY FORMS YOU HAVE TO FILL OUT TO INVOKE BS SECURITY PROTOCOL M33343?

A *DIRECT ATTACK* ON BLUE SUN HEADQUARTERS IN THE HEART OF NEW MAGISTRAR?

THAT WOULD BE *SUICIDE.*

THAT CAN'T BE HIS PLAN.

I DON'T KNOW HOW MUCH DIRECT EXPERIENCE YOU'VE HAD WITH REYNOLDS...

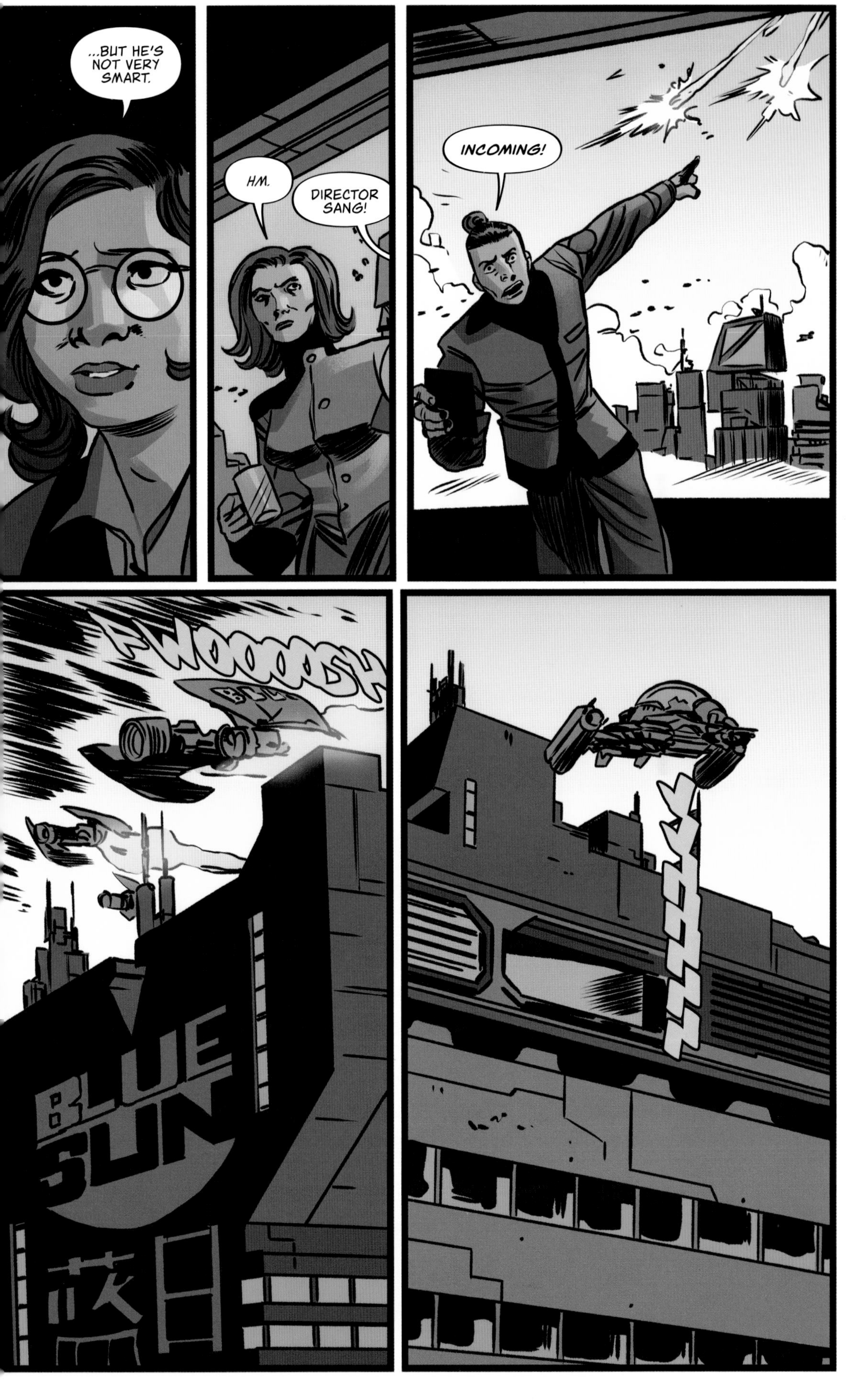
...BUT HE'S NOT VERY SMART.
HM.
DIRECTOR SANG!
INCOMING!
FWOOOOSH
BLUE SUN

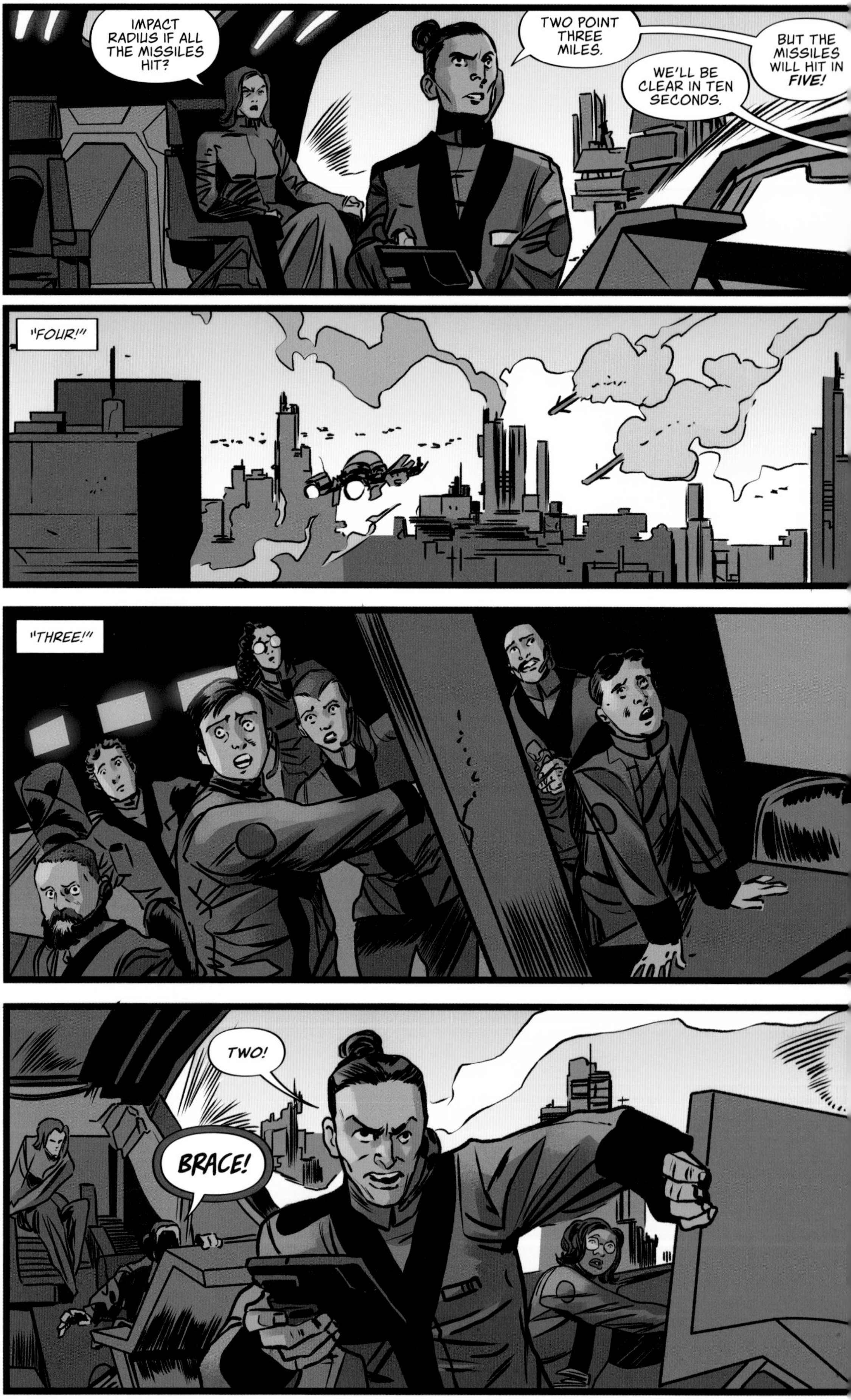
IMPACT RADIUS IF ALL THE MISSILES HIT?
TWO POINT THREE MILES.
BUT THE MISSILES WILL HIT IN FIVE!
WE'LL BE CLEAR IN TEN SECONDS.
"FOUR!"
"THREE!"
TWO!
BRACE!

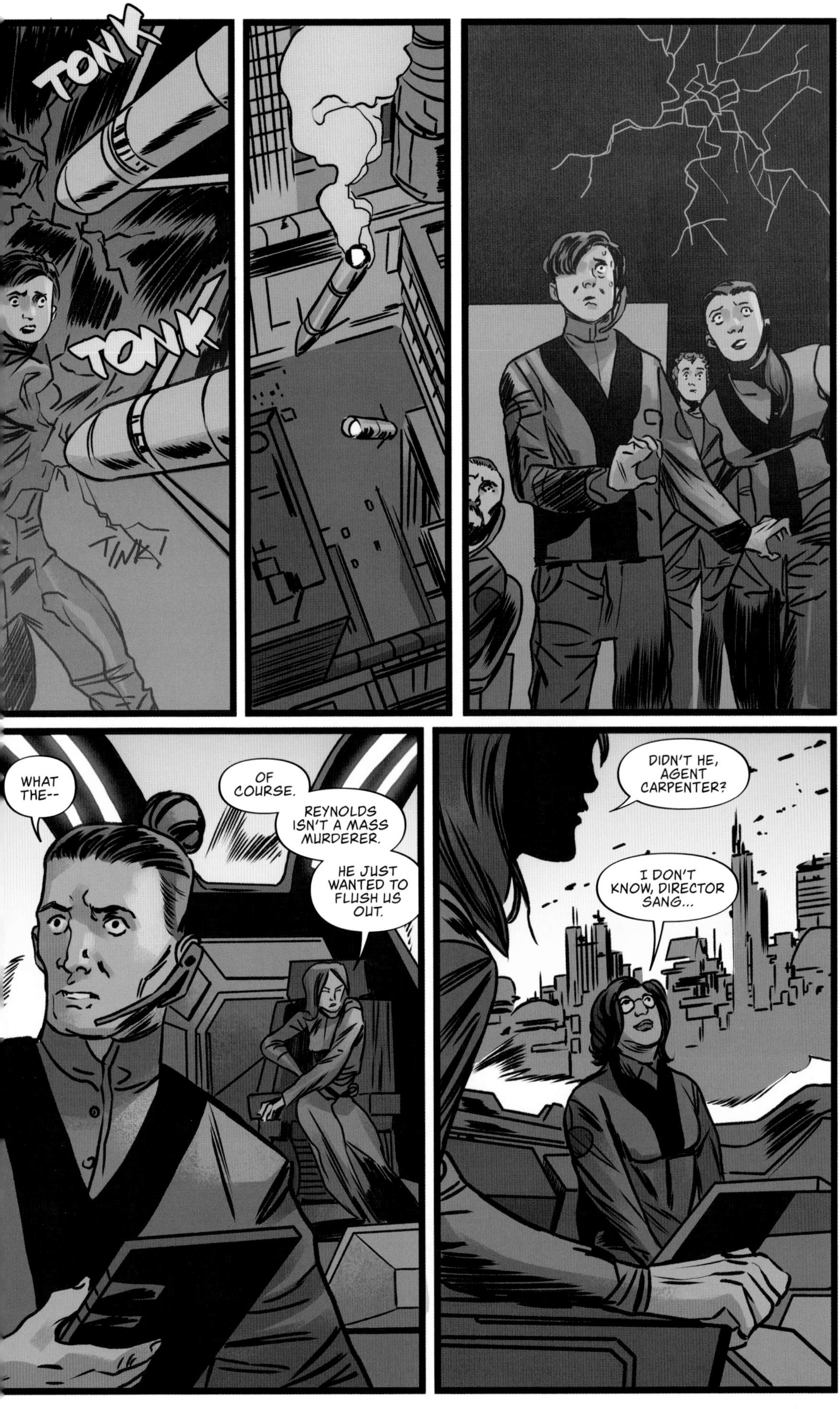
TONK
TONK
TINK!
WHAT THE--
OF COURSE.
REYNOLDS ISN'T A MASS MURDERER.
HE JUST WANTED TO FLUSH US OUT.
DIDN'T HE, AGENT CARPENTER?
I DON'T KNOW, DIRECTOR SANG...

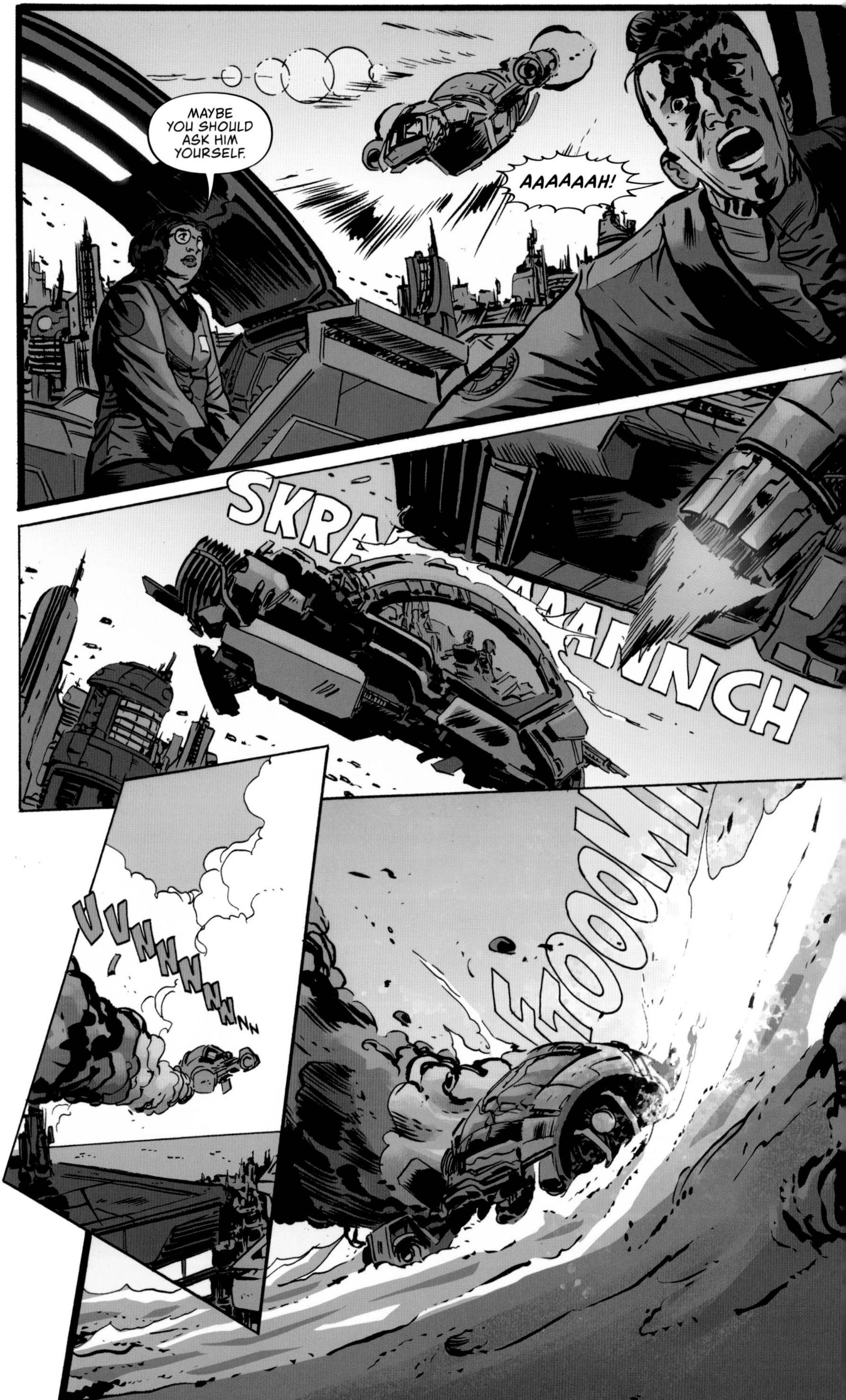
MAYBE YOU SHOULD ASK HIM YOURSELF.
AAAAAAH!
SKRAAAAAANNCH
VVNNNNNNNNnn
FOOOM

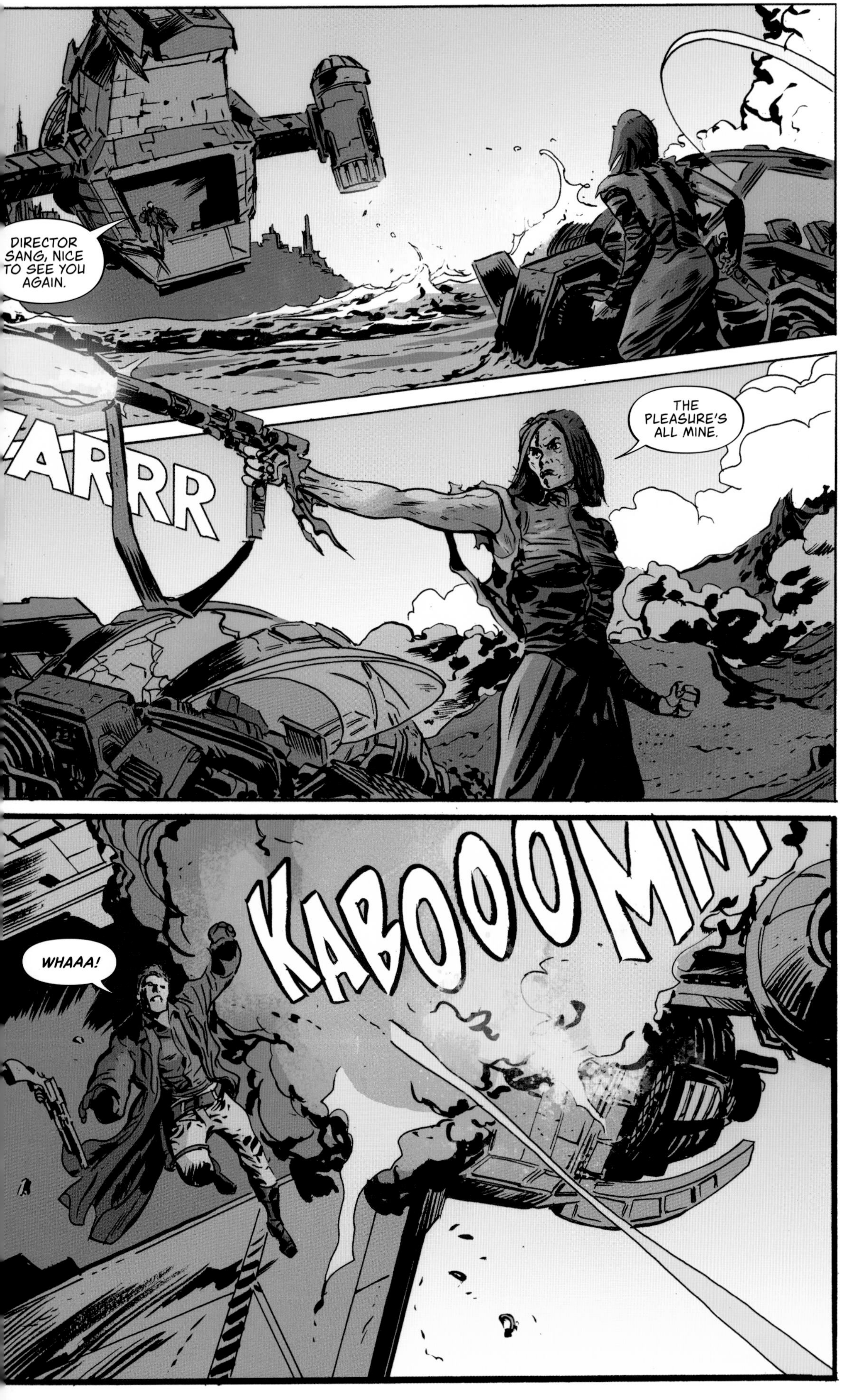
DIRECTOR SANG, NICE TO SEE YOU AGAIN.
THE PLEASURE'S ALL MINE.
ARRR
WHAAA!
KABOOOM

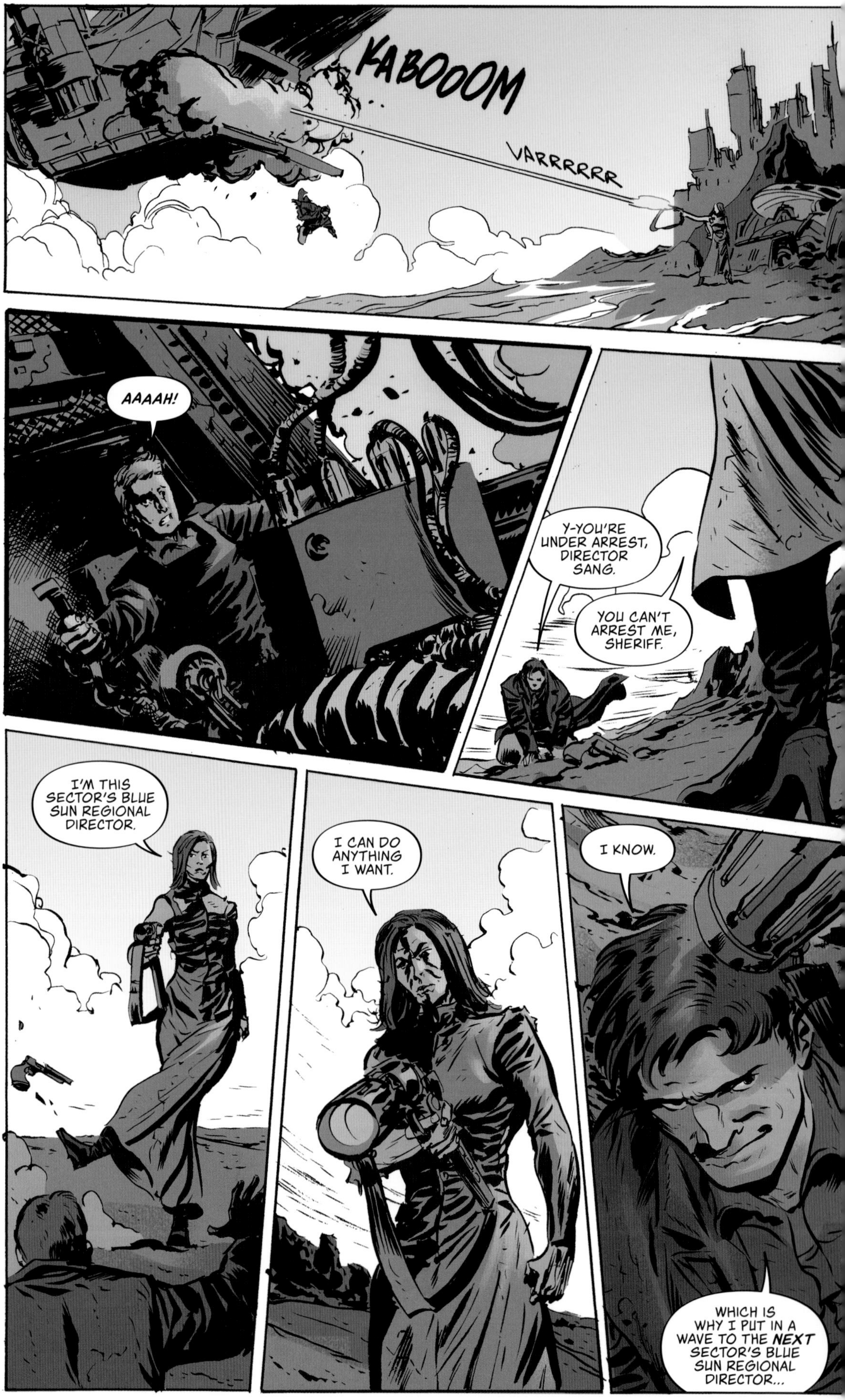
KABOOOM
VARRRRRR
AAAAH!
Y-YOU'RE UNDER ARREST, DIRECTOR SANG.
YOU CAN'T ARREST ME, SHERIFF.
I'M THIS SECTOR'S BLUE SUN REGIONAL DIRECTOR.
I CAN DO ANYTHING I WANT.
I KNOW.
WHICH IS WHY I PUT IN A WAVE TO THE *NEXT* SECTOR'S BLUE SUN REGIONAL DIRECTOR...

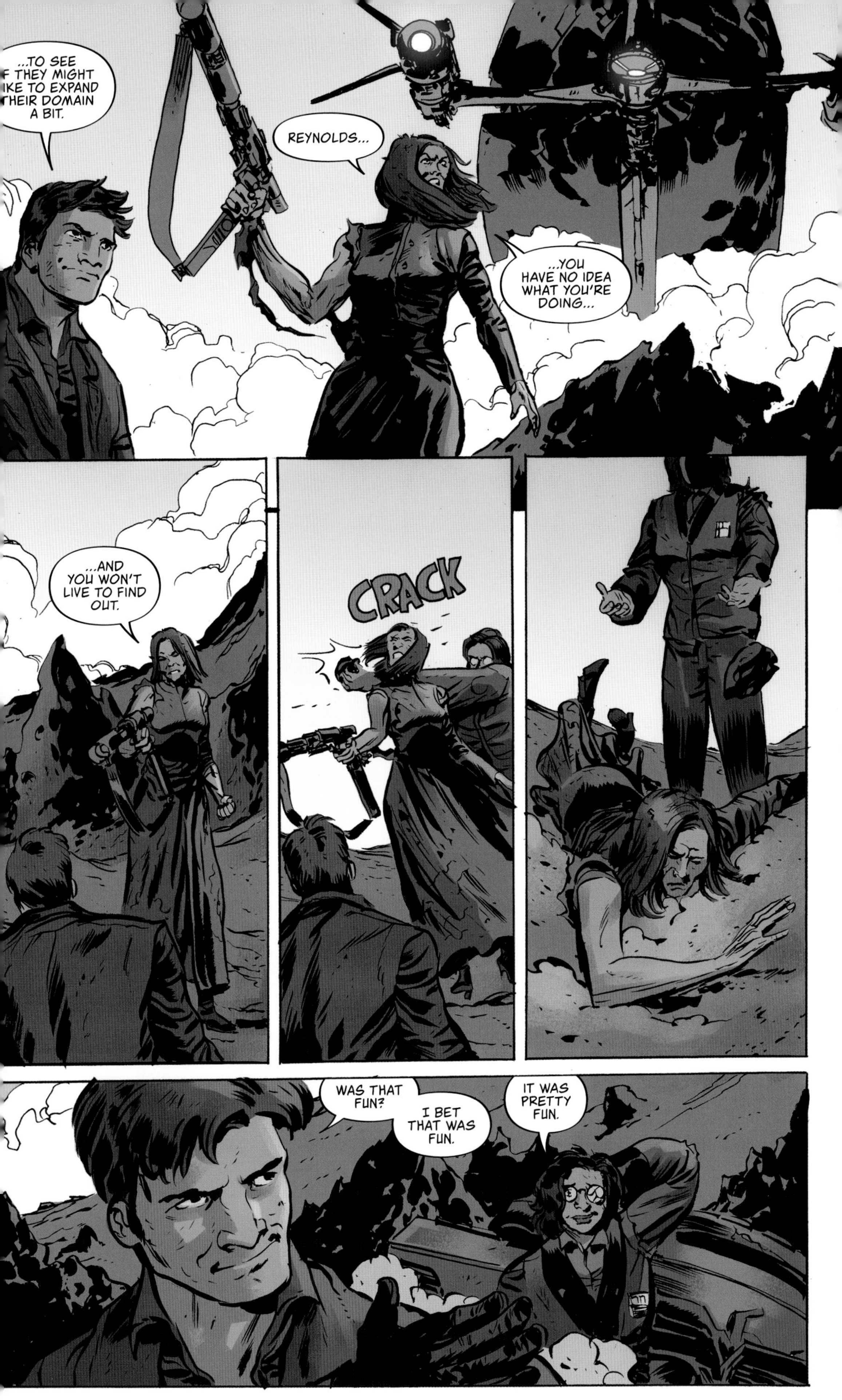
...TO SEE
F THEY MIGHT
IKE TO EXPAND
THEIR DOMAIN
A BIT.
REYNOLDS...
...YOU
HAVE NO IDEA
WHAT YOU'RE
DOING...
...AND
YOU WON'T
LIVE TO FIND
OUT.
CRACK
WAS THAT
FUN?
I BET
THAT WAS
FUN.
IT WAS
PRETTY
FUN.

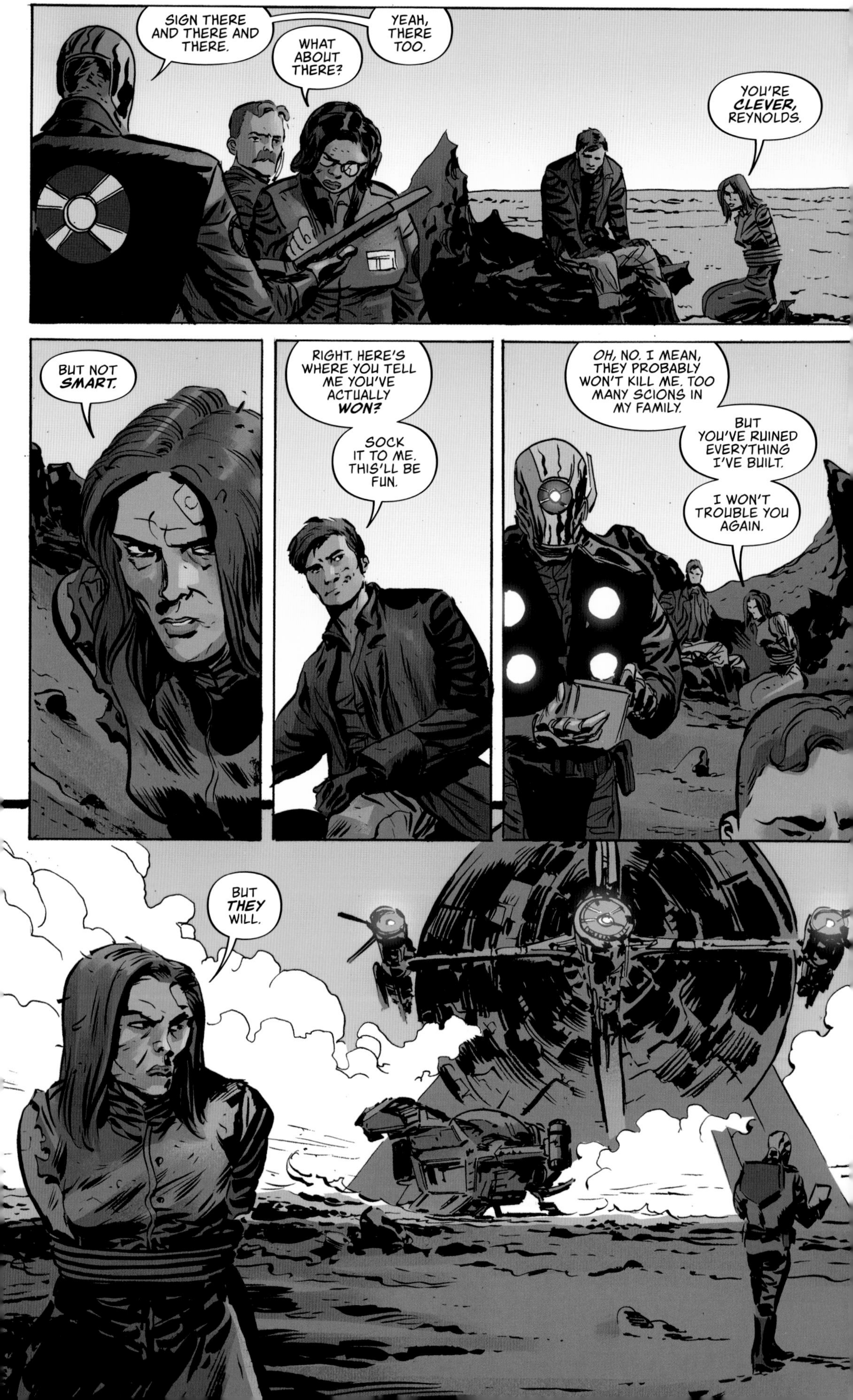
SIGN THERE AND THERE AND THERE.
WHAT ABOUT THERE?
YEAH, THERE TOO.
YOU'RE CLEVER, REYNOLDS.
BUT NOT SMART.
RIGHT. HERE'S WHERE YOU TELL ME YOU'VE ACTUALLY WON?
SOCK IT TO ME. THIS'LL BE FUN.
OH, NO. I MEAN, THEY PROBABLY WON'T KILL ME. TOO MANY SCIONS IN MY FAMILY.
BUT YOU'VE RUINED EVERYTHING I'VE BUILT.
I WON'T TROUBLE YOU AGAIN.
BUT THEY WILL.

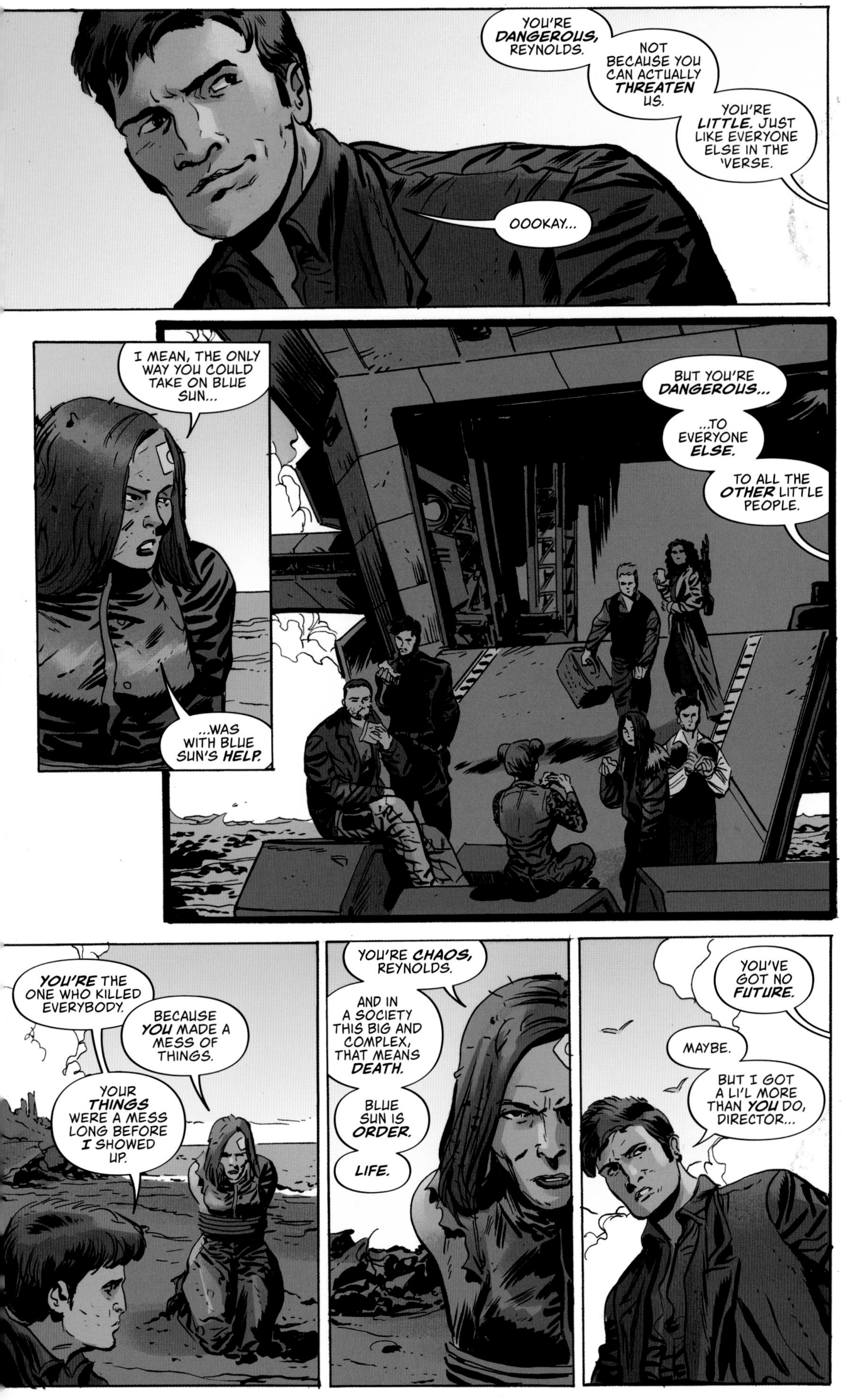
YOU'RE DANGEROUS, REYNOLDS.
NOT BECAUSE YOU CAN ACTUALLY THREATEN US.
YOU'RE LITTLE. JUST LIKE EVERYONE ELSE IN THE 'VERSE.
OOOKAY...
I MEAN, THE ONLY WAY YOU COULD TAKE ON BLUE SUN...
...WAS WITH BLUE SUN'S HELP.
BUT YOU'RE DANGEROUS...
...TO EVERYONE ELSE.
TO ALL THE OTHER LITTLE PEOPLE.
YOU'RE THE ONE WHO KILLED EVERYBODY.
BECAUSE YOU MADE A MESS OF THINGS.
YOUR THINGS WERE A MESS LONG BEFORE I SHOWED UP.
YOU'RE CHAOS, REYNOLDS.
AND IN A SOCIETY THIS BIG AND COMPLEX, THAT MEANS DEATH.
BLUE SUN IS ORDER.
LIFE.
YOU'VE GOT NO FUTURE.
MAYBE.
BUT I GOT A LI'L MORE THAN YOU DO, DIRECTOR...

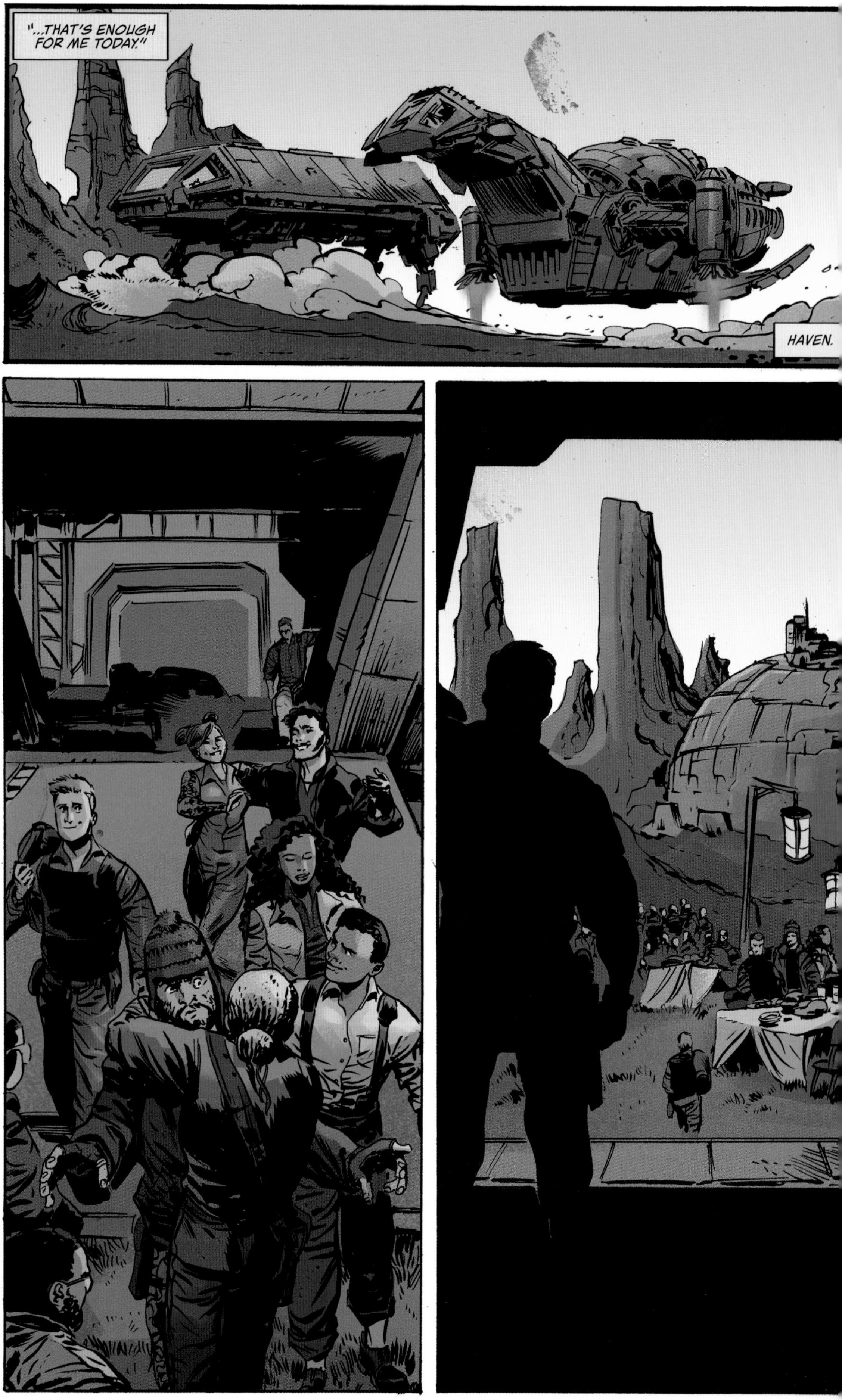
"...THAT'S ENOUGH FOR ME TODAY."
HAVEN.

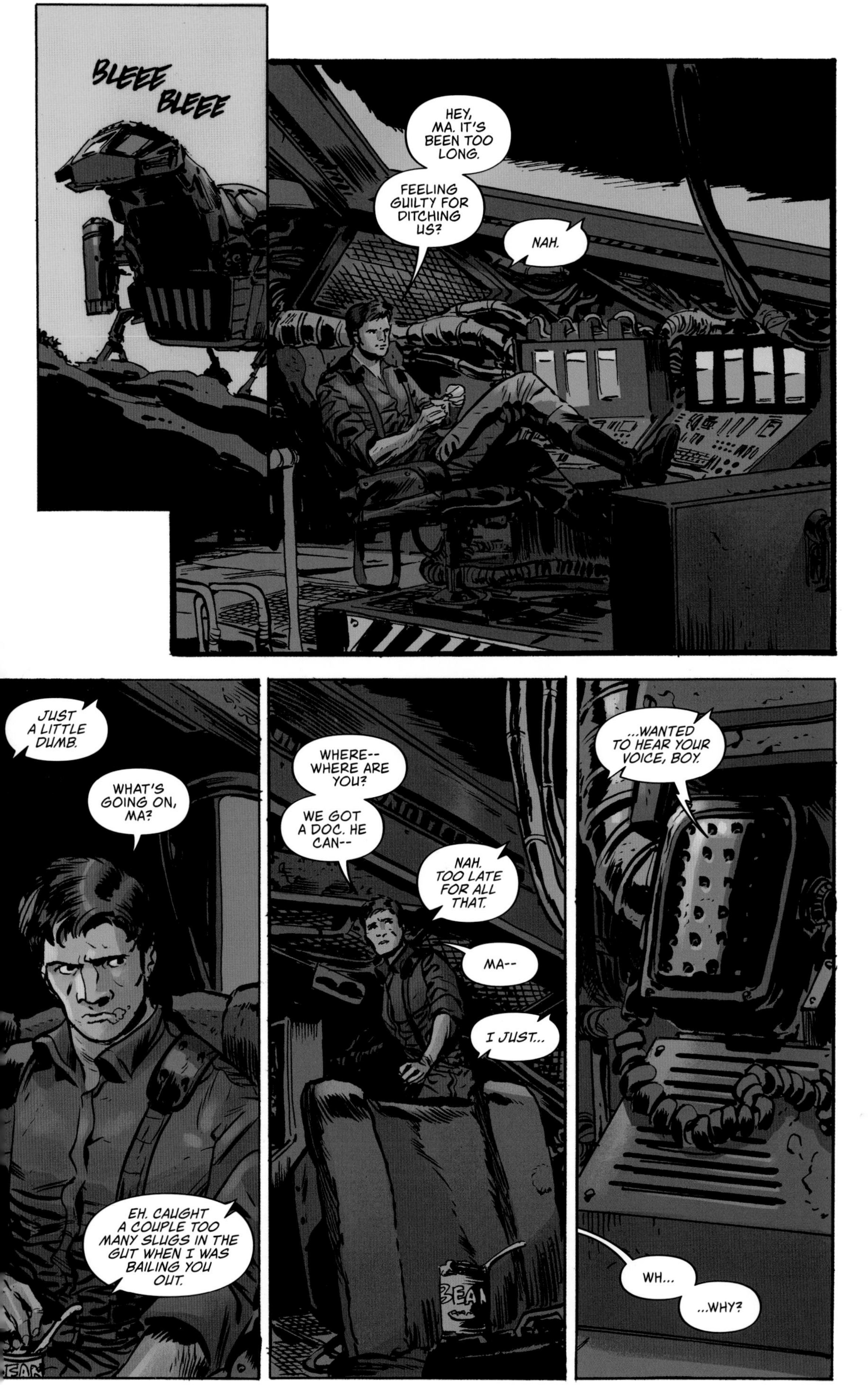
BLEEE BLEEE
HEY, MA. IT'S BEEN TOO LONG.
FEELING GUILTY FOR DITCHING US?
NAH.
JUST A LITTLE DUMB.
WHAT'S GOING ON, MA?
EH. CAUGHT A COUPLE TOO MANY SLUGS IN THE GUT WHEN I WAS BAILING YOU OUT.
WHERE-- WHERE ARE YOU?
WE GOT A DOC. HE CAN--
NAH. TOO LATE FOR ALL THAT.
MA--
I JUST...
...WANTED TO HEAR YOUR VOICE, BOY.
WH...
...WHY?

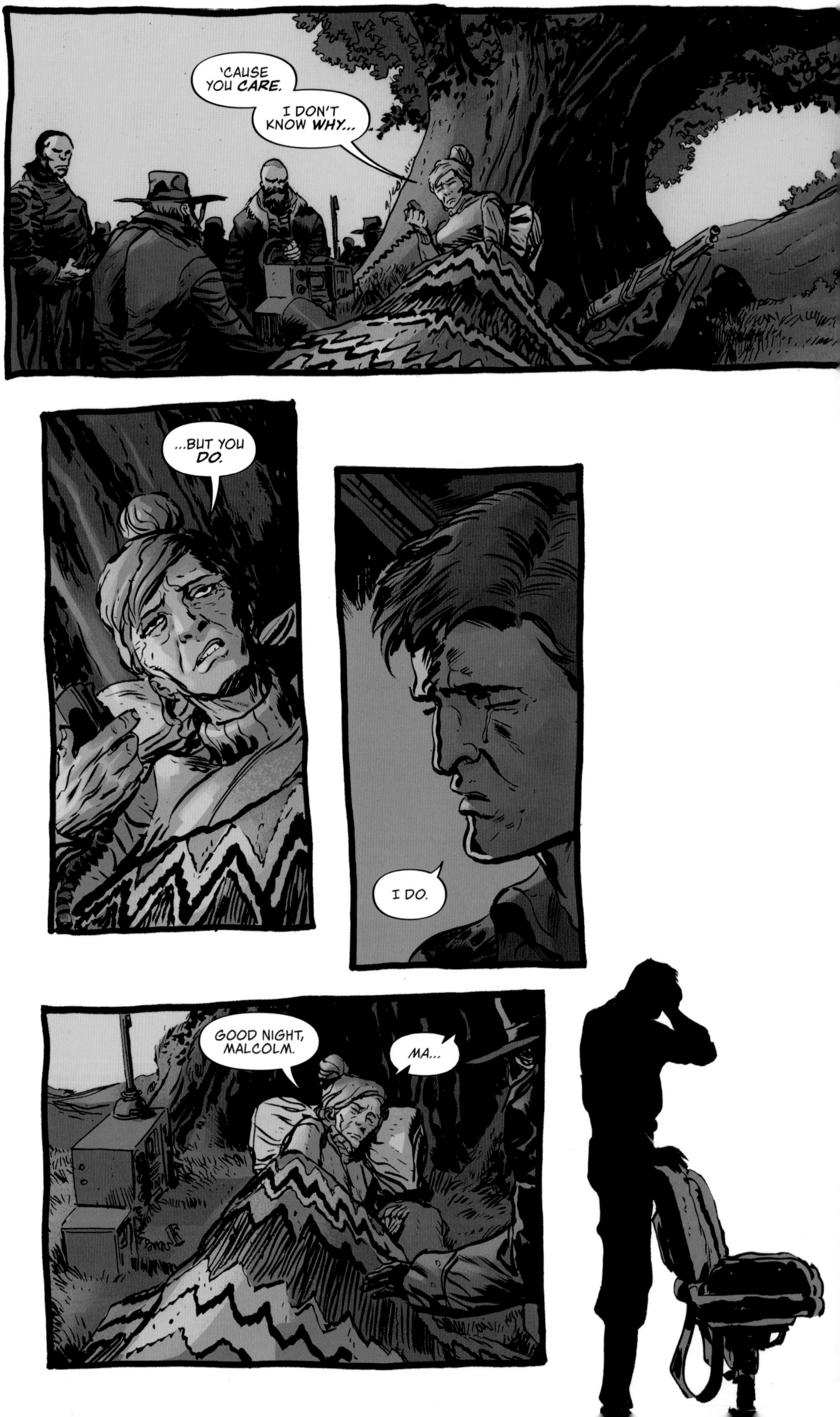
'CAUSE YOU CARE.
I DON'T KNOW WHY...
...BUT YOU DO.
I DO.
GOOD NIGHT, MALCOLM.
MA...

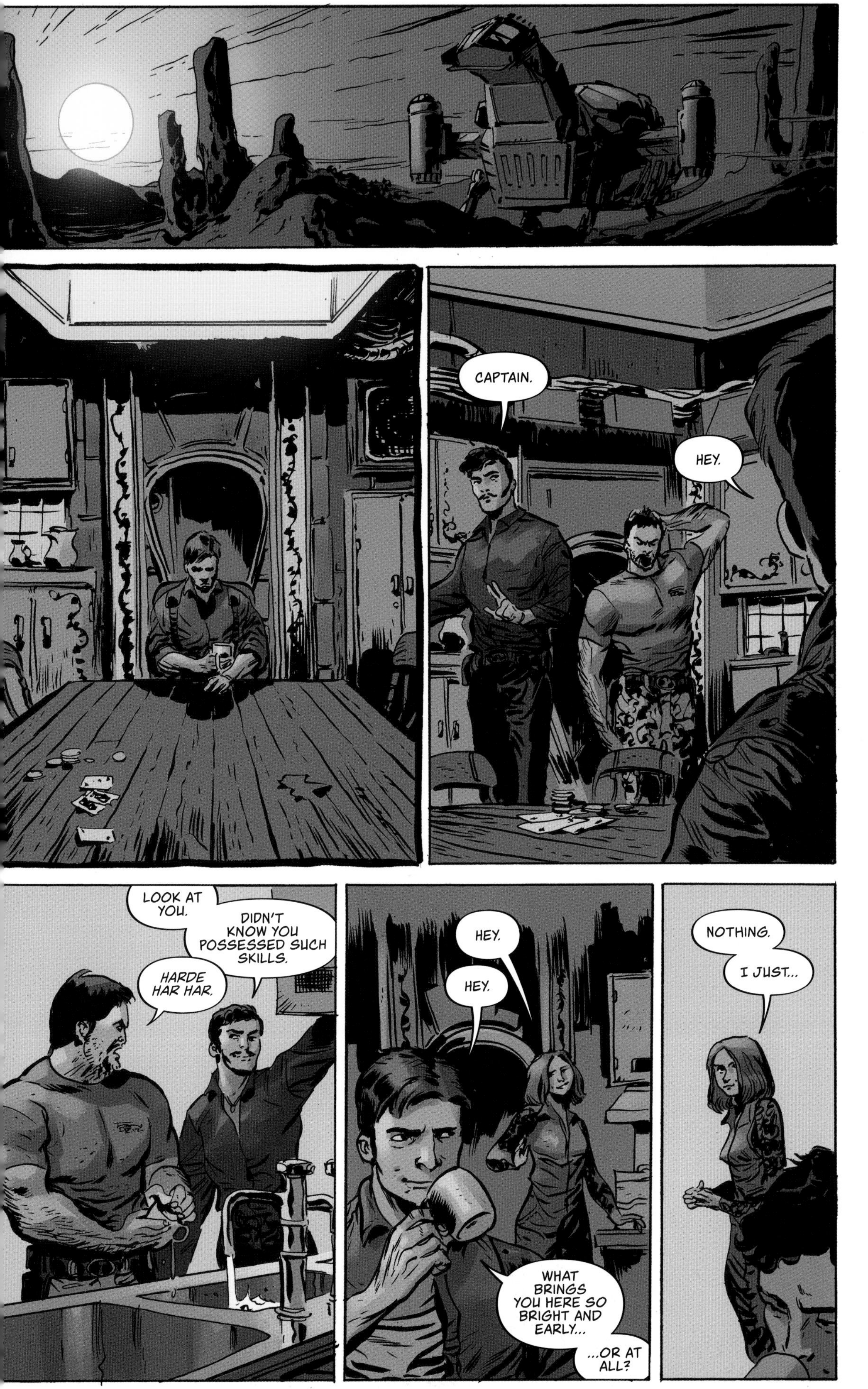
CAPTAIN.
HEY.
LOOK AT YOU.
DIDN'T KNOW YOU POSSESSED SUCH SKILLS.
HARDE HAR HAR.
HEY.
HEY.
WHAT BRINGS YOU HERE SO BRIGHT AND EARLY...
...OR AT ALL?
NOTHING.
I JUST...

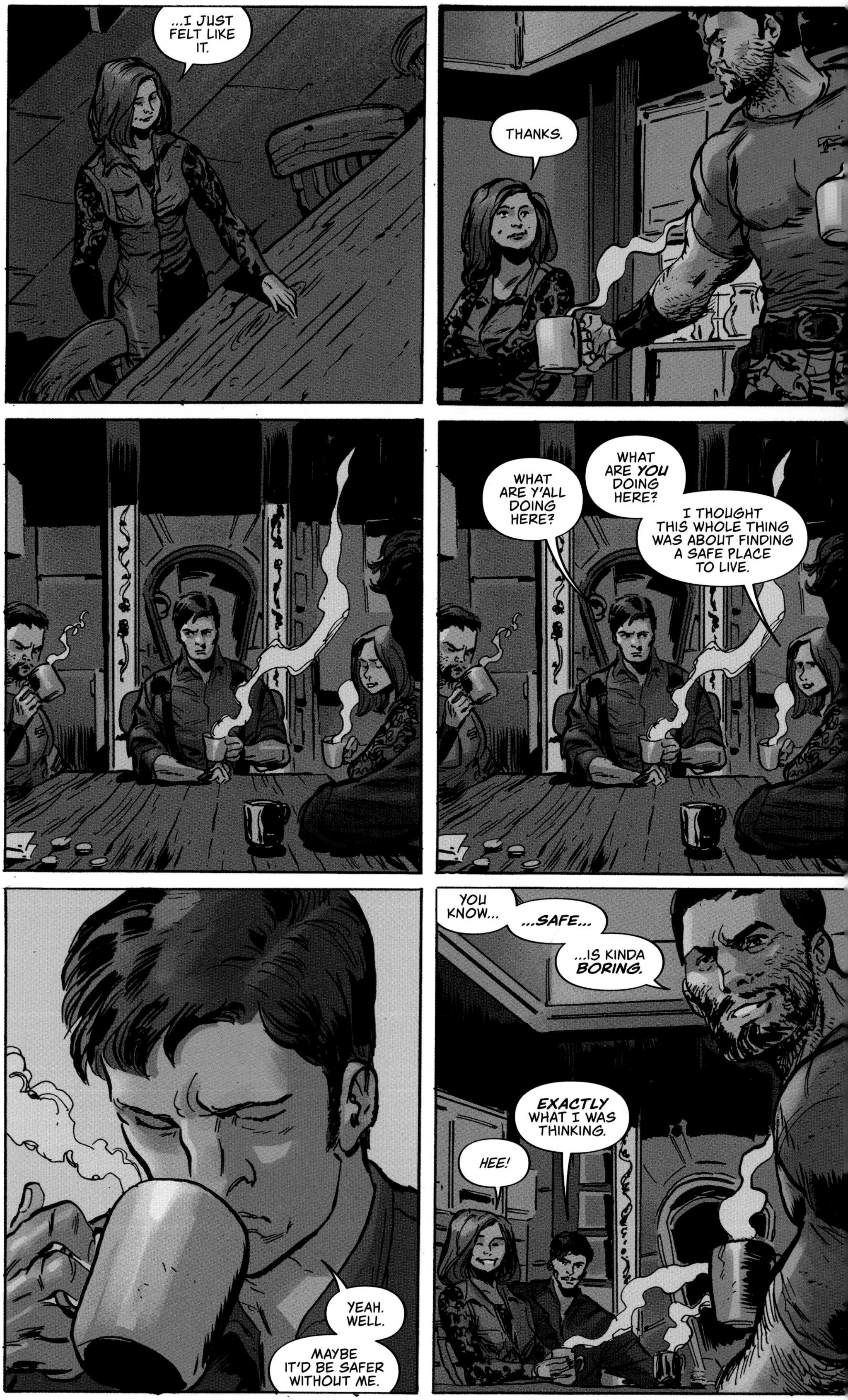

...I JUST FELT LIKE IT.
THANKS.
WHAT ARE Y'ALL DOING HERE?
WHAT ARE YOU DOING HERE?
I THOUGHT THIS WHOLE THING WAS ABOUT FINDING A SAFE PLACE TO LIVE.
YEAH. WELL.
MAYBE IT'D BE SAFER WITHOUT ME.
YOU KNOW...
...SAFE...
...IS KINDA BORING.
EXACTLY WHAT I WAS THINKING.
HEE!

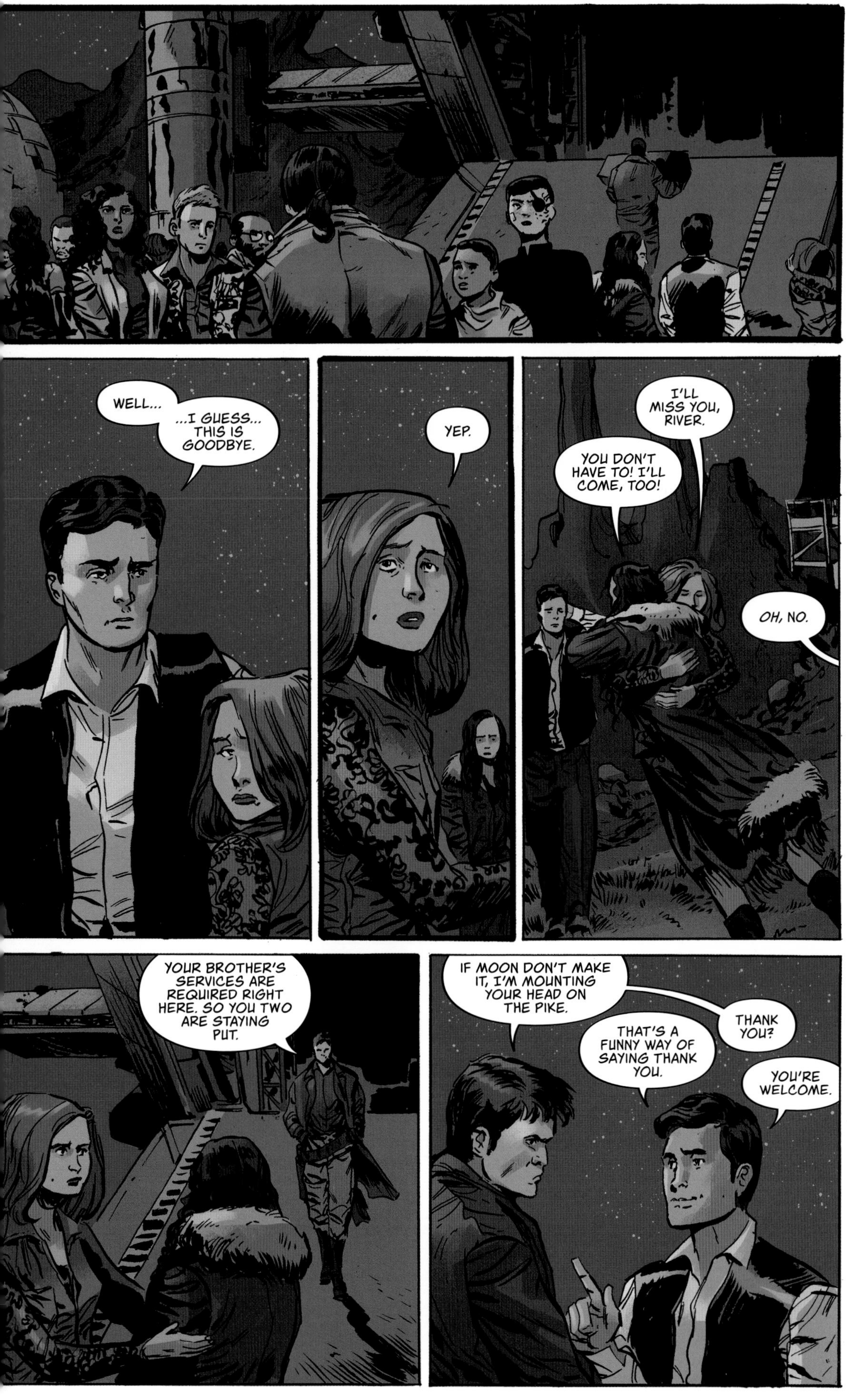
WELL...
...I GUESS... THIS IS GOODBYE.
YEP.
I'LL MISS YOU, RIVER.
YOU DON'T HAVE TO! I'LL COME, TOO!
OH, NO.
YOUR BROTHER'S SERVICES ARE REQUIRED RIGHT HERE. SO YOU TWO ARE STAYING PUT.
IF MOON DON'T MAKE IT, I'M MOUNTING YOUR HEAD ON THE PIKE.
THANK YOU?
THAT'S A FUNNY WAY OF SAYING THANK YOU.
YOU'RE WELCOME.

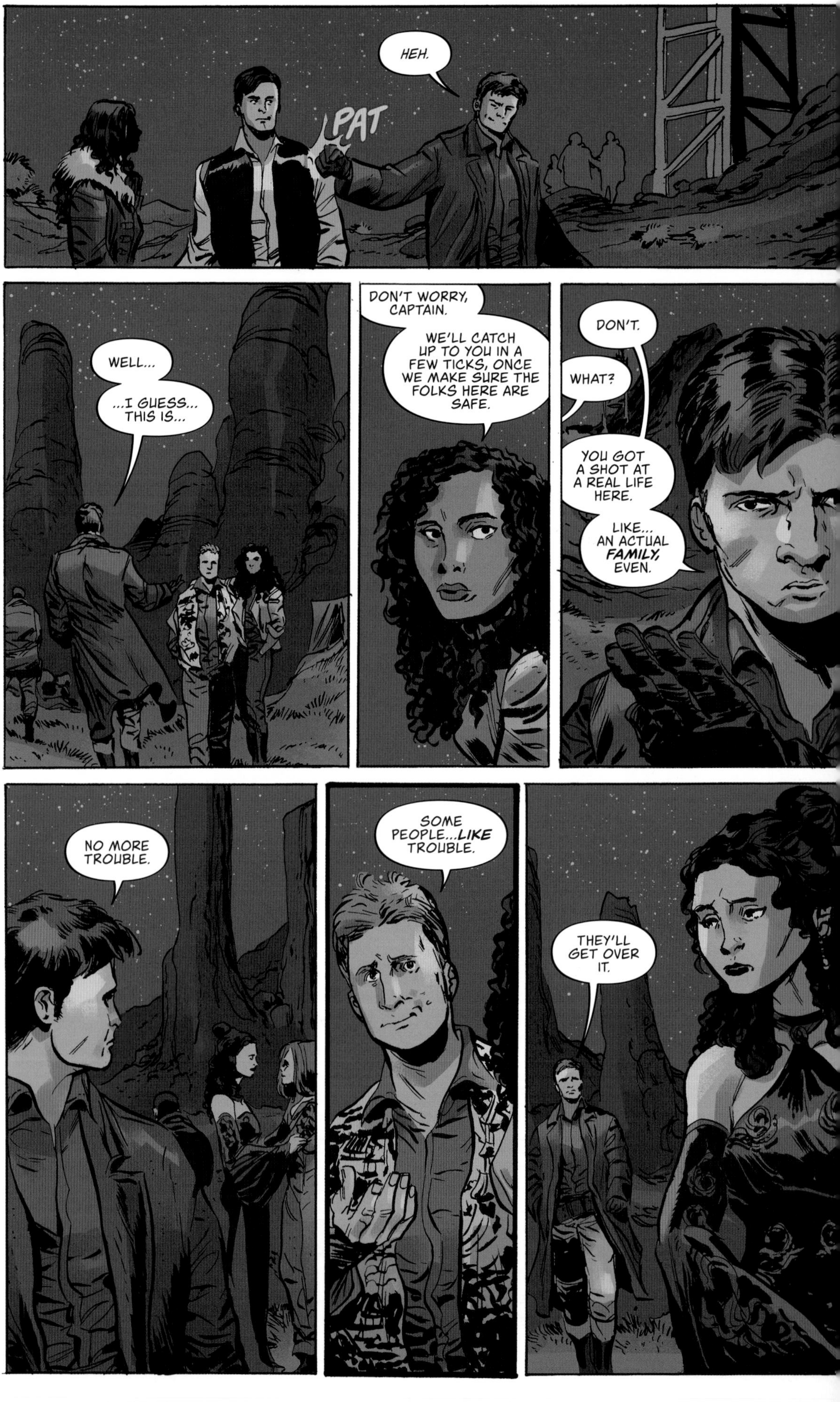
HEH.
PAT
WELL...
...I GUESS... THIS IS...
DON'T WORRY, CAPTAIN.
WE'LL CATCH UP TO YOU IN A FEW TICKS, ONCE WE MAKE SURE THE FOLKS HERE ARE SAFE.
DON'T.
WHAT?
YOU GOT A SHOT AT A REAL LIFE HERE.
LIKE... AN ACTUAL **FAMILY,** EVEN.
NO MORE TROUBLE.
SOME PEOPLE...**LIKE** TROUBLE.
THEY'LL GET OVER IT.

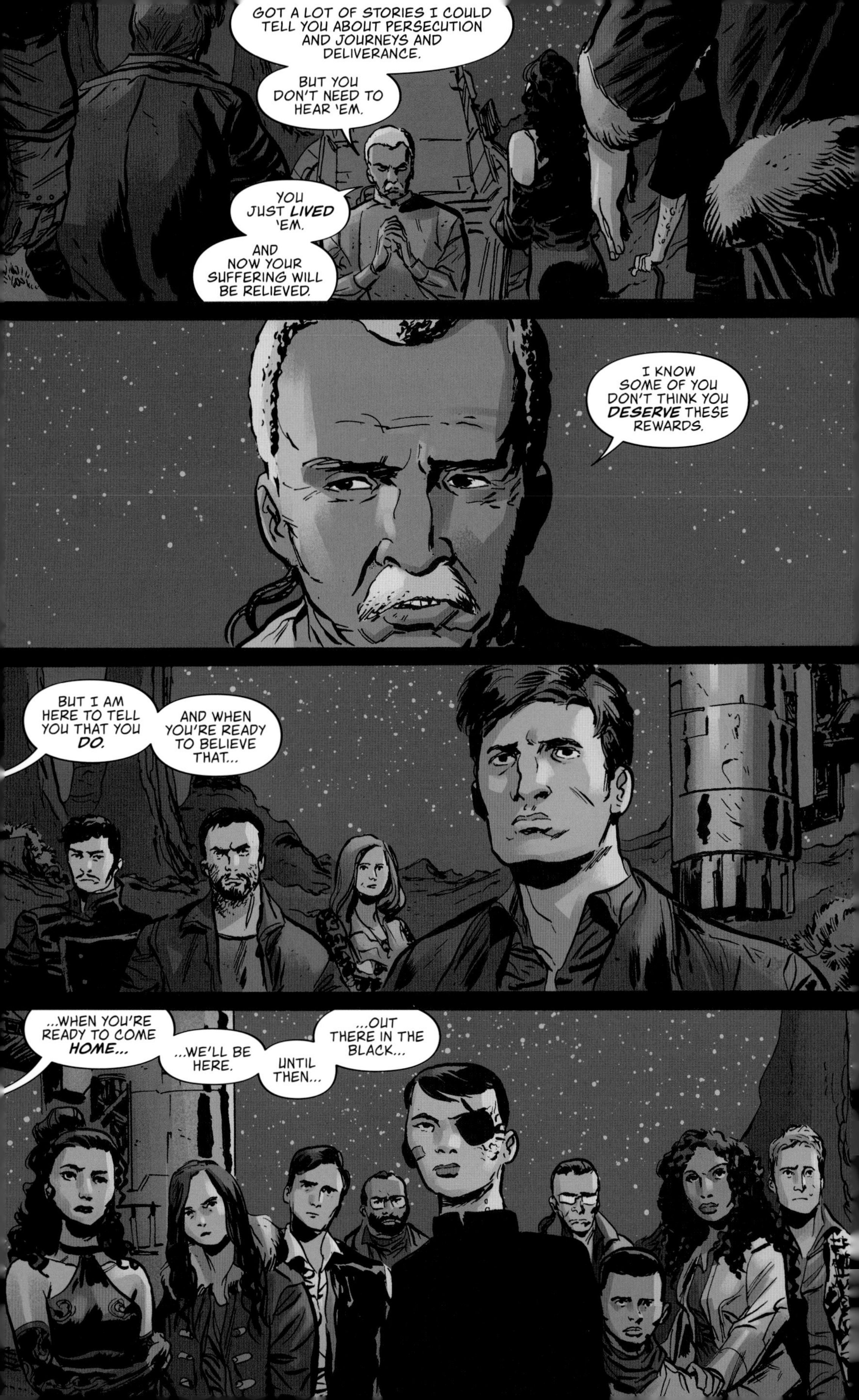
GOT A LOT OF STORIES I COULD TELL YOU ABOUT PERSECUTION AND JOURNEYS AND DELIVERANCE.
BUT YOU DON'T NEED TO HEAR 'EM.
YOU JUST **LIVED** 'EM.
AND NOW YOUR SUFFERING WILL BE RELIEVED.
I KNOW SOME OF YOU DON'T THINK YOU **DESERVE** THESE REWARDS.
BUT I AM HERE TO TELL YOU THAT YOU **DO.**
AND WHEN YOU'RE READY TO BELIEVE THAT...
...WHEN YOU'RE READY TO COME **HOME...**
...WE'LL BE HERE.
UNTIL THEN...
...OUT THERE IN THE BLACK...

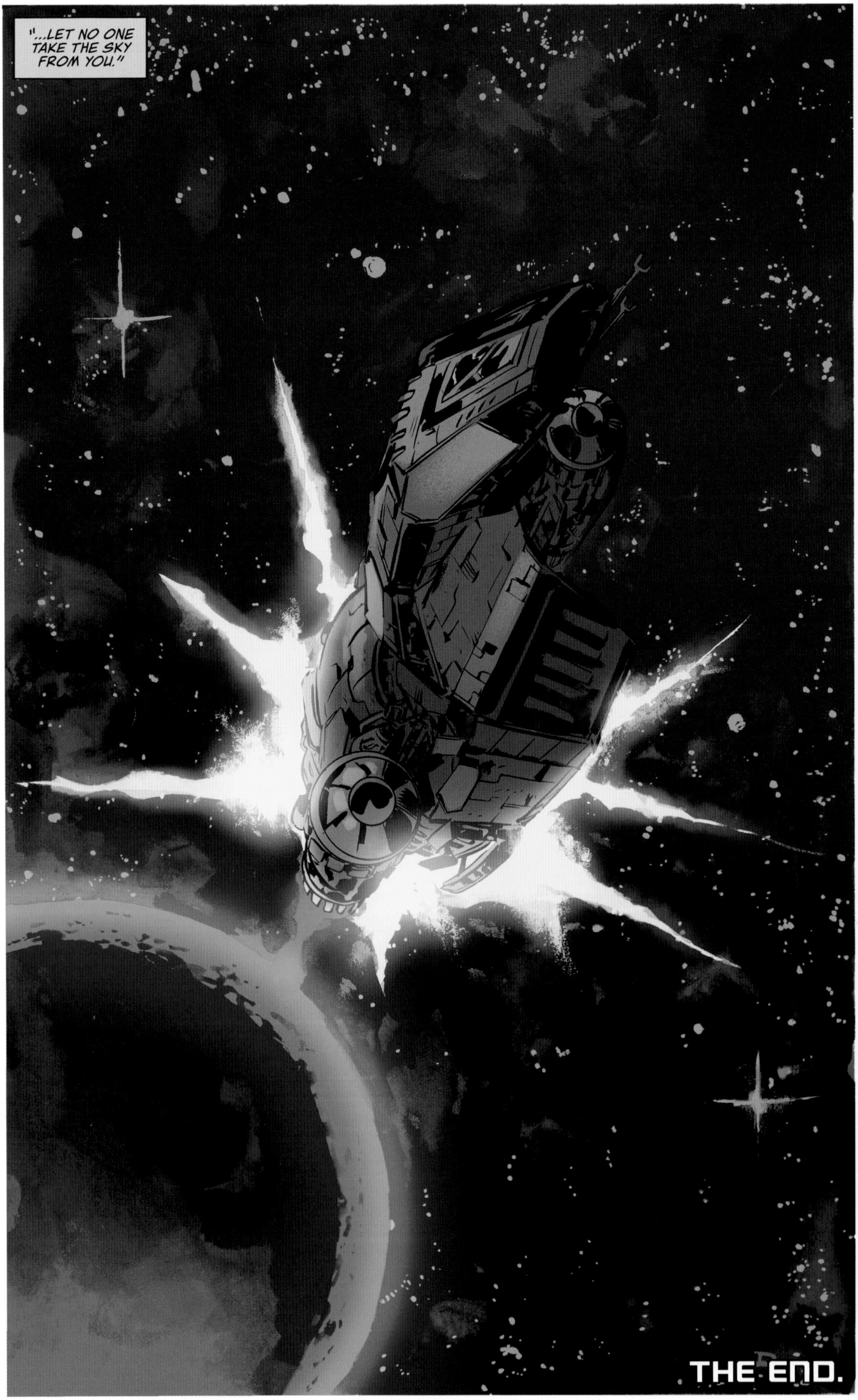
"...LET NO ONE TAKE THE SKY FROM YOU."
THE END.

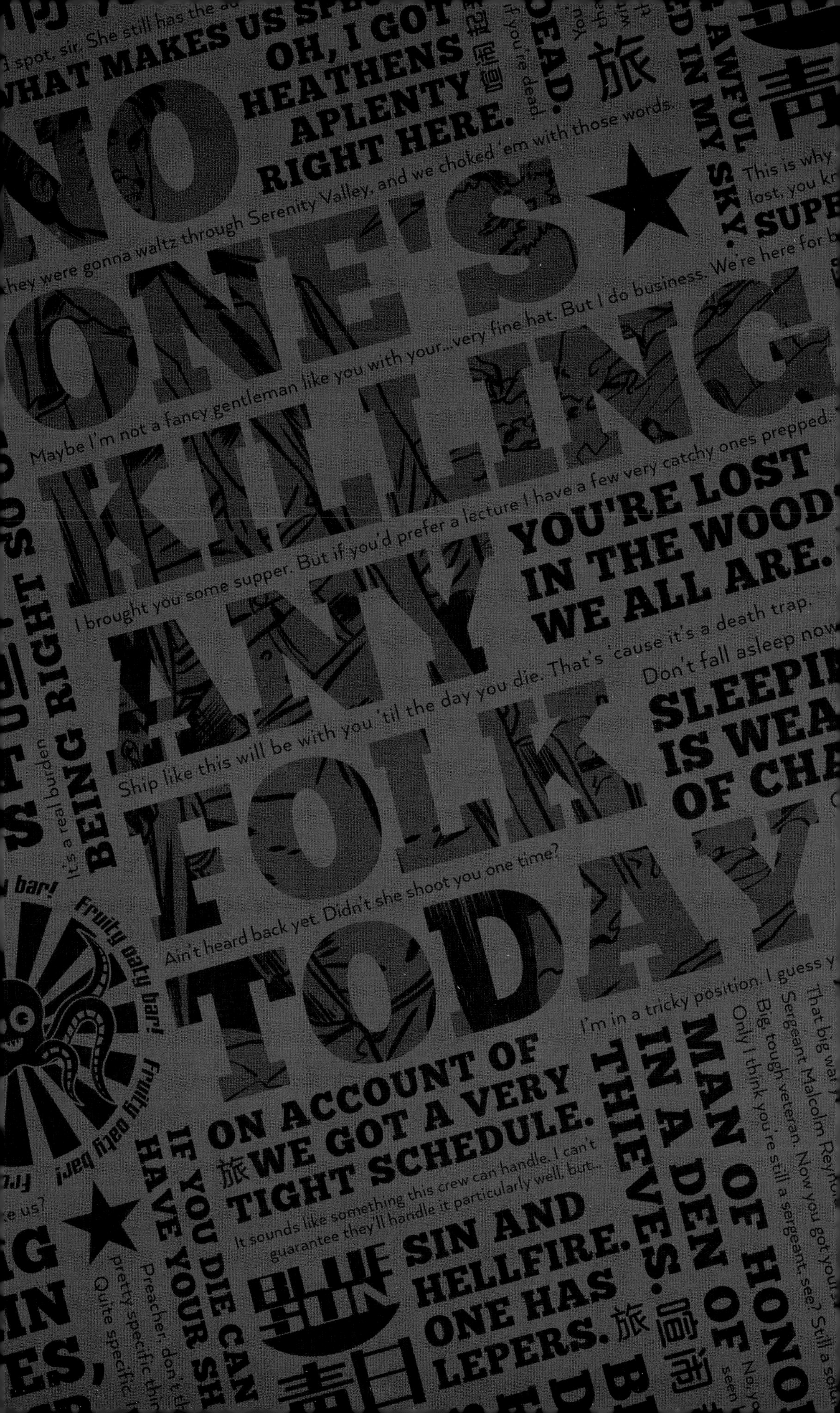

NO ONE'S KILLING ANY FOLK TODAY
OH, I GOT HEATHENS APLENTY RIGHT HERE.
WHAT MAKES US
if you're dead.
DEAD.
AWFUL IN MY SKY.
They were gonna waltz through Serenity Valley, and we choked 'em with those words.
Maybe I'm not a fancy gentleman like you with your...very fine hat. But I do business.
I brought you some supper. But if you'd prefer a lecture I have a few very catchy ones prepped.
YOU'RE LOST IN THE WOOD
WE ALL ARE.
Ship like this will be with you 'til the day you die. That's 'cause it's a death trap.
Don't fall asleep now
Ain't heard back yet. Didn't she shoot you one time?
It's a real burden
BEING RIGHT
Fruity oaty bar!
I'm in a tricky position.
ON ACCOUNT OF WE GOT A VERY TIGHT SCHEDULE.
It sounds like something this crew can handle. I can't guarantee they'll handle it particularly well, but...
SIN AND HELLFIRE. ONE HAS LEPERS.
IF YOU DIE
HAVE YOUR
THIEVES.
IN A DEN
MAN OF HONO
Sergeant Malcolm Reyno
Big, tough veteran. Now you got your
Only I think you're still a sergeant, see? Still a s
Preacher, don't
pretty specific
Quite specific

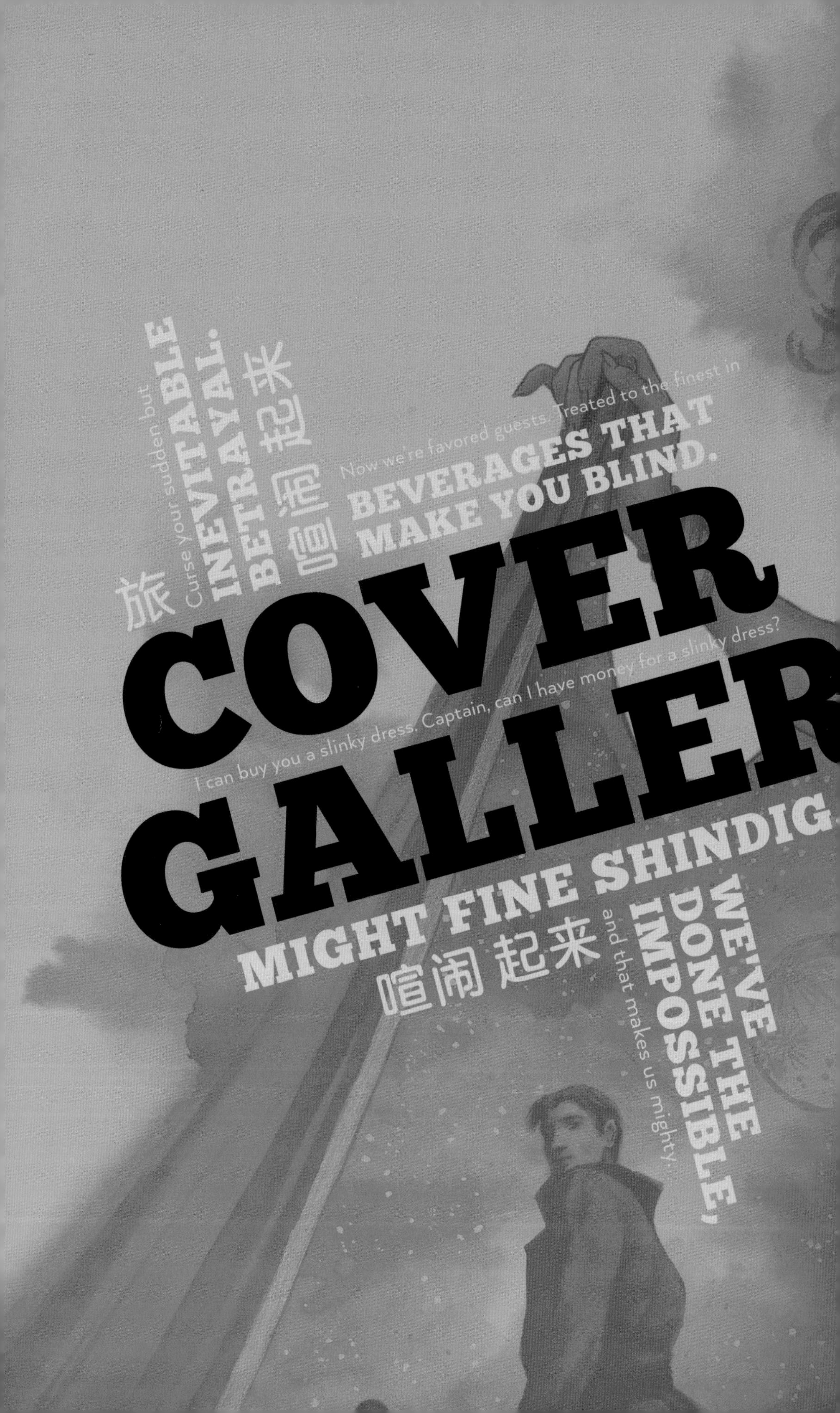
旅
Curse your sudden but
INEVITABLE
BETRAYAL.
喧闹 起来
Now we're favored guests. Treated to the finest in
BEVERAGES THAT
MAKE YOU BLIND.
COVER
I can buy you a slinky dress. Captain, can I have money for a slinky dress?
GALLER
MIGHT FINE SHINDIG
喧闹 起来
WE'VE
DONE THE
IMPOSSIBLE,
and that makes us mighty.

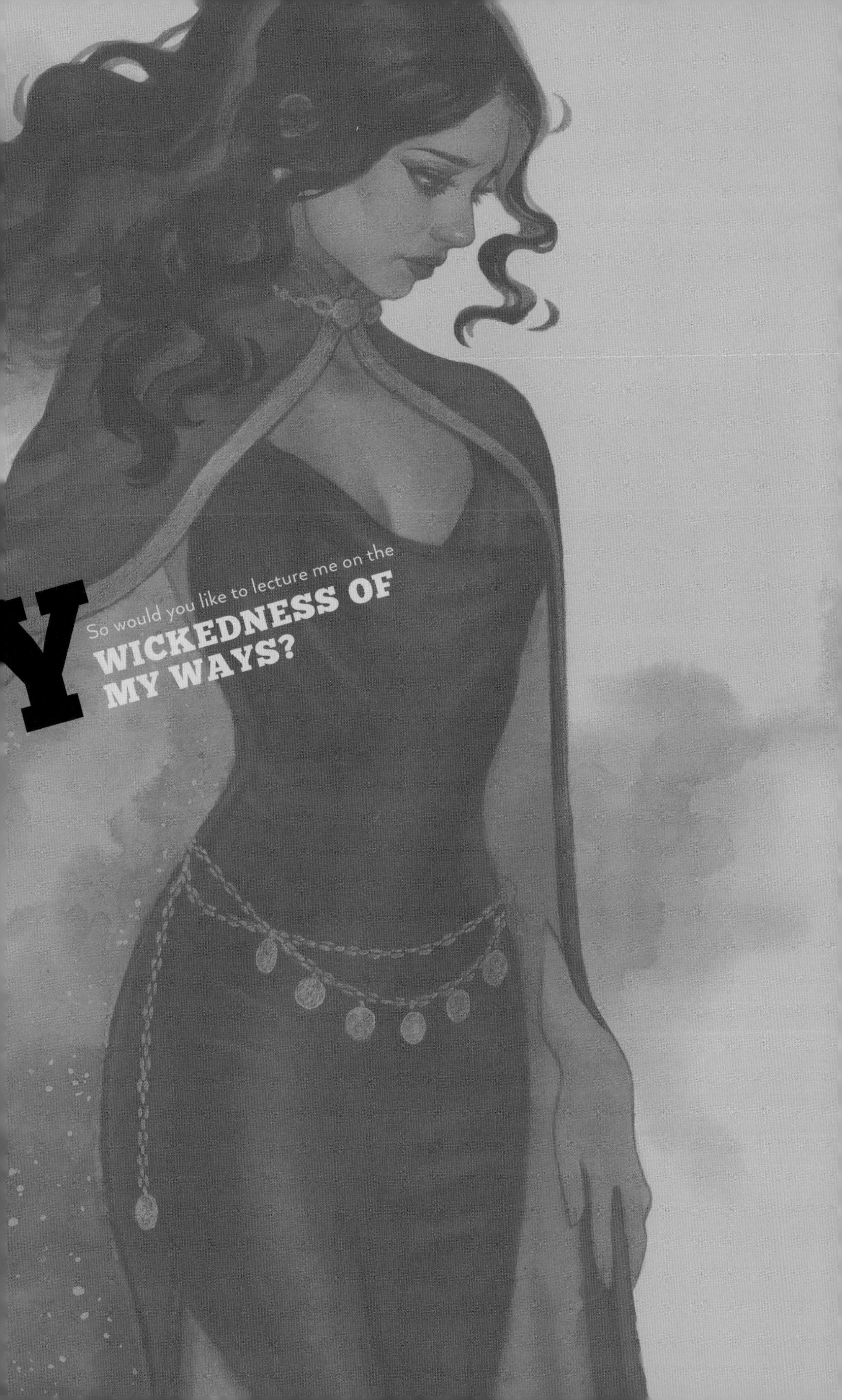
Y
So would you like to lecture me on the
WICKEDNESS OF
MY WAYS?

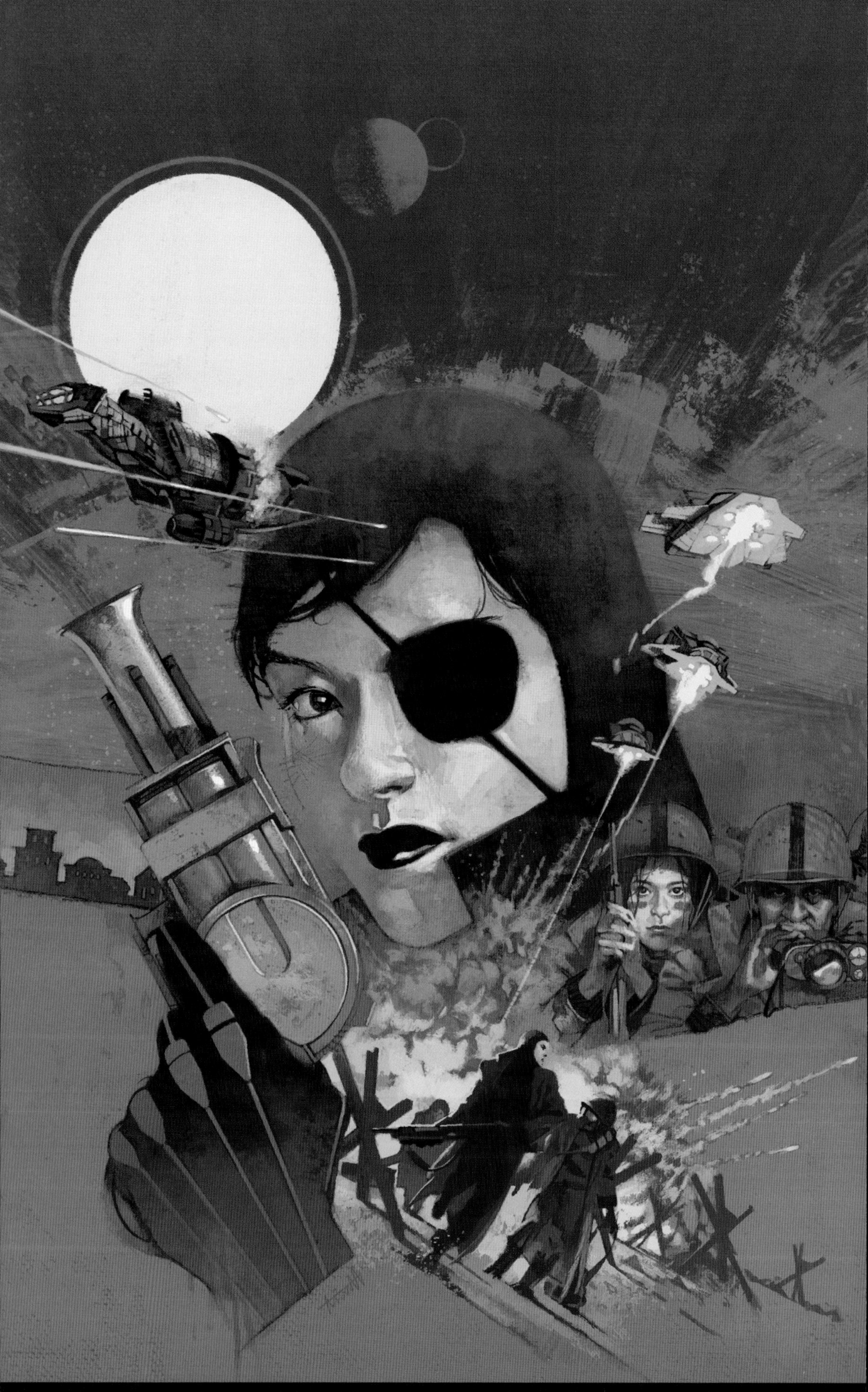

Firefly #23 Cover by **Marc Aspinall**

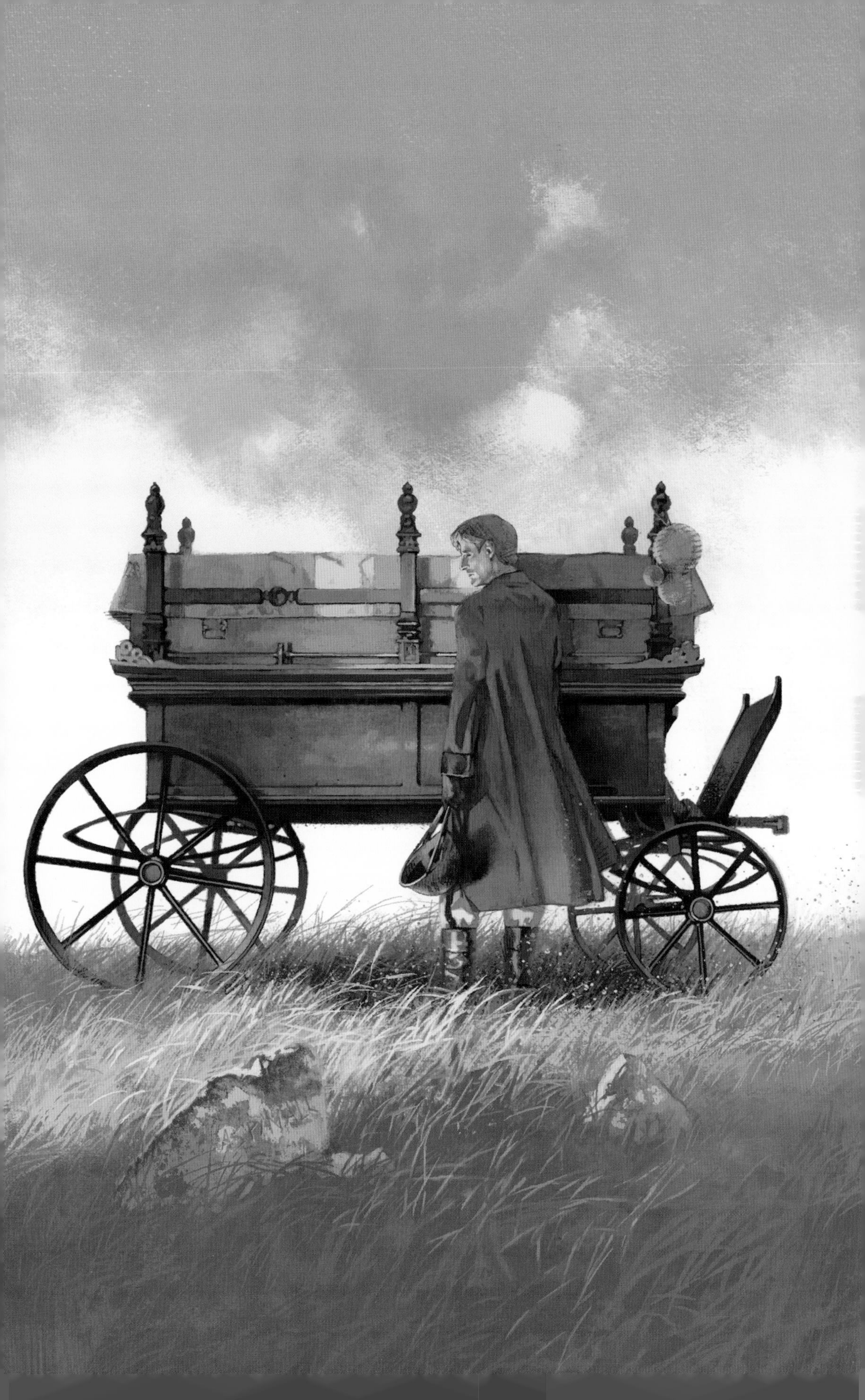

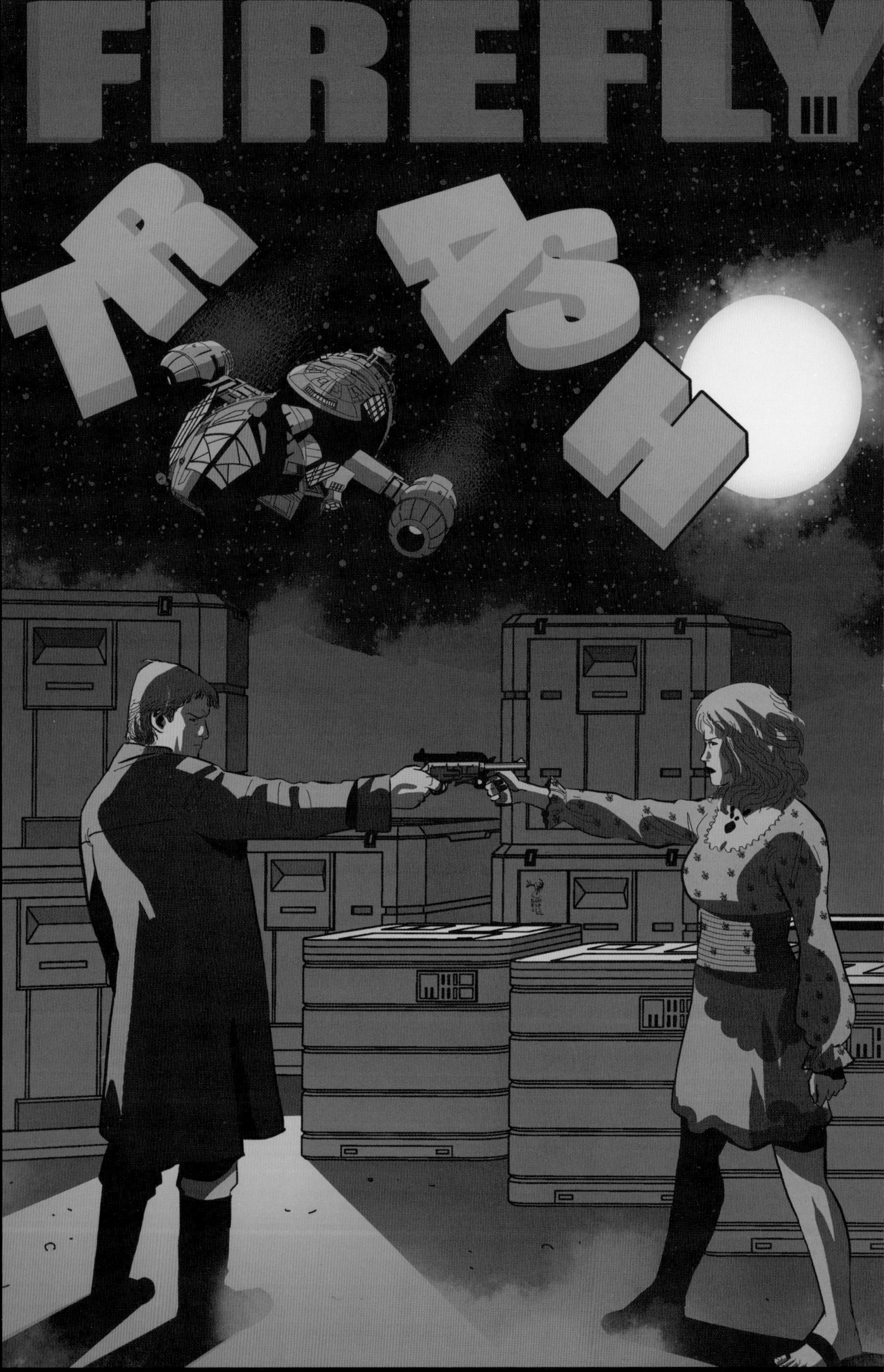
FIREFLY
TRASH

Firefly #23 Episode Cover by **George Kambadais** with colors by **Joana Lafuente**

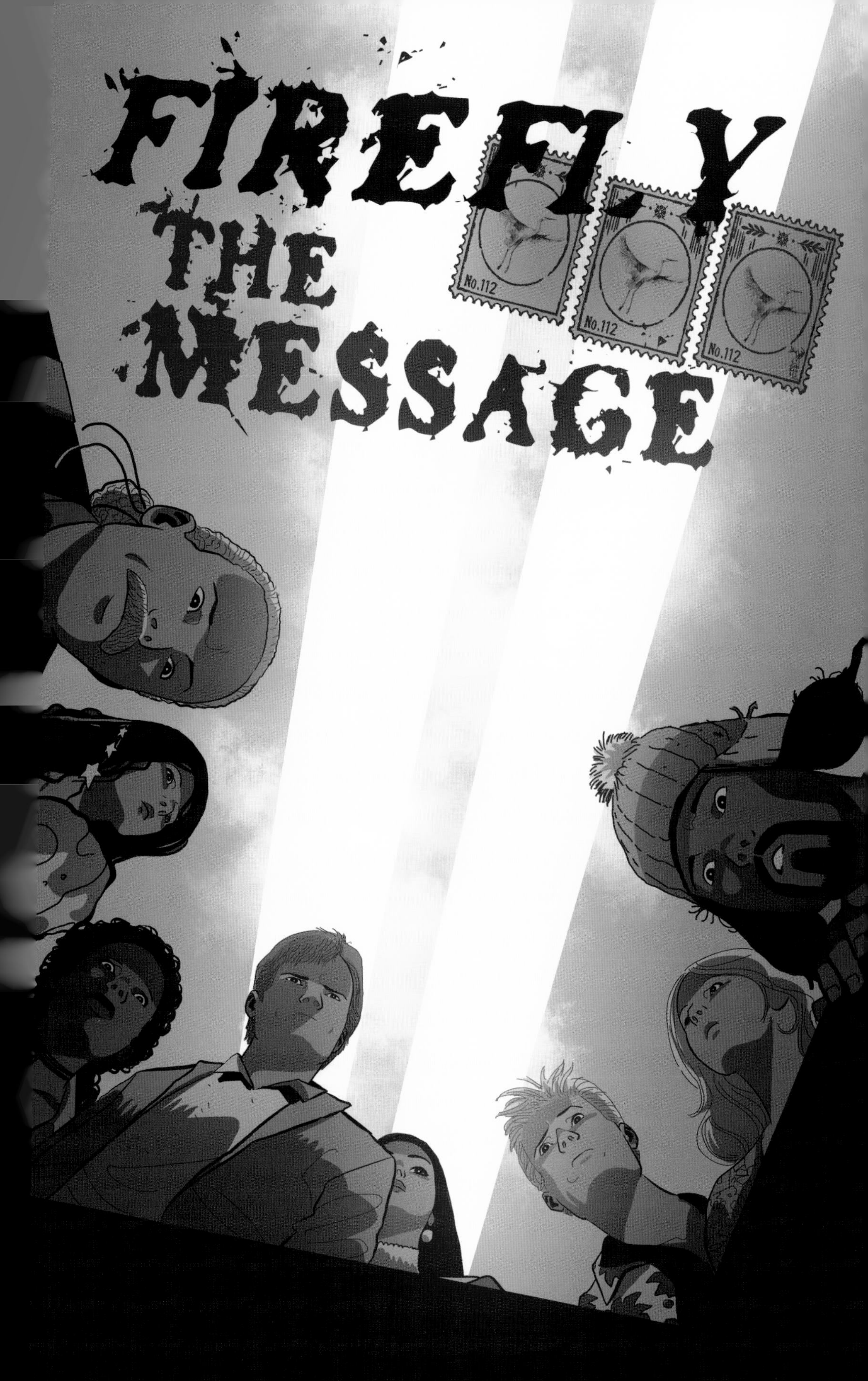
FIREFLY
THE MESSAGE
No.112
No.112
No.112

Firefly #24.5 Episode Cover by **George Kambadais** with colors by **Joana Lafuente**

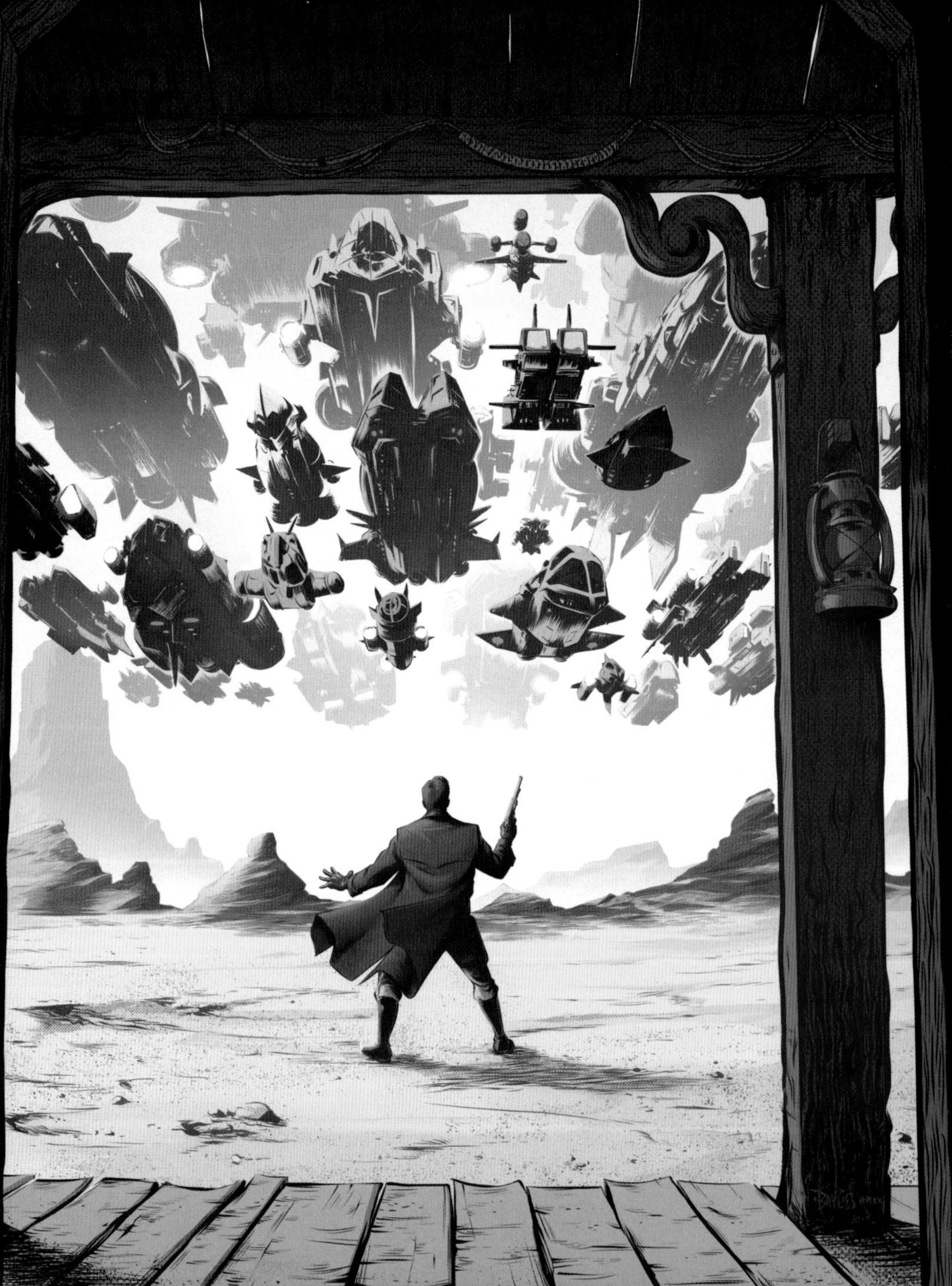

Firefly #23 Variant Cover by **Daneil Bayliss**

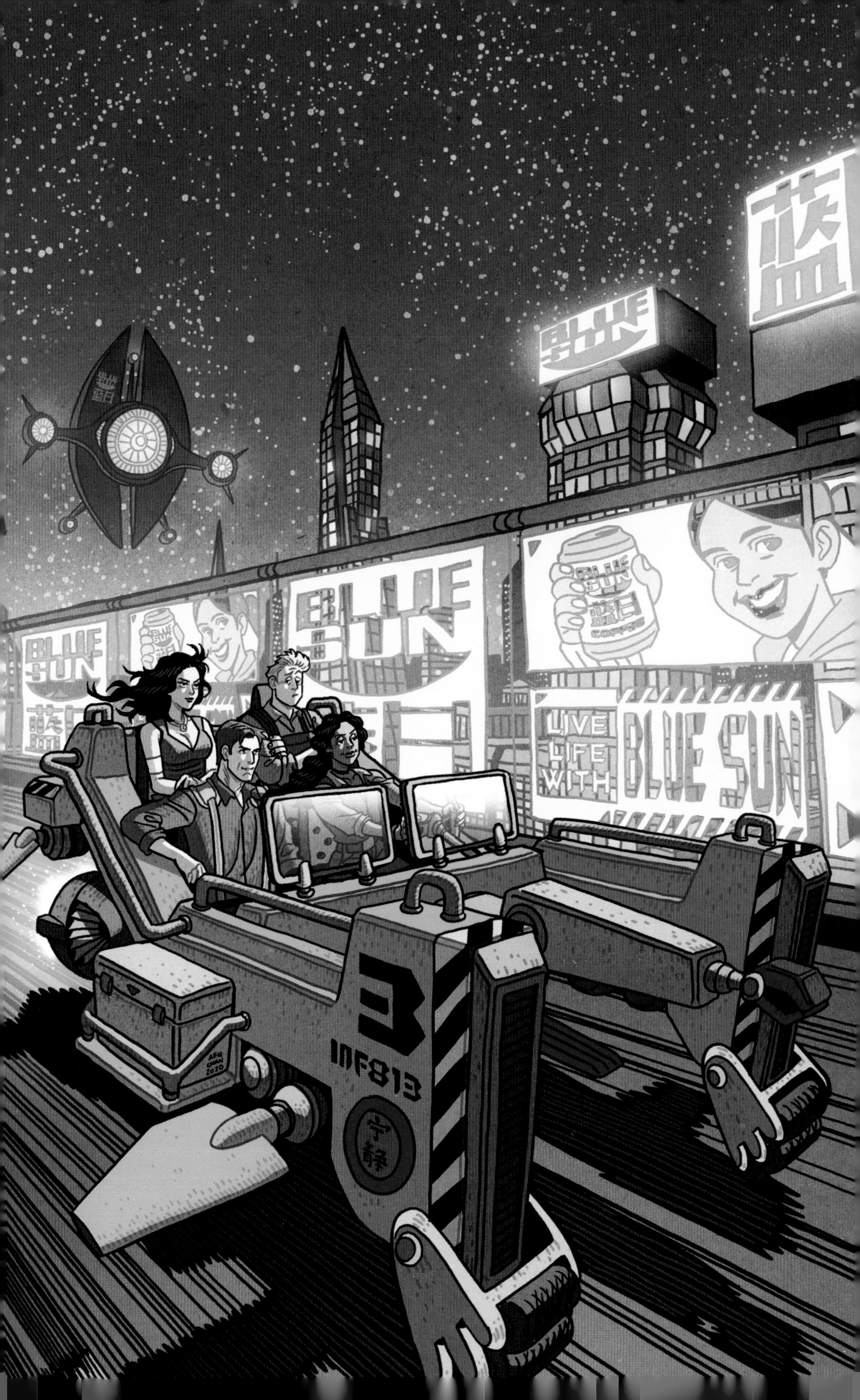
BLUE SUN
藍日
BLUE SUN
COFFEE
LIVE LIFE WITH
BLUE SUN
3

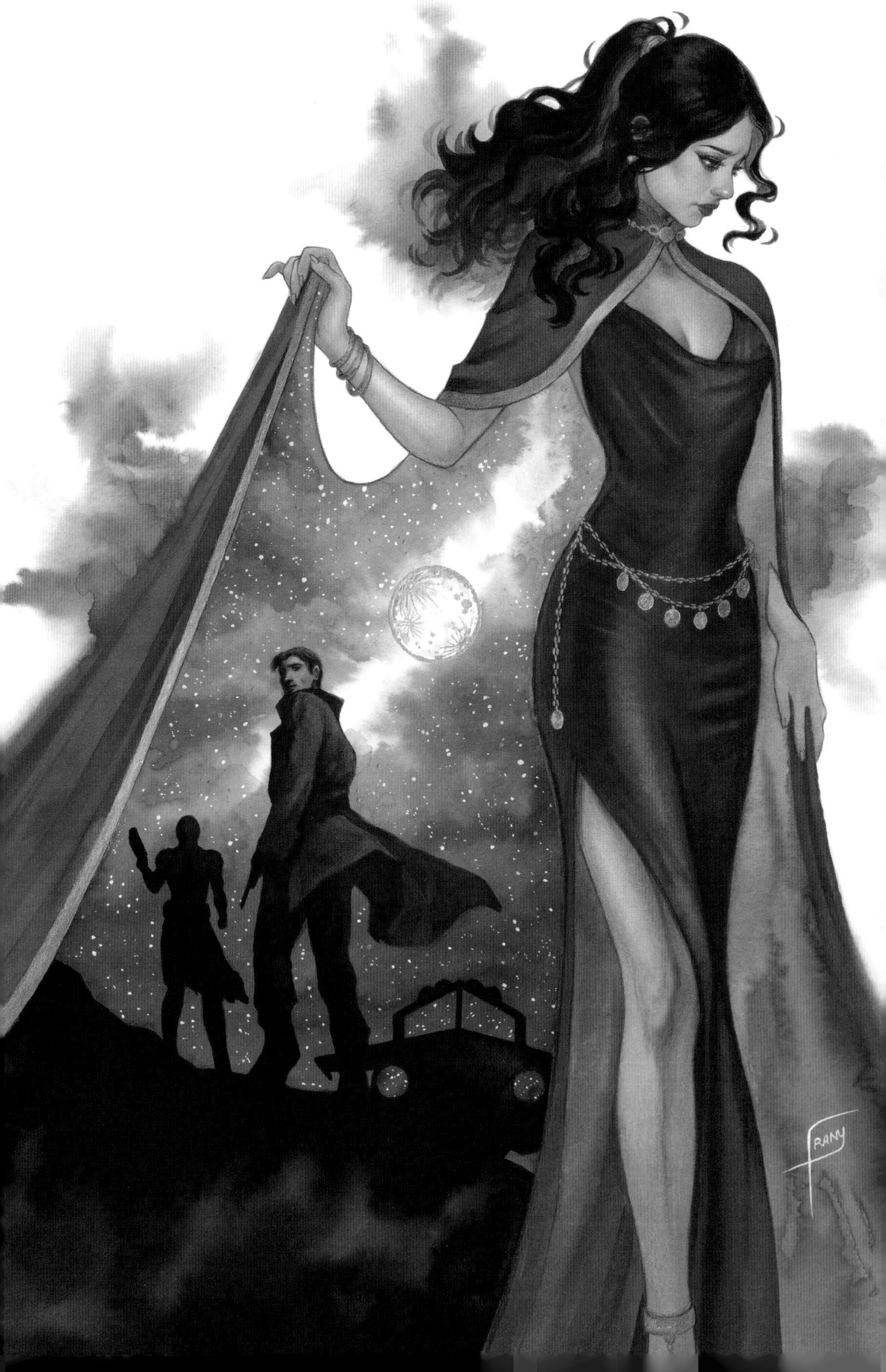
FRANY

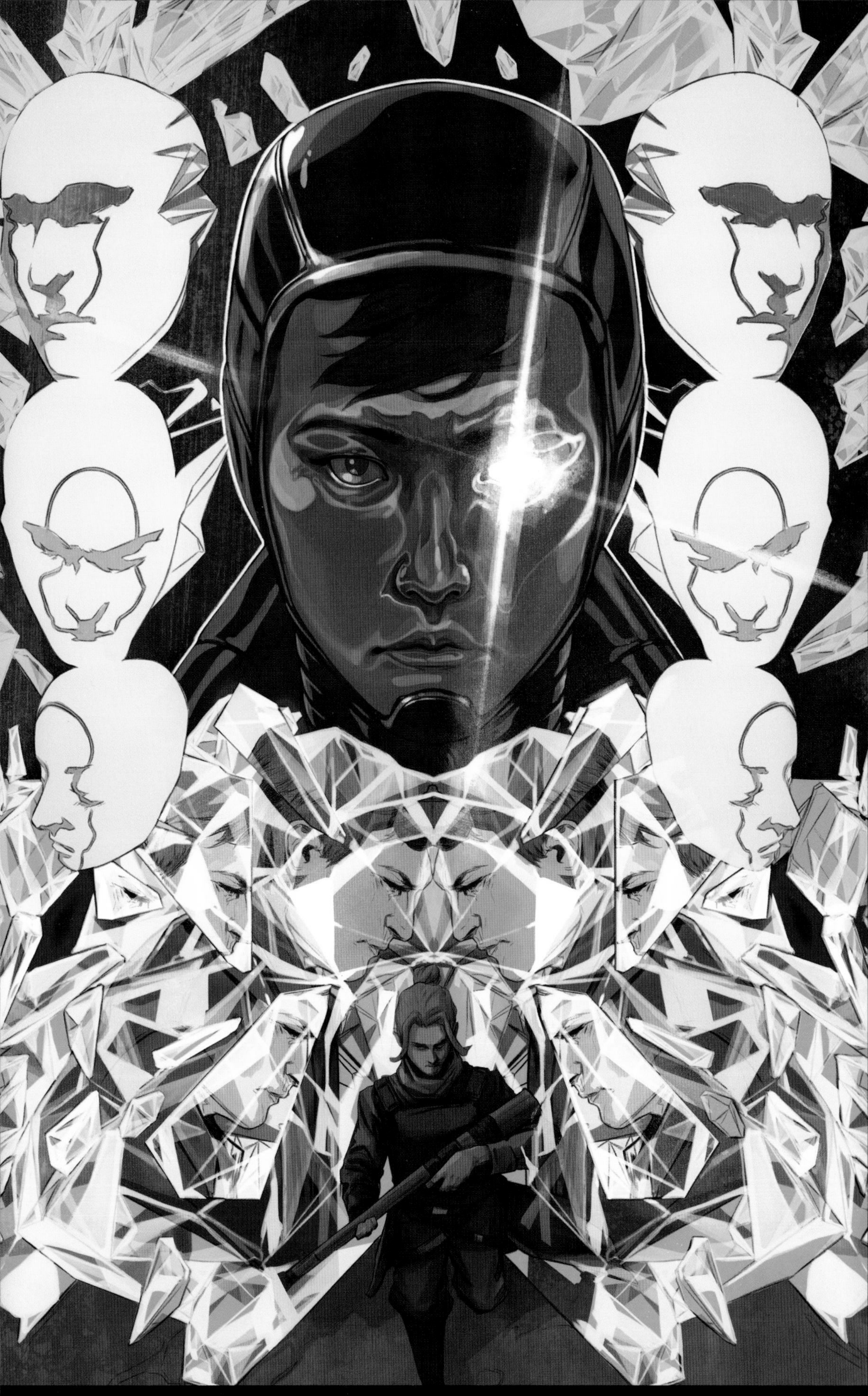

Firefly: Blue Sun Rising #1 Cover by **Nimit Malavia**

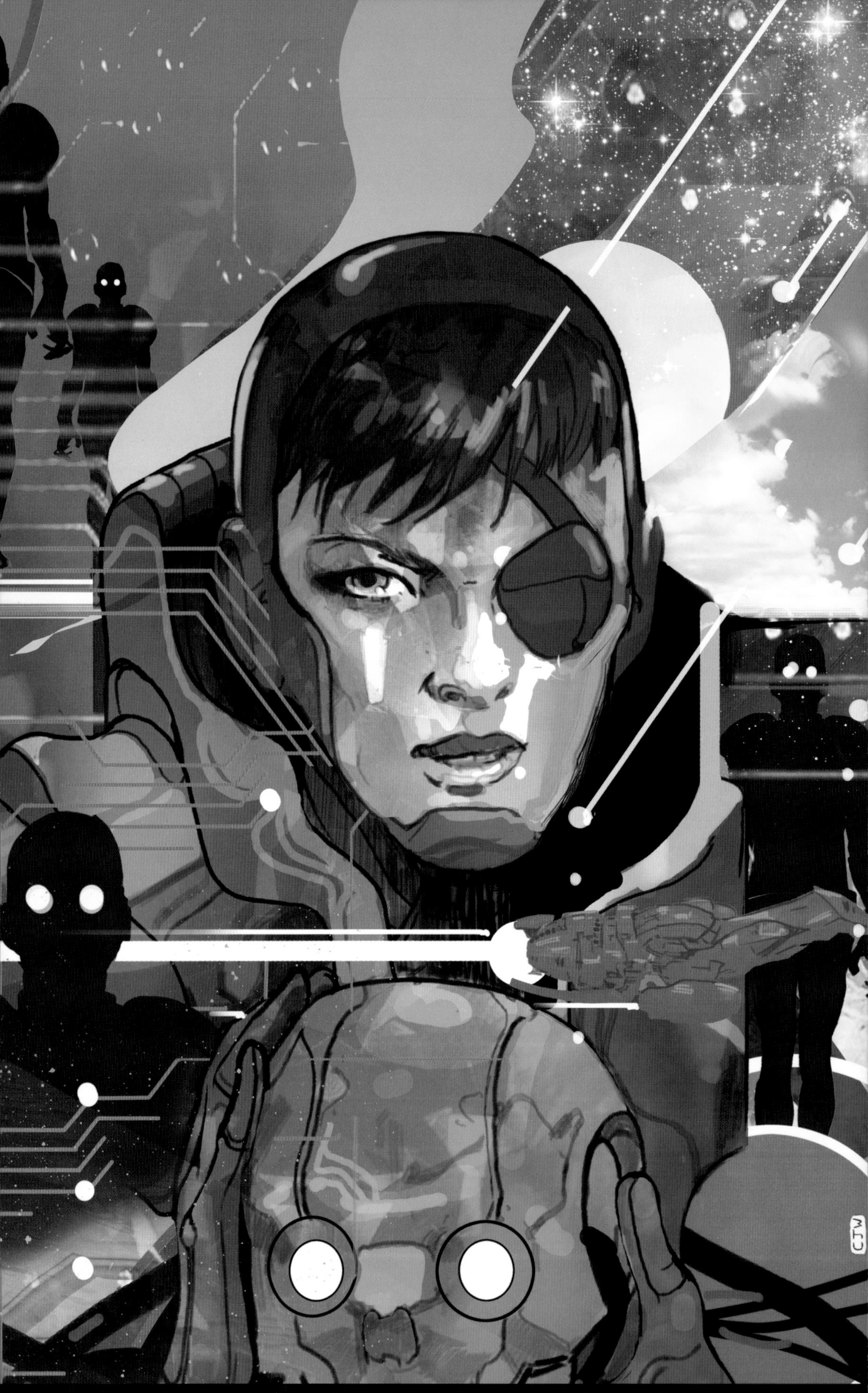

Firefly: Blue Sun Rising #1 Connecting Cover by **Christian Ward**

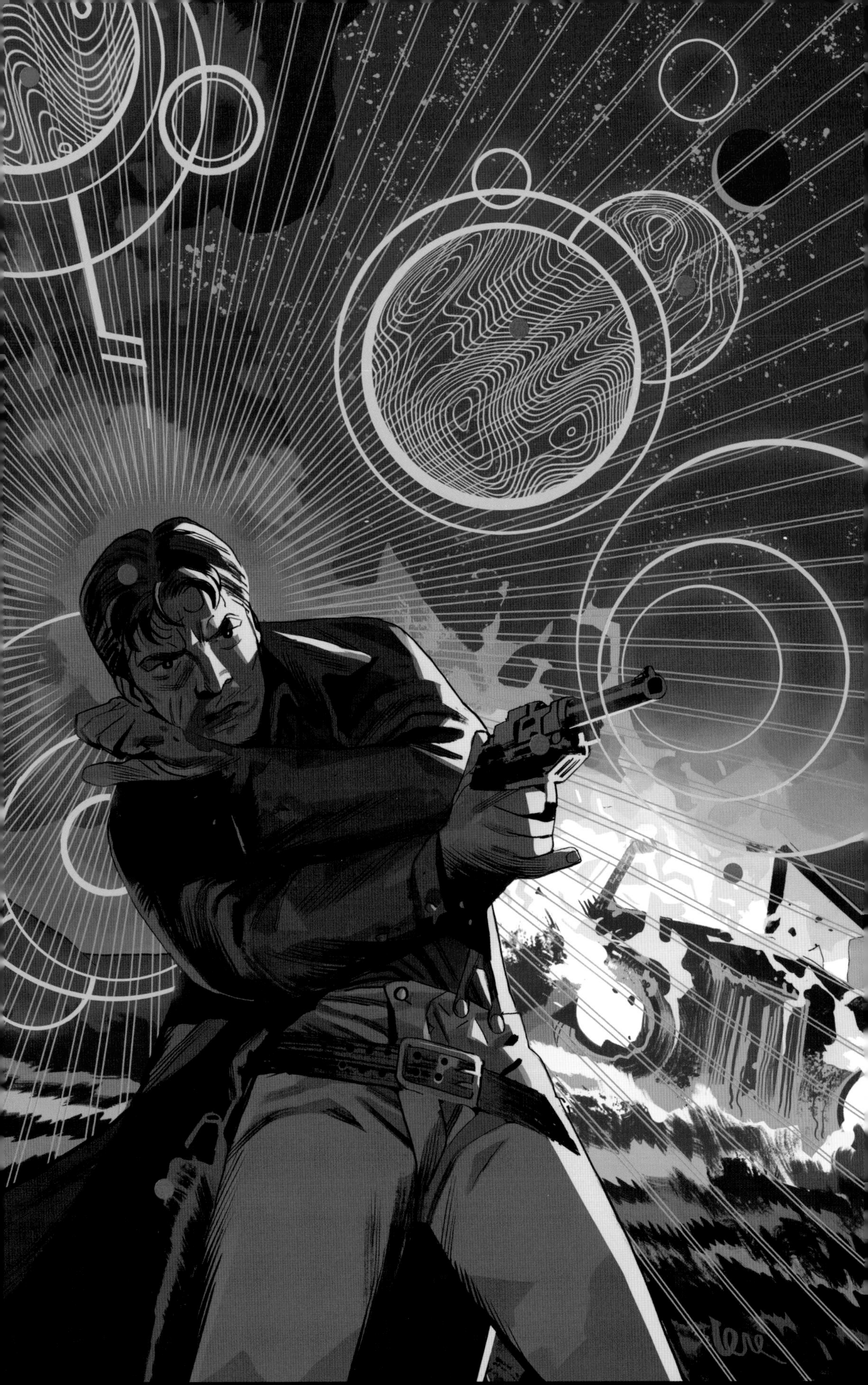

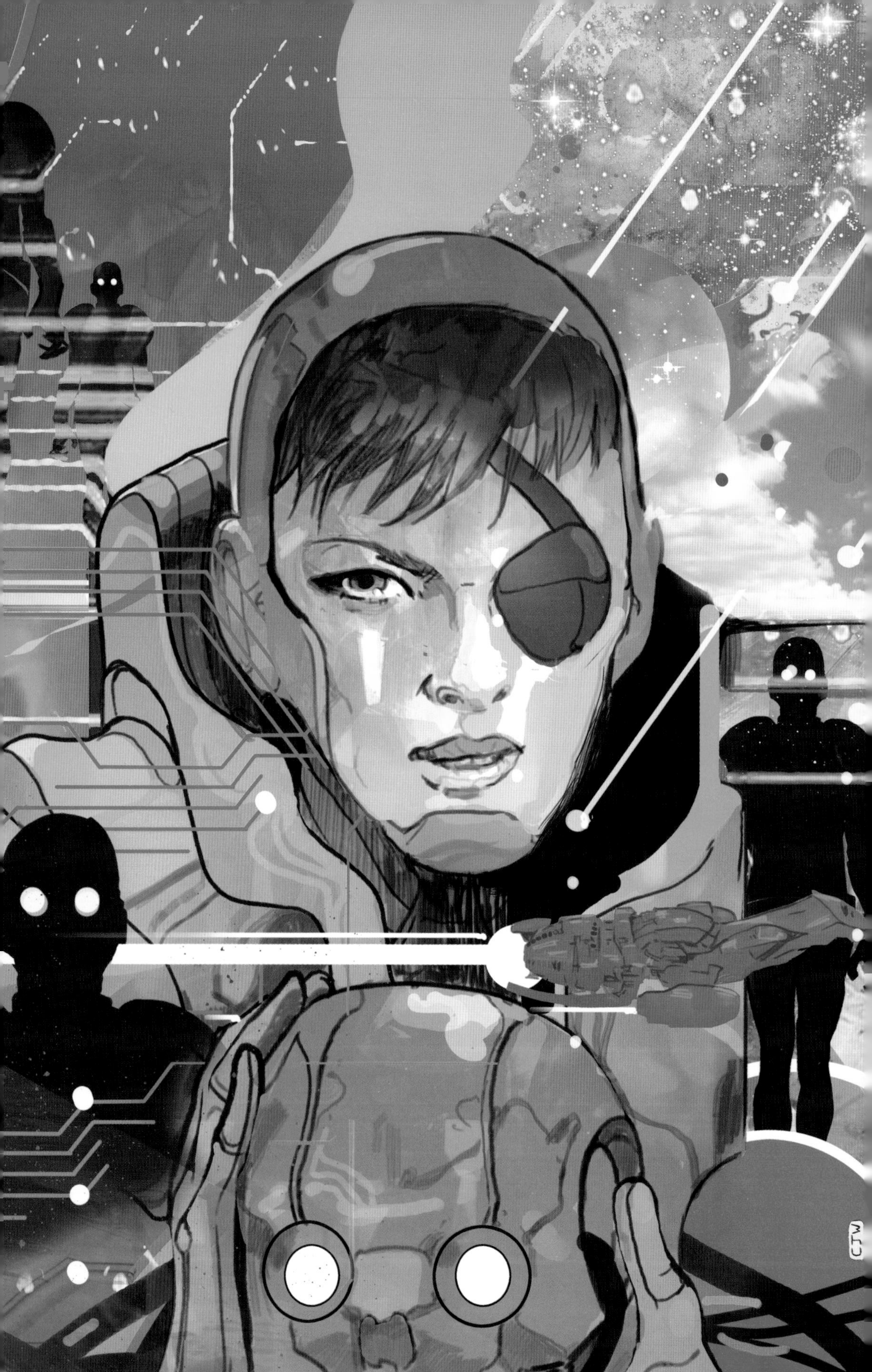
CJW

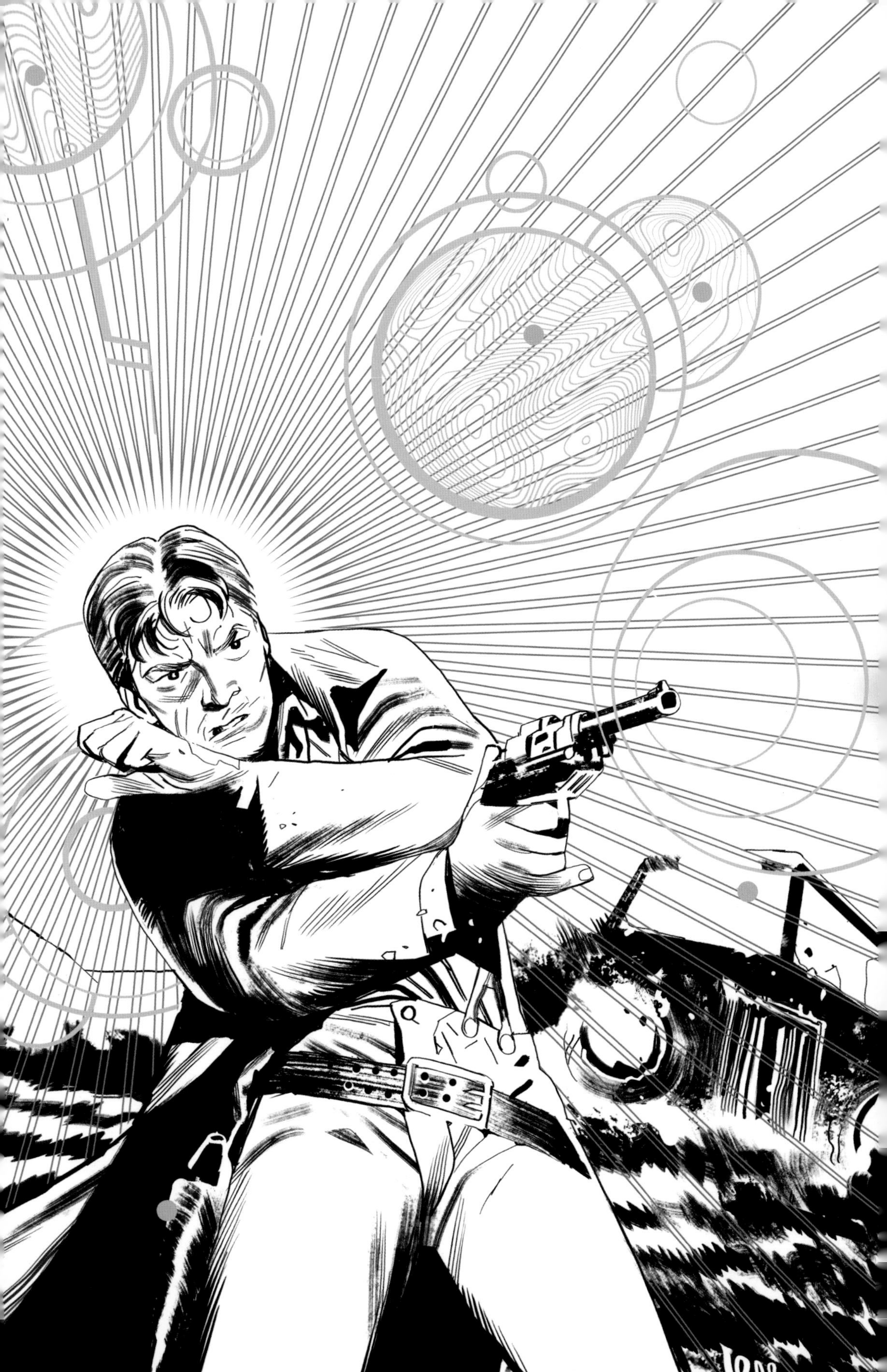

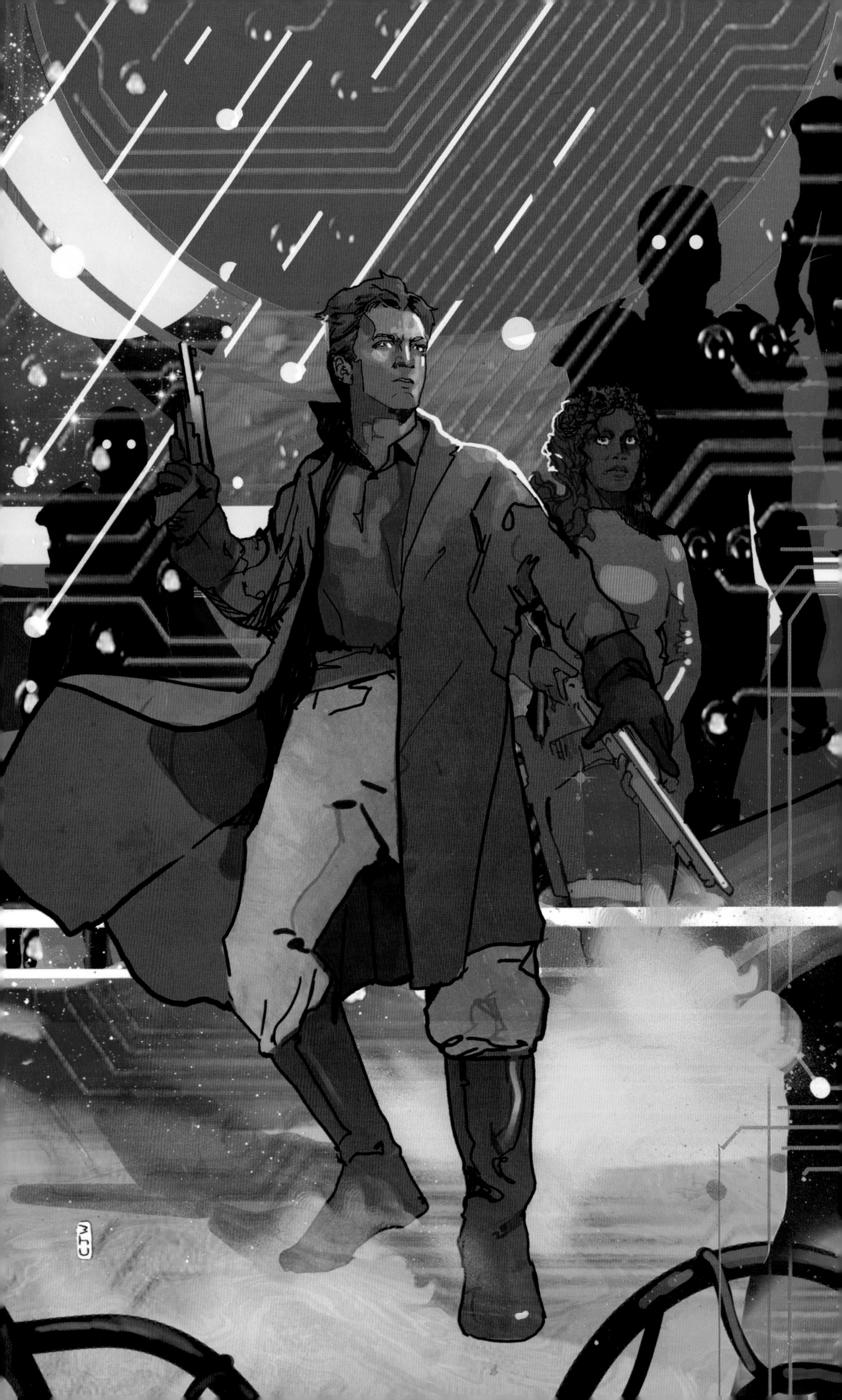

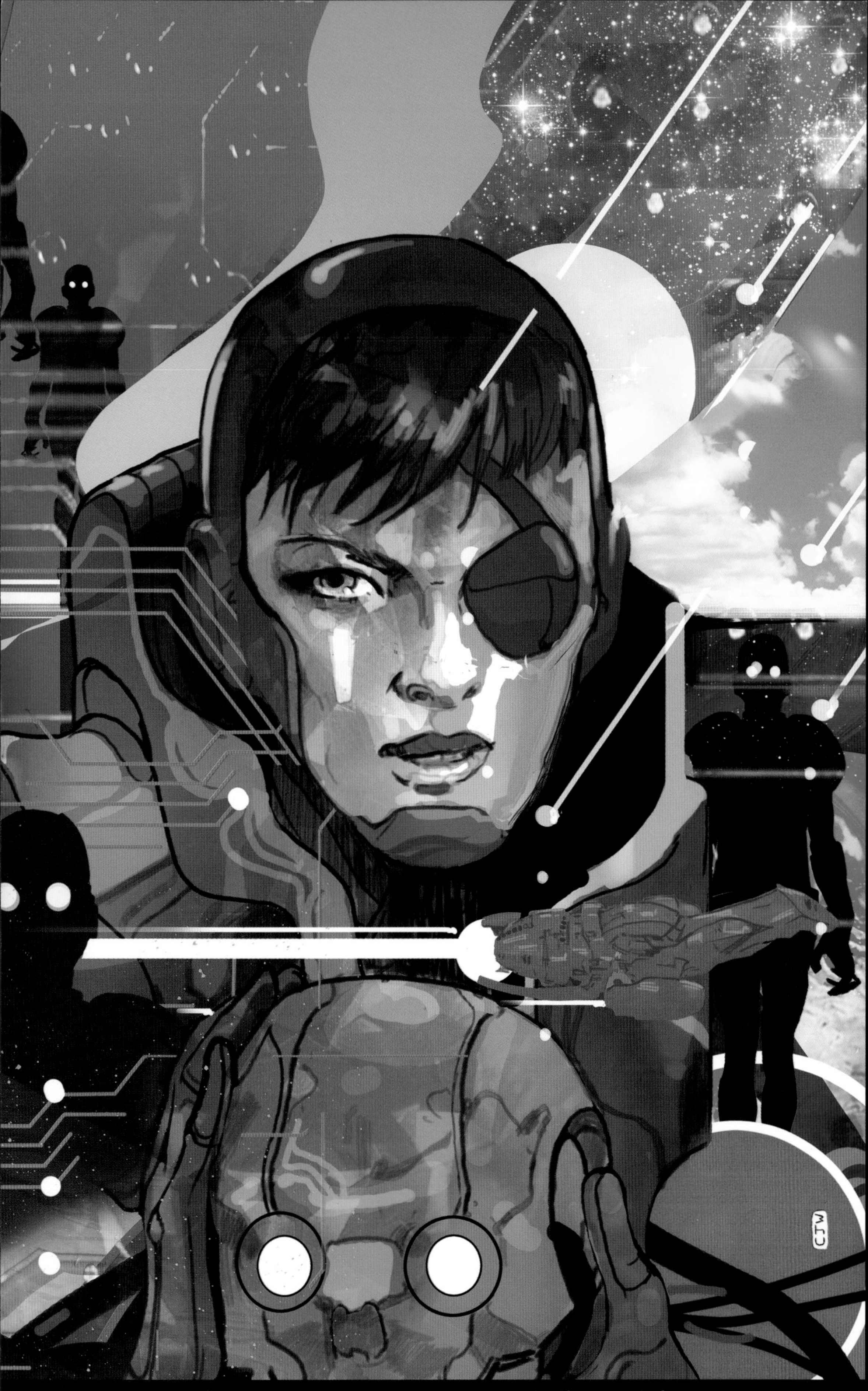
CTW

Firefly: Blue Sun Rising #0-1 Connecting Covers by **Christian Ward**

PREVIEW OF **BOOM!** ORIGINAL SERIES

WE ONLY FIND THEM WHEN THEY'RE DEAD™

Written by
Al Ewing

Illustrated by
Simone Di Meo
with Color Assists by **Mariasara Miotti**

Lettered by
AndWorld Design

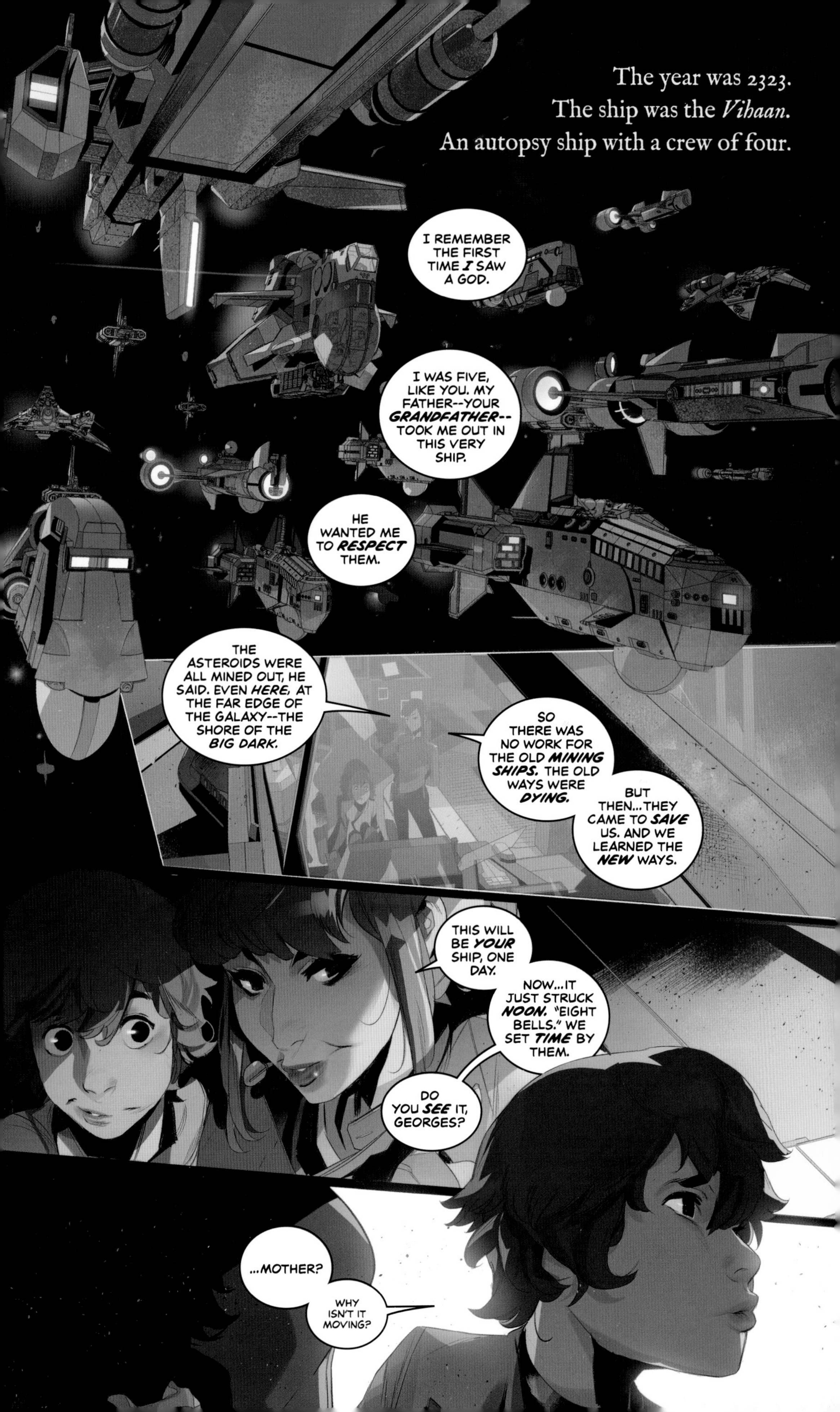
The year was 2323.
The ship was the *Vihaan*.
An autopsy ship with a crew of four.
I REMEMBER THE FIRST TIME *I* SAW A GOD.
I WAS FIVE, LIKE YOU. MY FATHER--YOUR *GRANDFATHER*--TOOK ME OUT IN THIS VERY SHIP.
HE WANTED ME TO *RESPECT* THEM.
THE ASTEROIDS WERE ALL MINED OUT, HE SAID. EVEN *HERE*, AT THE FAR EDGE OF THE GALAXY--THE SHORE OF THE *BIG DARK*.
SO THERE WAS NO WORK FOR THE OLD *MINING SHIPS*. THE OLD WAYS WERE *DYING*.
BUT THEN...THEY CAME TO *SAVE* US. AND WE LEARNED THE *NEW* WAYS.
THIS WILL BE *YOUR* SHIP, ONE DAY.
NOW...IT JUST STRUCK *NOON*. "EIGHT BELLS." WE SET *TIME* BY THEM.
DO YOU *SEE* IT, GEORGES?
...MOTHER?
WHY ISN'T IT MOVING?

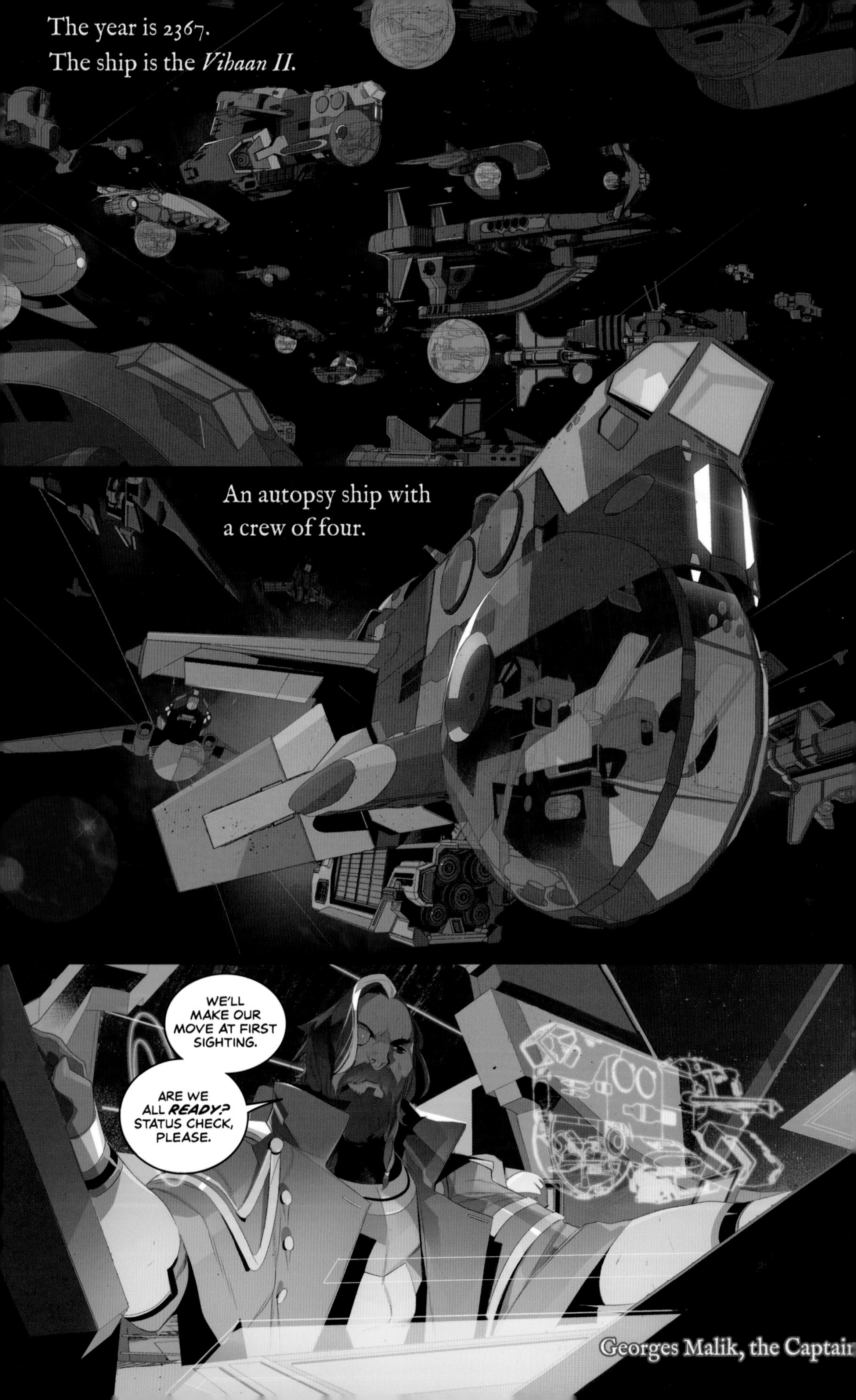
The year is 2367.
The ship is the *Vihaan II*.
An autopsy ship with a crew of four.
WE'LL MAKE OUR MOVE AT FIRST SIGHTING.
ARE WE ALL ***READY?*** STATUS CHECK, PLEASE.
Georges Malik, the Captain

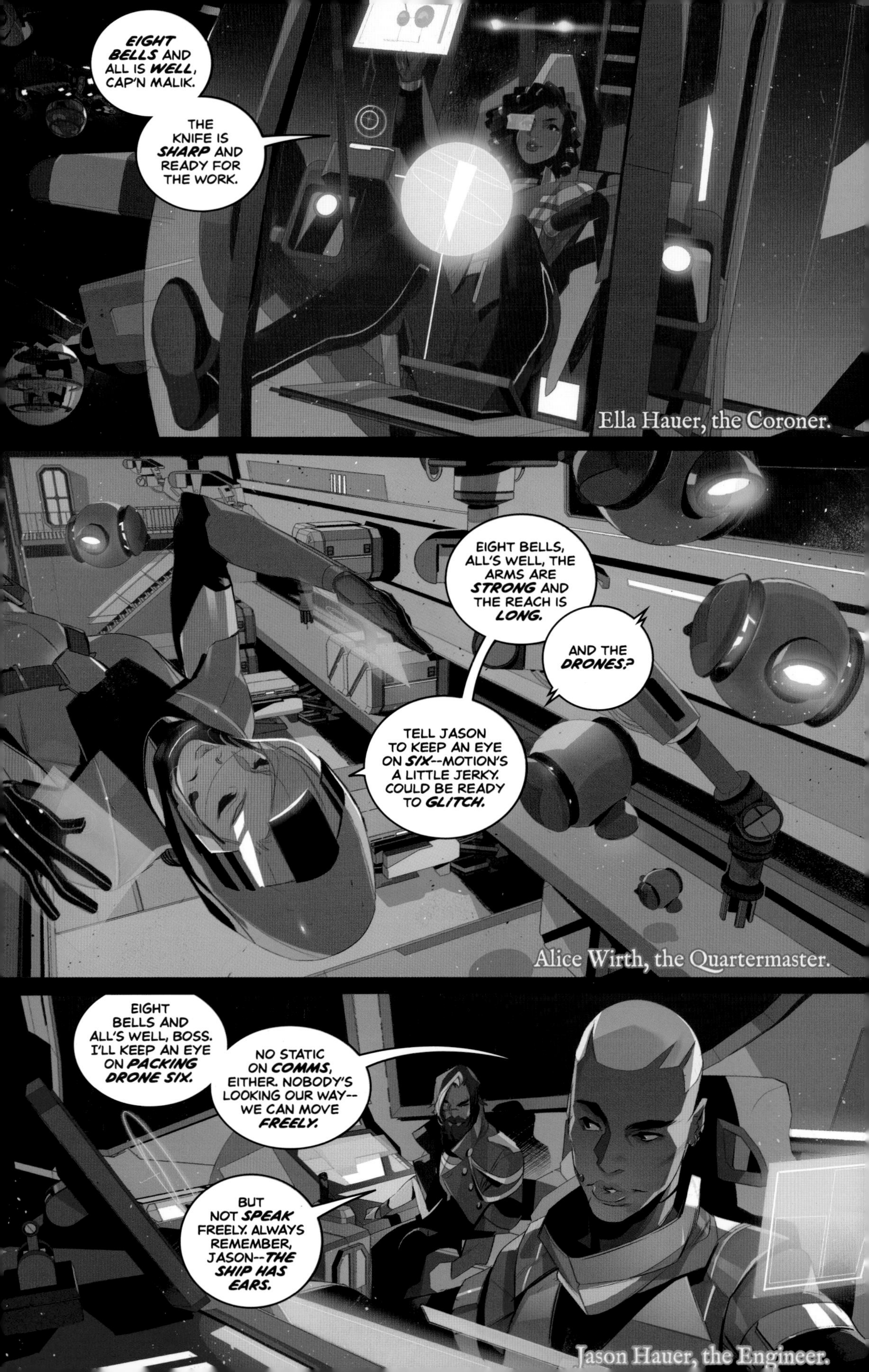
EIGHT BELLS AND ALL IS WELL, CAP'N MALIK.
THE KNIFE IS SHARP AND READY FOR THE WORK.
Ella Hauer, the Coroner.
EIGHT BELLS, ALL'S WELL, THE ARMS ARE STRONG AND THE REACH IS LONG.
AND THE DRONES?
TELL JASON TO KEEP AN EYE ON SIX--MOTION'S A LITTLE JERKY. COULD BE READY TO GLITCH.
Alice Wirth, the Quartermaster.
EIGHT BELLS AND ALL'S WELL, BOSS. I'LL KEEP AN EYE ON PACKING DRONE SIX.
NO STATIC ON COMMS, EITHER. NOBODY'S LOOKING OUR WAY-- WE CAN MOVE FREELY.
BUT NOT SPEAK FREELY. ALWAYS REMEMBER, JASON--THE SHIP HAS EARS.
Jason Hauer, the Engineer.

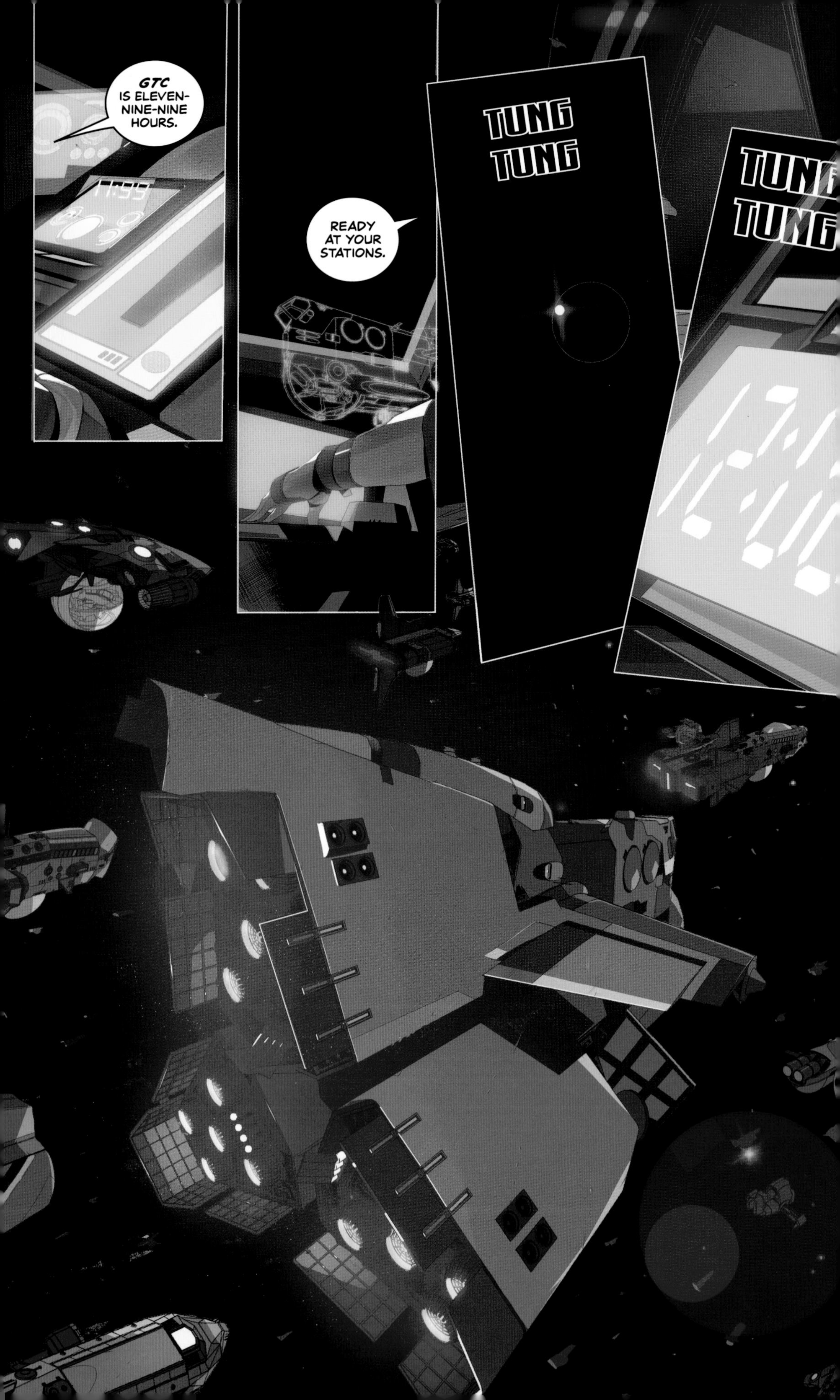
GTC IS ELEVEN-NINE-NINE HOURS.
READY AT YOUR STATIONS.
TUNG TUNG

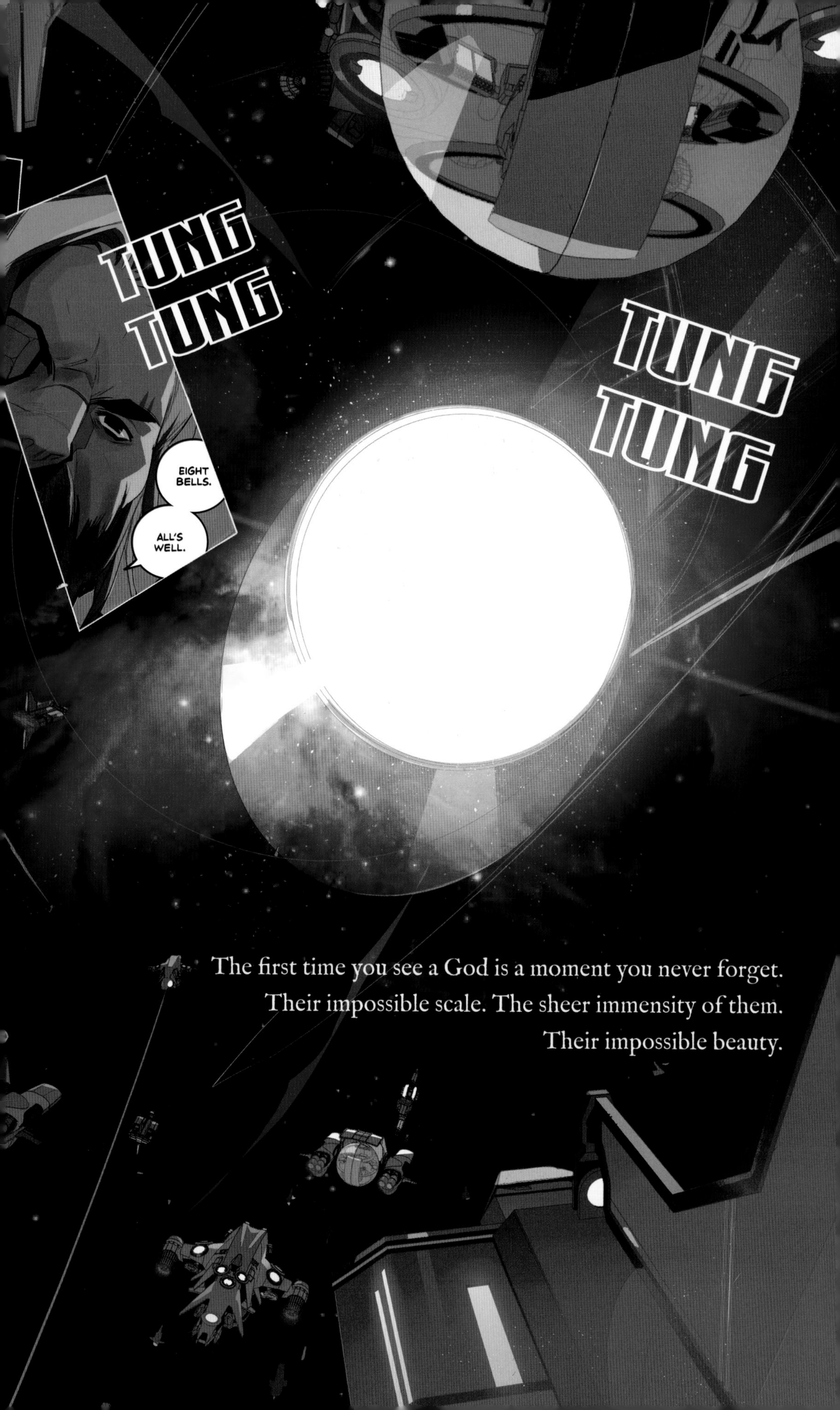
TUNG TUNG
EIGHT BELLS.
ALL'S WELL.
TUNG TUNG
The first time you see a God is a moment you never forget. Their impossible scale. The sheer immensity of them. Their impossible beauty.

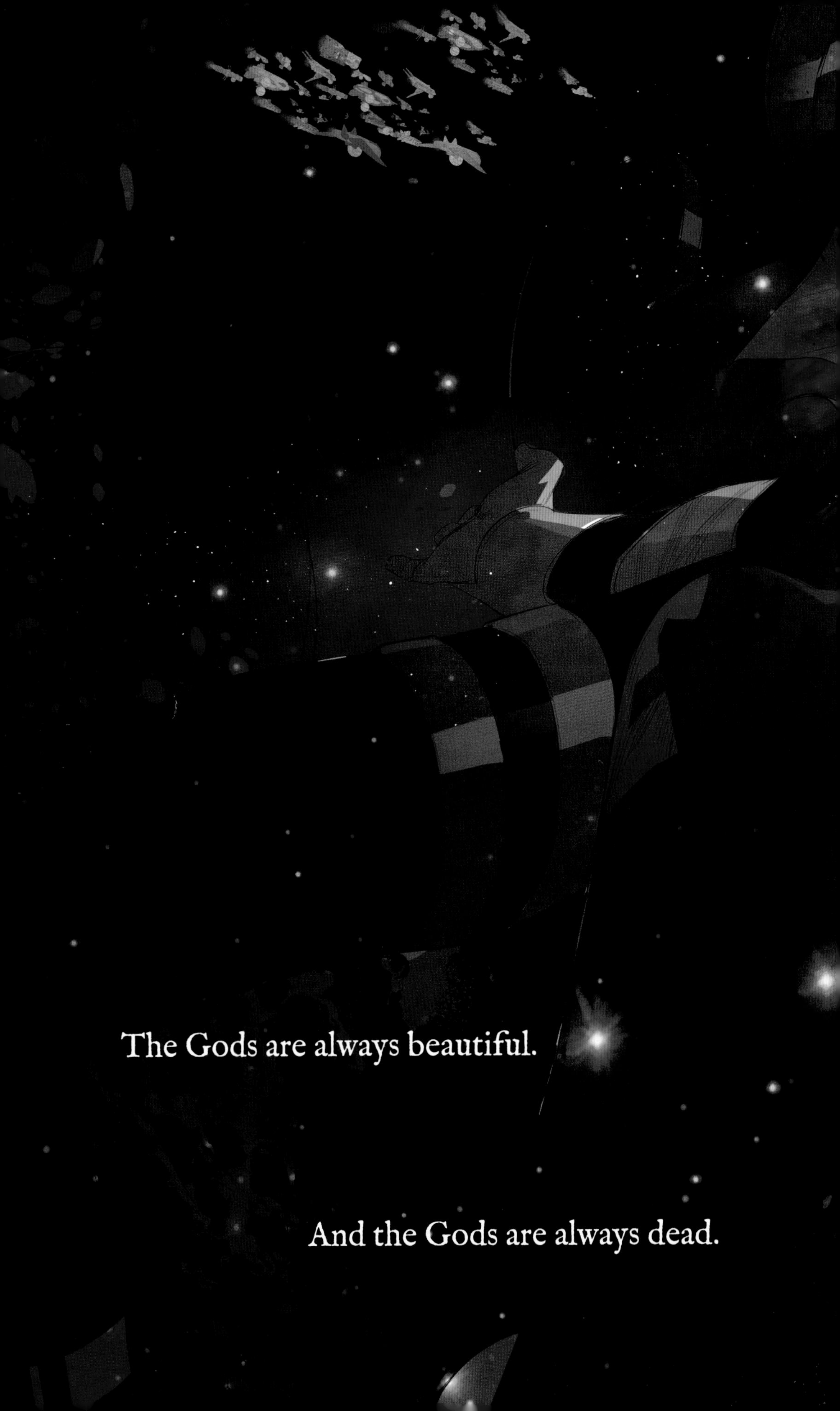
The Gods are always beautiful.
And the Gods are always dead.

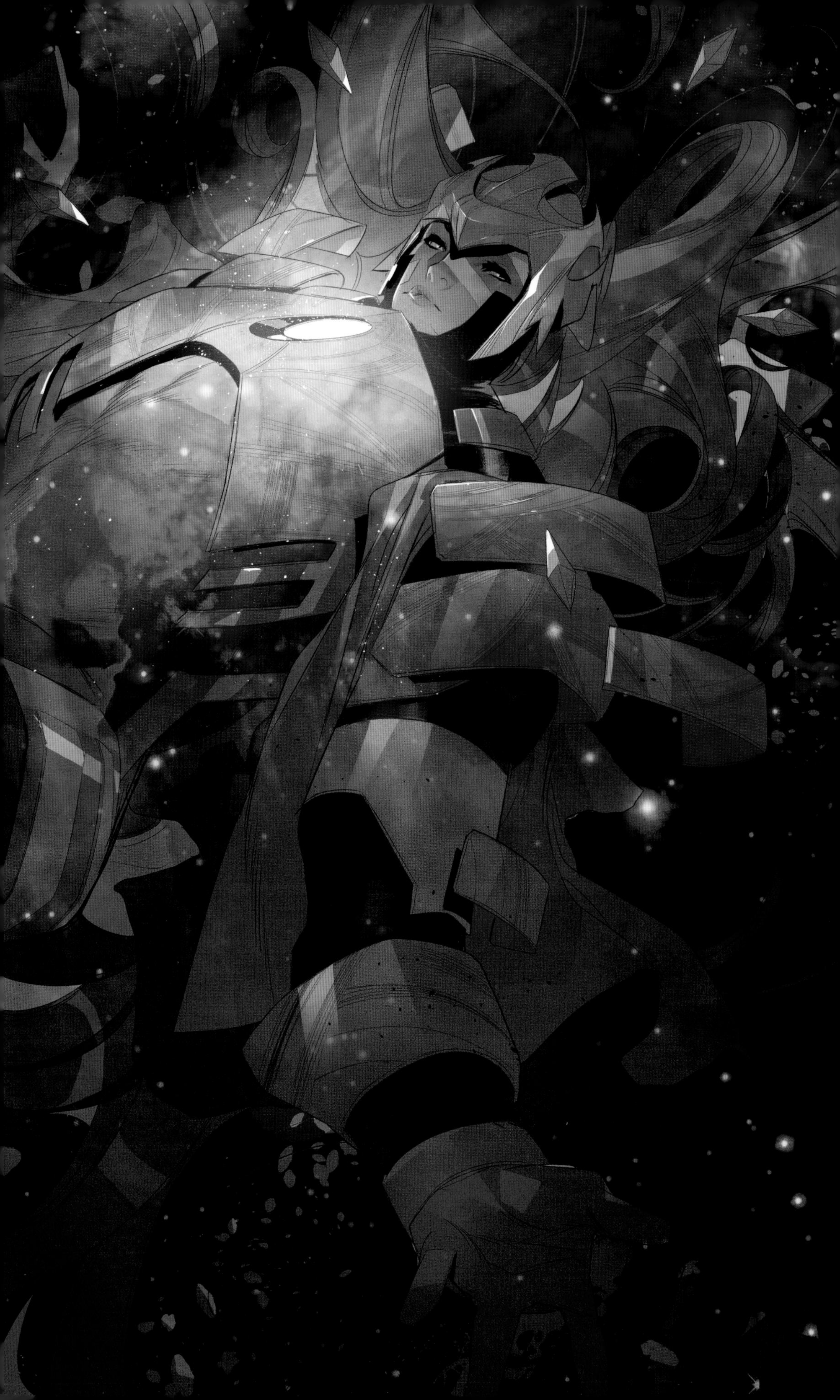

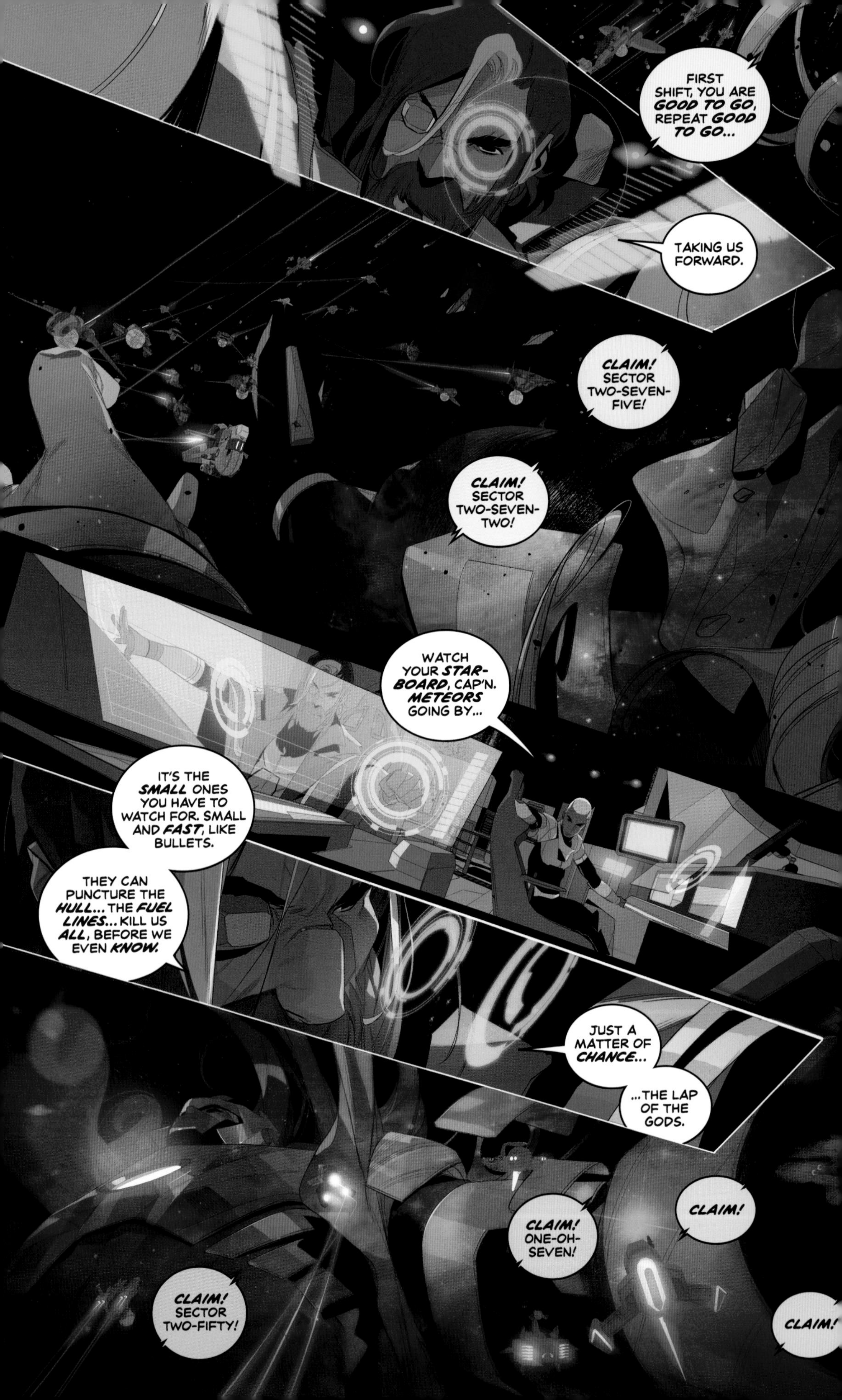
FIRST SHIFT, YOU ARE GOOD TO GO, REPEAT GOOD TO GO...
TAKING US FORWARD.
CLAIM! SECTOR TWO-SEVEN-FIVE!
CLAIM! SECTOR TWO-SEVEN-TWO!
WATCH YOUR STAR-BOARD, CAP'N. METEORS GOING BY...
IT'S THE SMALL ONES YOU HAVE TO WATCH FOR. SMALL AND FAST, LIKE BULLETS.
THEY CAN PUNCTURE THE HULL... THE FUEL LINES... KILL US ALL, BEFORE WE EVEN KNOW.
JUST A MATTER OF CHANCE...
...THE LAP OF THE GODS.
CLAIM!
CLAIM! ONE-OH-SEVEN!
CLAIM! SECTOR TWO-FIFTY!
CLAIM!

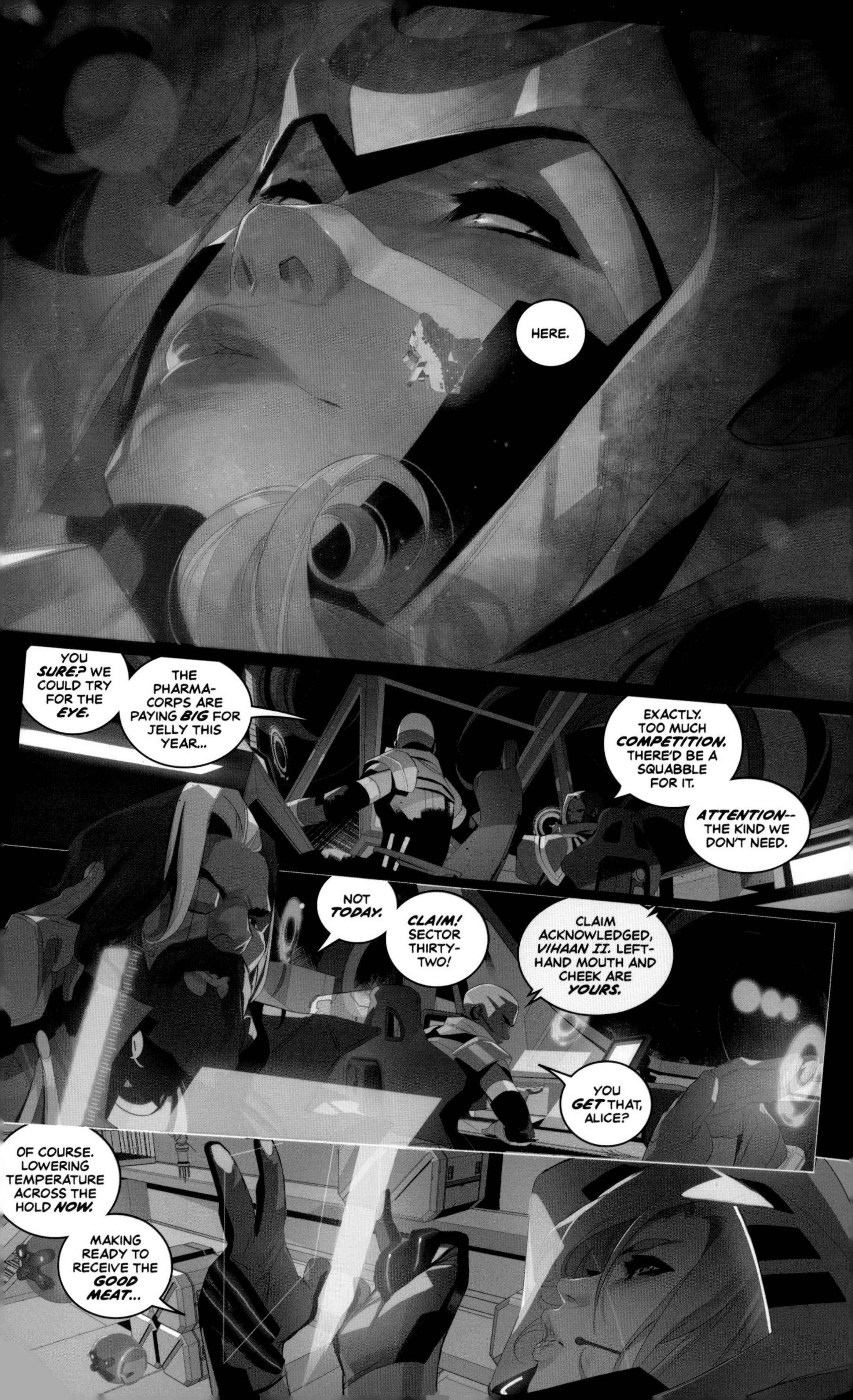
HERE.
YOU SURE? WE COULD TRY FOR THE EYE.
THE PHARMA-CORPS ARE PAYING BIG FOR JELLY THIS YEAR...
EXACTLY. TOO MUCH COMPETITION. THERE'D BE A SQUABBLE FOR IT.
ATTENTION-- THE KIND WE DON'T NEED.
NOT TODAY.
CLAIM! SECTOR THIRTY-TWO!
CLAIM ACKNOWLEDGED, VIHAAN II. LEFT-HAND MOUTH AND CHEEK ARE YOURS.
YOU GET THAT, ALICE?
OF COURSE. LOWERING TEMPERATURE ACROSS THE HOLD NOW.
MAKING READY TO RECEIVE THE GOOD MEAT...

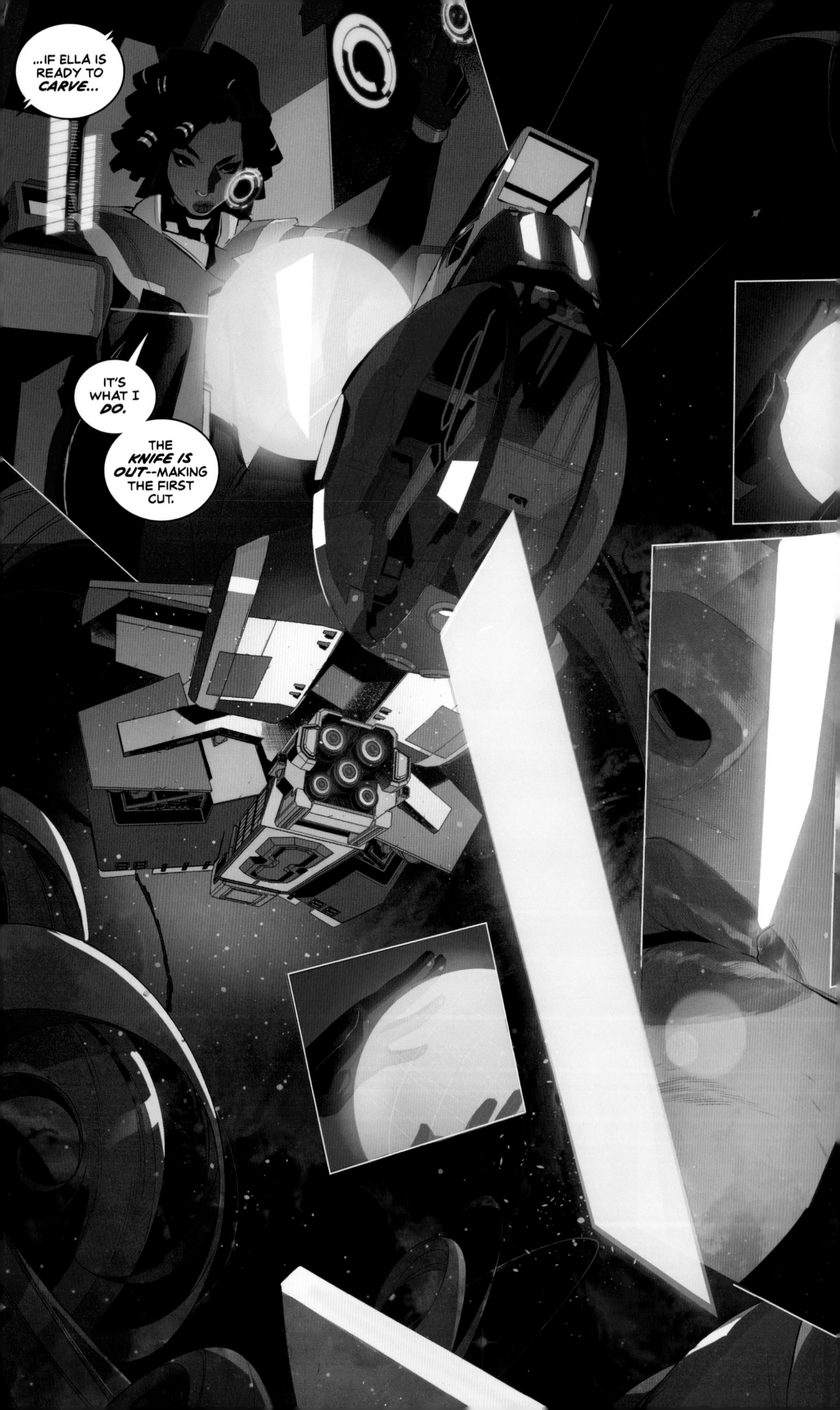
...IF ELLA IS READY TO CARVE...
IT'S WHAT I DO.
THE KNIFE IS OUT--MAKING THE FIRST CUT.

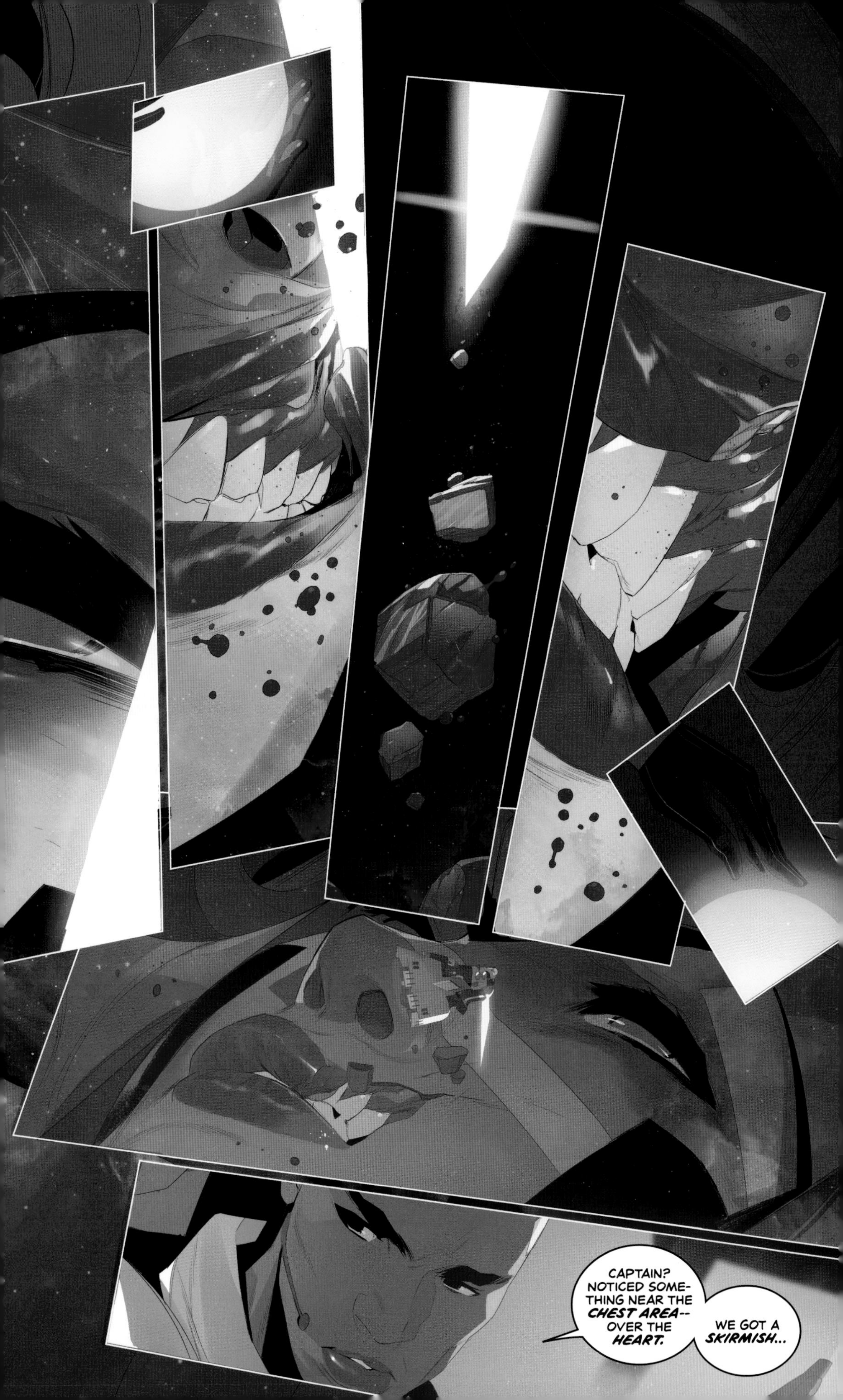
CAPTAIN? NOTICED SOMETHING NEAR THE CHEST AREA-- OVER THE HEART.
WE GOT A SKIRMISH...

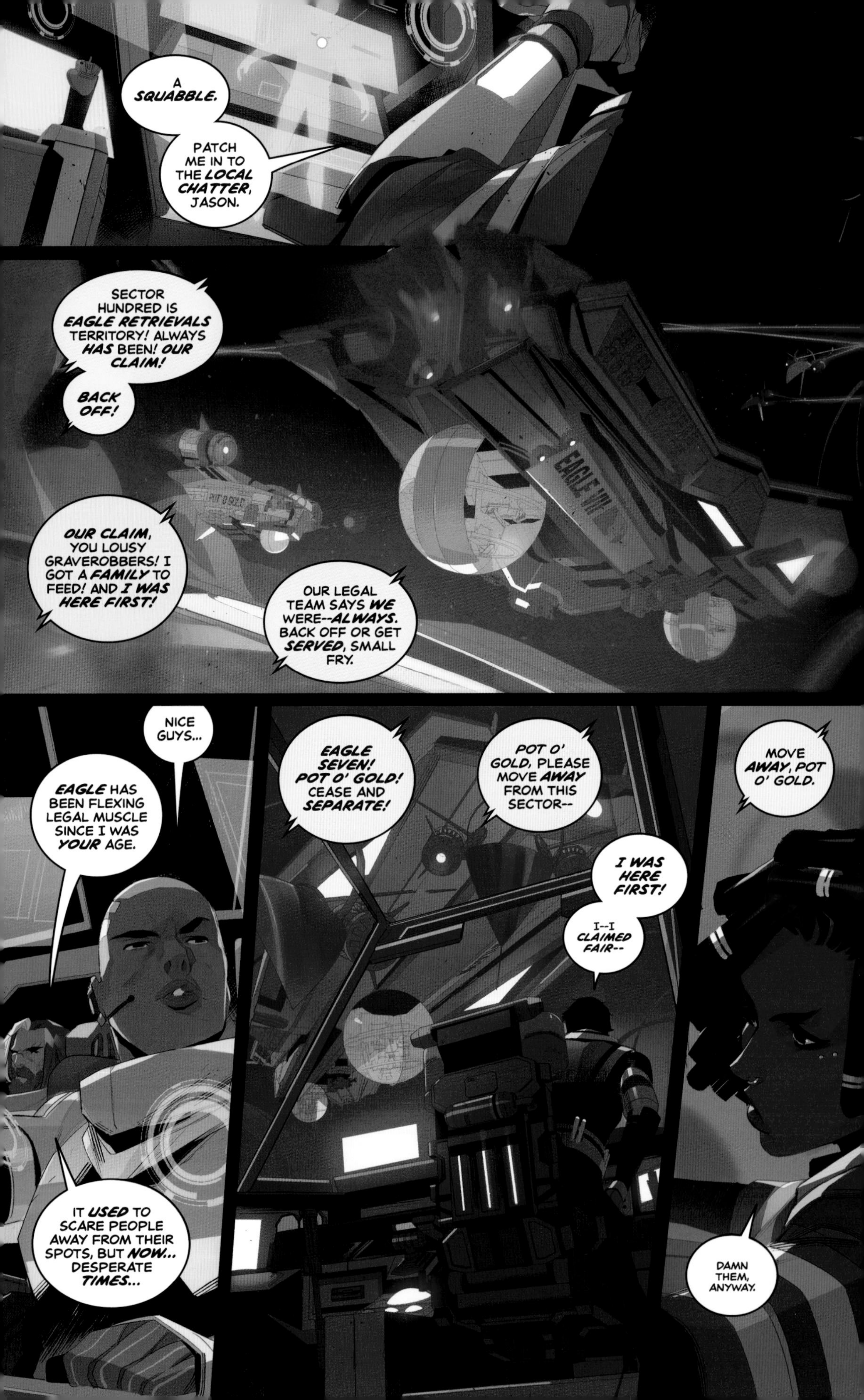
A SQUABBLE.
PATCH ME IN TO THE LOCAL CHATTER, JASON.
SECTOR HUNDRED IS EAGLE RETRIEVALS TERRITORY! ALWAYS HAS BEEN! OUR CLAIM!
BACK OFF!
POT O' GOLD
EAGLE VII
OUR CLAIM, YOU LOUSY GRAVEROBBERS! I GOT A FAMILY TO FEED! AND I WAS HERE FIRST!
OUR LEGAL TEAM SAYS WE WERE--ALWAYS. BACK OFF OR GET SERVED, SMALL FRY.
NICE GUYS...
EAGLE HAS BEEN FLEXING LEGAL MUSCLE SINCE I WAS YOUR AGE.
IT USED TO SCARE PEOPLE AWAY FROM THEIR SPOTS, BUT NOW... DESPERATE TIMES...
EAGLE SEVEN! POT O' GOLD! CEASE AND SEPARATE!
POT O' GOLD, PLEASE MOVE AWAY FROM THIS SECTOR--
I WAS HERE FIRST!
I--I CLAIMED FAIR--
MOVE AWAY, POT O' GOLD.
DAMN THEM, ANYWAY.

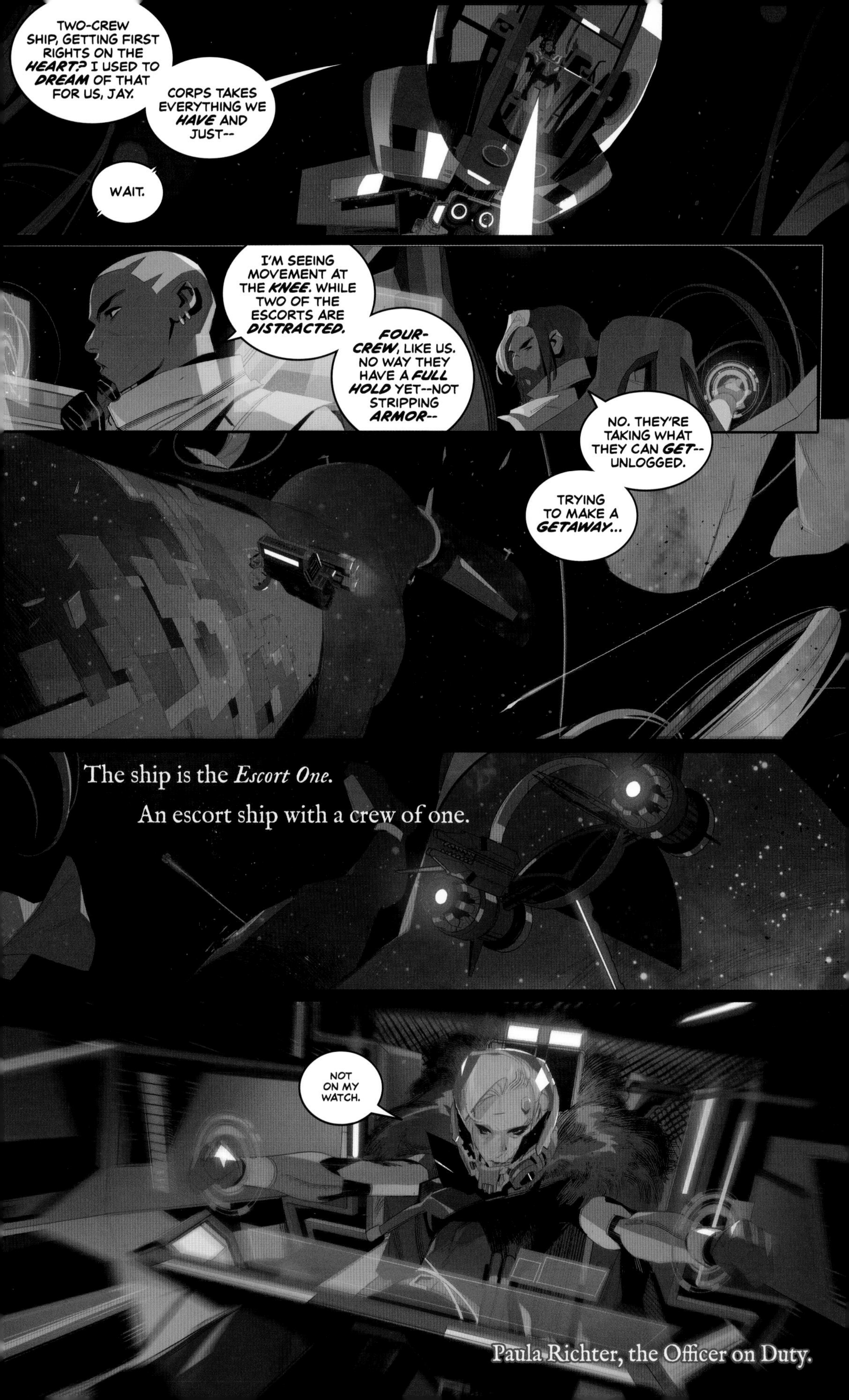

TWO-CREW SHIP, GETTING FIRST RIGHTS ON THE HEART? I USED TO DREAM OF THAT FOR US, JAY.
CORPS TAKES EVERYTHING WE HAVE AND JUST--
WAIT.
I'M SEEING MOVEMENT AT THE KNEE. WHILE TWO OF THE ESCORTS ARE DISTRACTED.
FOUR-CREW, LIKE US. NO WAY THEY HAVE A FULL HOLD YET--NOT STRIPPING ARMOR--
NO. THEY'RE TAKING WHAT THEY CAN GET-- UNLOGGED.
TRYING TO MAKE A GETAWAY...
The ship is the Escort One.
An escort ship with a crew of one.
NOT ON MY WATCH.
Paula Richter, the Officer on Duty.

VOLUME 1
ON SALE
NOW
AL EWING • SIMONE DI MEO
WE ONLY FIND THEM WHEN THEY'RE DEAD

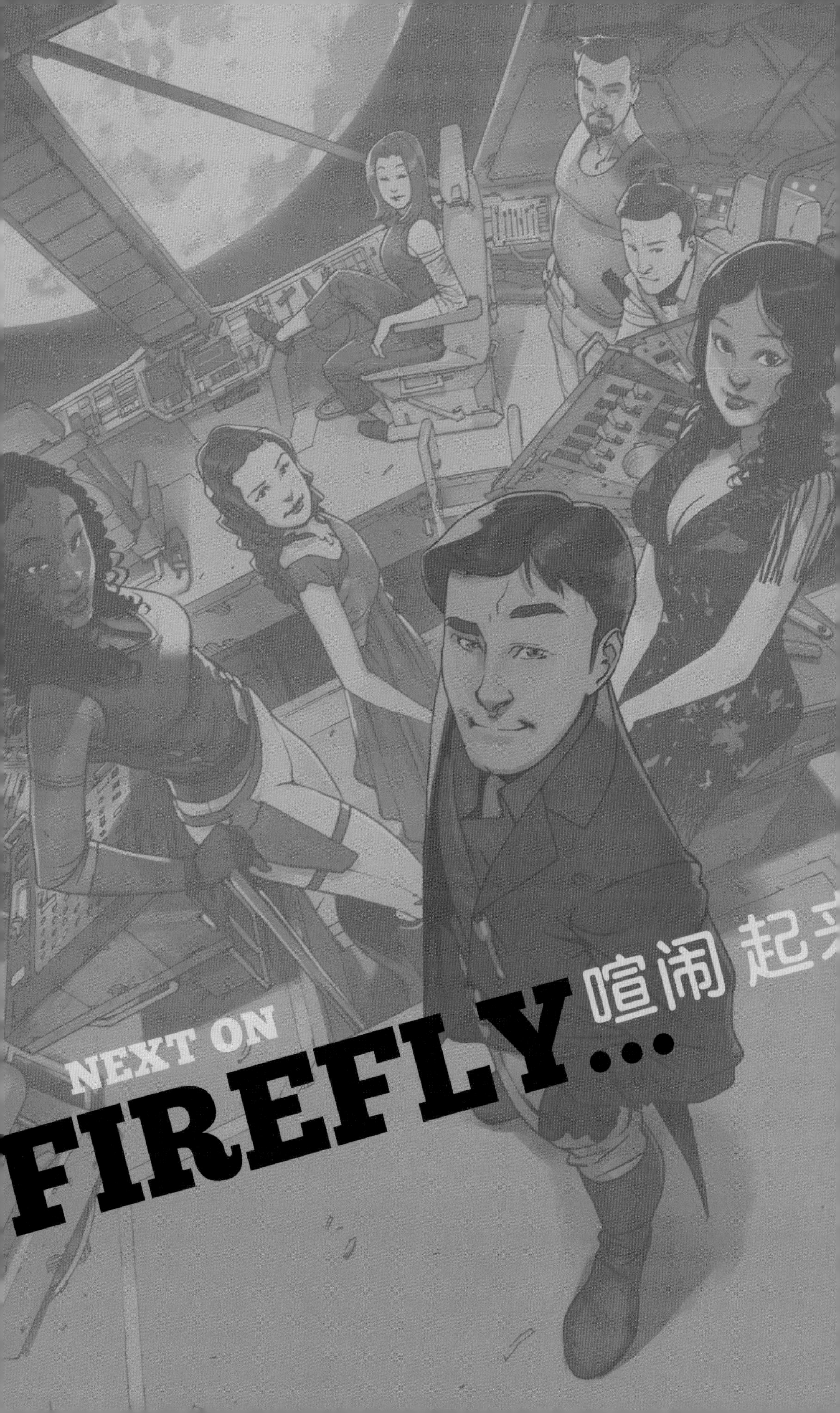
NEXT ON
FIREFLY...
喧闹起

DISCOVER
VISIONARY CREATORS

KIERON GILLEN DAN MORA
TAMRA BONVILLAIN
ONCE & FUTURE
VOLUME ONE
THE KING IS UNDEAD

JAMES TYNION IV
WERTHER DELL'EDERA
MIQUEL MUERTO
SOMETHING is KILLING the CHILDREN
VOLUME ONE
SCOTT SNYDER

Brian Azzarello · Maria Llovet
FAITHLESS

GRANT MORRISON
DAN MORA
Klaus
How Santa Claus Began

SIMON SPURRIER × MATÍAS BERGARA
CODA
VOLUME ONE
"This one is really special!"
—JEFF LEMIRE
(New York Times bestselling writer of Black Hammer)

matt kindt
tyler jenkins
GRASS KINGS

BOOM! STUDIOS™

AVAILABLE AT YOUR LOCAL COMICS SHOP AND BOOKSTORE

To find a comics shop in your area, visit www.comicshoplocator.com

WWW.**BOOM-STUDIOS**.COM

Once & Future
Kieron Gillen, Dan Mora
Volume 1
ISBN: 978-1-68415-491-3 | $16.99 US

Something is Killing the Children
James Tynion IV, Werther Dell'Edera
Volume 1
ISBN: 978-1-68415-558-3 | $14.99 US

Faithless
Brian Azzarello, Maria Llovet
ISBN: 978-1-68415-432-6 | $17.99 US

Klaus
Grant Morrison, Dan Mora
Klaus: How Santa Claus Began SC
ISBN: 978-1-68415-393-0 | $15.99 US
Klaus: The New Adventures of Santa Claus HC
ISBN: 978-1-68415-666-5 | $17.99 US

Coda
Simon Spurrier, Matias Bergara
Volume 1
ISBN: 978-1-68415-321-3 | $14.99 US
Volume 2
ISBN: 978-1-68415-369-5 | $14.99 US
Volume 3
ISBN: 978-1-68415-429-6 | $14.99 US

Grass Kings
Matt Kindt, Tyler Jenkins
Volume 1
ISBN: 978-1-64144-362-3 | $17.99 US
Volume 2
ISBN: 978-1-64144-557-3 | $17.99 US
Volume 3
ISBN: 978-1-64144-650-1 | $17.99 US

Bone Parish
Cullen Bunn, Jonas Scharf
Volume 1
ISBN: 978-1-64144-337-1 | $14.99 US
Volume 2
ISBN: 978-1-64144-542-9 | $14.99 US
Volume 3
ISBN: 978-1-64144-543-6 | $14.99 US

Ronin Island
Greg Pak, Giannis Milonogiannis
Volume 1
ISBN: 978-1-64144-576-4 | $14.99 US
Volume 2
ISBN: 978-1-64144-723-2 | $14.99 US
Volume 3
ISBN: 978-1-64668-035-1 | $14.99 US

Victor LaValle's Destroyer
Victor LaValle, Dietrich Smith
ISBN: 978-1-61398-732-2 | $19.99 US